National Policy-Making

Notions of social change are often divided into local versus international. But what actually happens at the national level—where policies are ultimately made and implemented—when policy-making is interdependent worldwide? How do policy-makers take into account the prior choices of other countries? Far more research is needed on the process of interdependent decision-making in the world polity.

National Policy-Making: domestication of global trends offers a unique set of hybrid cases that straddle these disciplinary and conceptual divides. The volume brings together well-researched case studies of policy-making from across the world that speak to practical issues but also challenge current theories of global influence in local policies. Distancing itself from approaches that conceive narrowly of policy transfer as a "one-way street" from powerful nations to weaker ones, this book argues instead for an understanding of national decision-making processes that emphasize cross-national comparisons and domestic field battles around the introduction of worldwide models.

The case studies in this collection show how national policies appear to be synchronized globally yet are developed with distinctly "national" flavors. Presenting new theoretical ideas and empirical cases, this book is aimed globally at scholars of political science, international relations, comparative public policy, and sociology.

Pertti Alasuutari is Academy Professor in the School of Humanities and Social Sciences at the University of Tampere, Finland.

Ali Qadir is a researcher in the School of Humanities and Social Sciences at the University of Tampere, Finland.

Routledge advances in sociology

National Policy-Making

Domestication of global trends

Edited by Pertti Alasuutari and Ali Qadir

Routledge
Taylor & Francis Group

LONDON AND NEW YORK

First published 2014 by Routledge

2 Park Square, Milton Park, Abingdon, Oxfordshire OX14 4RN
711 Third Avenue, New York, NY 10017

Routledge is an imprint of the Taylor & Francis Group, an informa business

First issued in paperback 2018

British Library Cataloguing in Publication Data
A catalogue record for this book is available from the British Library

Library of Congress Cataloging in Publication Data
National policy-making : domestication of global trends / edited by Pertti
Alasuutari and Ali Qadir.
    pages cm. – (Routledge advances in sociology)
    Includes bibliographical references and index.
    1. Policy sciences – Cross-cultural studies. 2. Decision making –
Cross-cultural studies. I. Alasuutari, Pertti. II. Qadir, Ali.
    H97.N38 2013
    320.6–dc23

2013022803

ISBN: 978-0-415-64123-4 (hbk)
ISBN: 978-1-138-37711-0 (pbk)

Typeset in Times New Roman
by Wearset Ltd, Boldon, Tyne and Wear

Contents

PART II
Domestic field battles and naturalization

Contributors

Editors

Pertti Alasuutari is Academy Professor in the School of Social Sciences and Humanities at the University of Tampere, Finland. He has published widely in the areas of social theory, cultural and media studies, and social research methodology. His current research focuses on the role of knowledge production in global governance. His books include *Researching Culture: Qualitative Method and Cultural Studies* (Sage, 1995), *An Invitation to Social Research* (Sage, 1998), *Rethinking the Media Audience* (Sage, 1999), and *Social Theory and Human Reality* (Sage, 2004). He has published in numerous international scientific journals, including *Journal of Educational Policy, Identities, Journal of Power, Cultural Studies—Critical Methodologies*, and *Acta Sociologica*.

Ali Qadir is a researcher in the School of Social Sciences and Humanities at the University of Tampere, Finland. He has a doctorate in Social Anthropology. His dissertation, *Tangential Modernity: Culture of Higher Education Reform in Pakistan*, was published by Tampere University Press. He has also published in *International Journal of Humanities, British Journal of Religious Education, Asian Journal of Communication, Media, Culture & Society*, and *Pakistan Journal of History and Culture*, besides contributing to books and writing policy reports. His research interests center on cultural aspects of globalization, including religion, multiple modernities, and philosophical hermeneutics.

Contributors

Stefan Bernhard has worked in the Institut für Arbeitsmarkt- und Berufsforschung (IAB) (Institute for Employment Research), Nürnberg, Germany, since October 2008. From October 2004 to September 2005 he worked as assistant at the chair of Sociology II in Bamberg. For the following three years he held a scholarship in the doctoral program "Markets and Social Systems in Europe." During that time he wrote a PhD on the sociology of European poverty and social exclusion policy.

Sebastian M. Büttner works in the Institute of Sociology, Friedrich-Alexander-Universität Erlangen-Nürnberg, Germany. His interests include the sociology of knowledge and culture, social government and social mobilization, transnationalization and regionalization in contemporary Europe. His publications include *Mobilizing Regions, Mobilizing Europe: Expert Knowledge and Scientific Planning in European Regional Development* (Routledge, 2012); and 'Transnationality', pp. 537–570, in: Stefan Immerfall and Göran Therborn (eds) *Handbook of European Societies* (Springer 2010) (co-authored).

Selina Gallo-Cruz works in the Department of Sociology and Anthropology, College of the Holy Cross, USA. Her research centers on the spread of global culture in social movements and political change. Her dissertation research examines the development and role of INGOs in globalizing nonviolent protest tactics. She has additional publications in health care movements, globalization theories, and Latin American social movements.

Anu Kantola works in the Media and Communication Studies Department, University of Helsinki, Finland. She has worked in the departments of communication and political science at the University of Helsinki. Her research interests include political communication and in particular the politics of globalization. She has published textbooks, journal articles and book chapters in her research fields.

Daniel Maman works in the Department of Sociology and Anthropology, Ben-Gurion University of the Negev, Israel. His areas of interest include economic sociology, political sociology, institutional analysis, and networks analysis. He is the co-author with Zeev Rosenhek of *The Israeli Central Bank: Political Economy, Global Logics and Local Actors* (Routledge, 2011) and *The Bank of Israel: Political Economy in the Neoliberal Era* (Van Leer Jerusalem Institute/Hakibbutz Hameuchad Publishing House, 2009, in Hebrew). He is now studying the Israeli financial system's restructuring from a comparative perspective.

Marjaana Rautalin works in the School of Social Sciences and Humanities, University of Tampere, Finland. Her research interests include governmentality and world polity research and in more particular, the role of the OECD in global governance. She is currently preparing her doctoral thesis in sociology on the role of the OECD PISA Study in Finnish education policy. Her recently published articles include: Rautalin and Alasuutari (2007) "The curse of success: The impact of the OECD's Programme for International Student Assessment on the discourses of the teaching profession in Finland," *European Educational Research Journal, 6*: 348–63; and Rautalin and Alasuutari (2009) "The uses of the national PISA results by Finnish officials in central government," *Journal of Education Policy, 24*: 539–56.

Zeev Rosenhek works in the Department of Sociology, Political Science and Communication, The Open University of Israel. His fields of research include state–society relations, the political economy of the welfare state, labour migration, and institutional change. He has published numerous articles on these topics, and is co-author, with Daniel Maman, of *The Israeli Central Bank: Political Economy, Global Logics and Local Actors* (Routledge, 2011), and *The Bank of Israel: Political Economy in the Neoliberal Era* (Van Leer Jerusalem Institute/Hakibbutz Hameuchad Publishing House, 2009, in Hebrew). He is currently studying from a comparative perspective the practices of sense making employed by the US Federal Reserve and the European Central Bank during the global financial crisis.

Jukka Syväterä works in the School of Social Sciences and Humanities, University of Tampere, Finland. His research interests include relations between bioscience and governmentality, specifically global governance of developments in the life sciences and biomedicine. He is currently writing his doctoral thesis on the institutionalization of bioethics.

Keita Takayama works in the Faculty of the Professions, School of Education, University of New England, USA. His recent writings have appeared in *Asia Pacific Journal of Education, British Journal of Sociology of Education, Comparative Education, Comparative Education Review, Global Crises, Social Justice, and Education* (2010, edited by Michael Apple), and *Routledge International Handbook for Critical Education* (2009, edited by Michael Apple, Wayne Au, and Luis Gandin). His article in 2010 won the Comparative and International Education Society's George Bereday Award, given to the most outstanding article in a year out of all articles in *Comparative Education Review*.

Acknowledgments

Any volume, more so an edited one, naturally has a story to it. This book has its origins in 2009, when Pertti Alasuutari was appointed Academy Professor by the Academy of Finland. As part of his five-year research project "The Moderns: A Study on the Governmentality of World Society," together with his research team and scholars from other countries he planned to put together an edited book on local–global interaction and on the domestication of global trends in local contexts. Pursuing this plan, in 2010 he organized a stream of sessions on the local–global interfaces for the "Power and Knowledge" international conference held at the University of Tampere. That conference was crucial for the realization of the dream. Several papers given in it later evolved into chapters in this book. Furthermore, Ali Qadir's presentation led into his joining the Moderns project and becoming a co-editor of this volume.

Instead of first acknowledging our intellectual debts to particular individuals, we want to begin by acknowledging our collective debt to our colleagues in the Moderns project and to the entire Tampere Research Group for Cultural and Political Sociology (TCuPS). The theoretical framework of domestication introduced in this book has been developed as a long-lasting enterprise that has benefited greatly from the weekly seminar in which participants have presented and commented on each other's work related to it, including the Introduction and several other chapters of this book. Our special thanks go to Jari Aro, Johanna Hiitola, Matti Kortesoja, Lauri Lepistö, Jari Luomanen, Elina Mikola, Virve Peteri, Ajay Saini, Leena Tervonen-Gonçalves, Tatiana Tiaynen, Laura Valkeasuo, Oscar Miranda Villanueva, Valtteri Vähä-Savo, and Li Wang.

For several years TCuPS has also held joint seminars with the Helsinki Research Group for Political Sociology, in which we have received valuable feedback from a group of researchers with similar research interests but a somewhat different approach. We especially want to thank Risto Alapuro, Eeva Luhtakallio, and Tuomas Ylä-Anttila. In this instance we also want to thank Karin Creutz, Peter Holley, and Markku Lonkila, who have served as double agents and links between these two groups.

We are also grateful to Risto Heiskala, Anne Kovalainen, Risto Kunelius, and Seppo Poutanen for their contribution in our joint effort in putting together a research application on a related topic. The ideas presented in this book have greatly benefited from their comments and criticism during the intensive process through which the application assumed its final shape.

We are also greatly indebted to the community of scholars developing world society theory, to which this book aims to make a contribution. We particularly thank Ann Hironaka, Evan Schofer, and George Thomas for their hospitality, kind help, and support, and for the many discussions we have had with them.

We are, of course, immensely grateful to the contributors of this volume for their patience, cooperation, and effort. Thanks are also due to Gerhard Boom-gaarden, Emily Briggs, and the production team at Routledge for realizing this project in an enviably smooth publishing process.

Work on this book was primarily funded by the Academy of Finland (code 218200). This funding is gratefully acknowledged, as is support received from the University of Tampere. Ali Qadir's participation was partially financed by the Kone Foundation, whose assistance is also appreciated.

Abbreviations

BoI	Bank of Israel
CCE	Central Council of Education (Japan)
CEC	Commission of the European Communities
CEU	Council of the European Union
CNE	Commission on National Education (Pakistan)
DG Regio	Directorate-General for Regional Policy (European Commission)
EAD	Economic Affairs Division (Government of Pakistan)
EAPN	European Anti-Poverty Network
EC	European Commission
ECB	European Central Bank
ETENE	National Advisory Board on Health Care Ethics (Finland)
ETLA	*Elinkeinoelämän tutkimuslaitos*: Research Institute of the Finnish Economy
EU	European Union
FAO	Food and Agriculture Organization (United Nations)
FARC	Revolutionary Armed Forces of Colombia
FEANTSA	European Federation of National Organisations Working with the Homeless
Fed	Federal Reserve Bank (USA)
FMA	Finnish Medical Association (FMA)
GDP	Gross domestic product
HEC	Higher Education Commission (Pakistan)
HRW	Human Rights Watch
ILO	International Labour Organization (ILO)
IMF	International Monetary Fund
INGO	International Non-Governmental Organization
MEXT	Ministry of Education, Culture, Sports, Science and Technology (Japan)
MoF	Ministry of Finance (Israel)
MP	Member of Parliament (Finland)
NBC	National Bioethics Committee (Finland)
NBE	National Board of Education (Finland)
NGO	Non-Governmental Organization

NIER	National Institute for Educational Policy Research (Japan)
OECD	Organisation for Economic Co-operation and Development
OMC	Open Method of Coordination (European Union)
PISA	Programme for International Student Assessment (OECD)
PoF	Parliament of Finland
RDS	Regional Development Strategy (Poland)
TFHES	Task Force on Higher Education and Society (UNESCO)
TFIHE	Task Force on Improvement of Higher Education (Pakistan)
UNESCO	United Nations Educational, Scientific and Cultural Organization
UNHCR	United Nations High Commissioner for Refugees
VNK	*Valtioneuvoston kanslia* (Prime-Minister's Office, Finland)

1 Introduction

Pertti Alasuutari and Ali Qadir

Interdependent national policy-making

The rise and rise of neoliberal economic policy over 40 years is an outstanding example of how global ideas surge and spread across the world. As David Harvey (2005) tells it in his brief history of neoliberalism, the late 1970s were a major turning point in nation-states' economic policy throughout the world. In 1978 Deng Xiaoping took the first steps to liberalize the Chinese communist-ruled economy, with the plan to transform China from a closed periphery to an open, dynamic, and rapidly growing economy. The next year Paul Volcker took command in the Federal Reserve of the USA and by the end of 1979 dramatically changed monetary policy. In Britain Margaret Thatcher was elected prime minister in May 1979, starting a new economic policy that emphasized deregulation of the financial sector, flexible labor markets, the privatization of state-owned companies, and reducing the power and influence of trade unions. Then, in 1980 Ronald Reagan was elected President of the USA, and in line with Volcker's moves turned the course toward supply-side economic policies that comprised reducing tax rates to spur economic growth, controlling the money supply to reduce inflation, deregulating the economy, and reducing government spending. The tremor of these acts by separate powerful nation-states seemingly spread and resounded to form a wave that swept throughout the globe, "to remake the world around us in a totally different image" (Harvey, 2005, p. 1).

These parallel developments in China, Britain, and the USA in the late 1970s and the sweeping popularity of liberalization policies that ensued throughout the world (Simmons et al., 2008) illustrate the inadequacy of methodological nationalism, which views the world as divided into self-contained entities called nation-states (Beck and Sznaider, 2006; Chernilo, 2006), making policy decisions independently of each other. Instead, the rise of neoliberalism as a global policy fashion attests to the fact that national decision-making is interdependent, and that the globe should be viewed as a single world society. The institutional infrastructure of this world society can be seen when we consider the way the globe is divided into some 200 nation-states. They are institutionally more or less copies of each other with a government, a similar set of ministries and many other private and public institutions, although there is no world government or leader who has ordered them to be organized in such a homogeneous manner. Furthermore, in their policy reforms these states and institutions often adopt the same models so that they appear like a shoal of fish, making the same turns and adjusting their movements to each other, yet never becoming a single fish. This global governance without a governor is evident in waves of policies that spread relatively quickly throughout the world, of which it is characteristic that governments act of their own free will, not because they are forced to adopt a particular model.

The paradigm change from independent to interdependent decision-making has opened up a new, rapidly growing field of research. In this scholarship, typically *operationalized* as policy diffusion, researchers have identified four factors behind the spread of policies: coercion, competition, learning, and emulation. Empirical research has found some evidence of all four mechanisms, although several studies stress that mere coercion is seldom the main process underlying policy diffusion and that learning is conditioned by belief patterns, suggesting that simple learning models do not depict the process accurately (Simmons, Dobbin, and Garrett, 2008). In the much-cited accounts by DiMaggio and Powell (1983) and Powell and DiMaggio (1991), organizations also could be seen as conforming to each other by way of coercion or mimesis, sometimes to the extent that their leaders are not even aware of their purposeful agency in copying.

This research tradition leads to many insights, most importantly to the neoinstitutionalist view of the constitution of nation-states and national actors by a world culture (Meyer, 2010; Meyer, Boli, Thomas, and Ramirez, 1997; Thomas, 2009). However, the operationalization of the idea of interdependence by way of diffusion has also limited the scope of such analyses. The dominant research design in this tradition comprises statistical analysis of the diffusion of a particular policy to different countries, leading to disaggregated criteria and patterns of diffusion. That is, the research has typically asked variants of the general question: what diffuses, from where and under what conditions? While such research has revealed much about diffusion, this has meant that the *practices* through which policy-makers actually end up making their decisions have been largely overlooked. What takes place within the nation-state to get to specific policy outcomes is left as a black box, perhaps filled up with speculative assumptions about unthinking conformism.

Following the diffusion research tradition into policy-making thus leaves somewhat of a mystery in many cases. What actually happens at the national level, where policies are ultimately made and implemented, in a worldwide condition of interdependent policy-making? How do policy-makers take into account the prior choices of other countries? And, through what process does that lead to policies that appear rhetorically as natural evolutions of solutions to national needs but yet maintain global isomorphism? Far more research is needed on the *process* of interdependent decision-making in the world polity.

Our aim in this book is to unpack some of these processes by way of case examination at the *receiving end*, so to speak. That is, we do not begin with the standard, top-down approach that identifies particular policies and then traces where they diffuse, thereby explaining isomorphism by variables considered as self-evident proof of causal mechanisms at play. Rather, we take a bottom-up perspective, which scrutinizes national decision-making in a particular reform process, identifying the ways in which local actors relate to the world society and engage in a field battle through which global trends and ideas are tamed to the local context. Such a change in perspective can add considerably to explanations about how global isomorphism is in fact an *outcome* of local decision-making. The contributions in this volume exploit this insight in a variety of settings that, collectively, illustrate the utility of this vantage point.

In this introduction we develop further this bottom-up perspective of national policy-making as the domestication of global trends. We begin by briefly listing the patterns of translocal interaction that we seek to explain, i.e. isomorphism coupled with a sense of national sovereignty in policy-making. We then quickly review the strengths of neoinstitutionalist explanations, including the body of literature known as world polity theory, which in our view comes closest to capturing these patterns, as well as some gaps left by most such accounts. We move on to introduce the analytical advantages in thinking about global changes as synchronization, as an outcome of national processes rather than as an external force to be contended with. This provides the theoretical basis and premises of our subsequent elaboration of national policy-making as the domestication of global trends, and we then discuss at some length what this entails. We end the introduction by previewing the chapters of this book and relating their contributions to the framework of domestication.

Neoinstitutionalism and the world polity

The remarkable similarity in the world society without a single state is paralleled by apparent national sovereignty. These two seemingly contradictory phenomena are difficult to explain by "realist" social scientific theories, and call for a neoinstitutionalist view.

Isomorphism and neoinstitutionalism

Similarities between national policies are a central focus of theories on the global system. However, as world polity theorists point out, most standard sociological explanations falter when encountering "patterns of influence and conformity that cannot be explained solely as matters of power relations or functional rationality" (Meyer et al., 1997, p. 145). Not only the administrative and political apparatuses of policy-making across the world but also actual policies themselves appear to be guided by the incorporation of worldwide models or blueprints. Thus, we see across the world very similar trends related, among others, to mass schooling (Meyer, Ramirez, and Soysal, 1992), higher education (Schofer and Meyer, 2005), development-oriented economic policy (Hall, 1986), and environmental policies (Frank, Hironaka, and Schofer, 2000). In this volume, case studies of subnational regional development by Büttner (Chapter 5), central bank independence in Israel by Maman and Rosenhek (Chapter 7), and the National Bioethics Committee in Finland by Syväterä and Alasuutari (Chapter 10), all begin with and analyze the spread of such global models of "rationality." In general, the more principally *universalist* are the norms in question, the more practically *universal* they appear to be. Thus, there is great conformity throughout the world polity on the constitutional forms balancing state authority with individual rights (Boli, 1987), on human rights in general (Elliott, 2007; Meyer, 2007), and on women's rights in particular (Bradley and Ramirez, 1996; Ramirez and Weiss, 1979).

These pieces of evidence lead to the conception of isomorphism, by which we denote "a world whose societies, organized as nation-states, are structurally similar in many unexpected dimensions and change in unexpectedly similar ways" (Meyer et al., 1997, p. 145). Explaining this worldwide pattern, world polity theory underlines that state and non-state actors enact the same worldwide models because they are constituted as agents and identities by a shared rationalistic "world culture."

The key to the diffusion of worldwide models in this approach is the influence of international governmental and non-governmental organizations (Boli and Thomas, 1999), which policy-makers often promote in their "double agent" roles and identities as national citizens and members of transnational communities or professions. These associations are seen as helping to diffuse the global models that are, in turn, "ritually enacted" by nation-states. Consequently, world polity theorists argue, the scripts comprising world culture, crystallized in the idea of the modern formal organization, permeate the whole world, structuring all organizations and nation-states accordingly so that all entities eventually look the same. As Drori et al. (2006, p. 14) put it, "much of the sovereignty and legitimacy of older national and local cultures are undercut so that their capacity to sustain more traditional organizational forms is weakened."

While we take distance from this last point about diffusion and its concomitant sense of *growing* "rationalization," the basic premises of world polity theory appear to adequately capture the phenomenon of global isomorphism. Rooted in a neoinstitutionalist perspective, world polity theory shifts the focus of attention from a state-centered approach common to standard analyses of independent decision-making to the globally shared rules of the game. The transnational institutional and cultural context becomes central. In other words, "Nation-states are similar because they adopt the same identity (of being a nation-state) and they thereby adopt similar practices" (Thomas, 2009, p. 118).

This line of thinking draws heavily on neoinstitutionalism, which stresses the importance of "patterns that constrain and empower very agentic, autonomous, bounded and purposive actors" (Meyer, 2010, p. 3). Rather than conceiving of national actors as bounded entities independent of participation in institutional orders, the sociological variant of neoinstitutionalism stresses that actors' agency and boundaries are legitimated by their participation in the wider institutional environment. Actors are not seen as natural entities prior to social life, but rather as constructed entities thoroughly embedded in the wider system that gives their own actions meaning. The discussion on the Open Method of Coordination in the European Union (EU) by Bernhard in this volume (Chapter 4) is a particularly striking example of how a web of inter-state expectations shapes social policy in European nations.

Such a perspective has proven remarkably useful in accounting for the similarity so evident across much of the world, especially as regards national policies. However, once again world polity theory operationalizes the notion of interdependence, or embeddedness in an institutionalized world polity, by way of diffusion. As a result, it elides roles of local actors in adopting such worldwide models, which after all are seldom just "copied" mindlessly, but rather instituted at the own will and desire of national leaders and decision makers. World polity theory treats what happens in the nation-state as a black box and, by implication, as less relevant than the institutional order. It thus remains a mystery how policymakers and national leaders can appear to be hypocrite conformists or "Babbits" (Meyer, 2004), almost like idolizing teenagers following the latest fashions. Furthermore, world polity theory does not account for, or even seek to explain, the persistent sense of national ownership in policy-making, which, in turn, leads to analyses of national differences trumping global homogeneity. Partly for these reasons, world polity theory is not without challenges and is still not the mainstream way of thinking about the world.

Community construction as a world cultural feature

To better capture the way in which world society functions, we need to pay more attention to the role of nation-states and national decision-making in hiding from view the world society as an isomorphic totality. As world polity theory stresses, agency in world society is "tamed" by world culture—that is, similar ideas appeal to national decision-makers because they are constituted as actors by the same global cultural ideas and principles. However, it is important to stress that the nation as a self-evident community and object of identification is one such world model. Accordingly, the adoption of new ideas takes place within nation-state containers, in which reforms drawing on cross-national comparisons, experiences gained and models applied in other countries are introduced and debated by constructing "us" and appealing to "our" interest as a nation. The policy formed as the outcome of a national law-making process, perhaps devised and promoted as an ideal combination of the strengths of existing solutions, is therefore viewed as "our" model, as an organic product of national politics. It is no wonder then that if the general public or policy analysts relate it to policies adopted in other countries, the focus is on the differences, not on the similarities. The shifting use of policy catchwords in Japanese education reforms in the wake of the results of the cross-national comparison by the Organisation for Economic Co-operation and Development (OECD) of student learning outcomes, discussed in this book by Takayama (Chapter 8), is one instance of this.

This "natural attitude" toward the nation can be detected behind the public and scholarly discussions regarding the exigencies of globalization, which typically boils down to the questions whether world cultures are becoming increasingly homogeneous or hybrid, and whether nation-states will retain or have already lost their sovereignty. Whichever way discussants have answered these questions, in practically all cases they are sympathetic toward sovereignty of local cultures and identities. That is, critical voices like, say, George Ritzer (1996, 2004) point out in a pessimistic or nostalgic tone that authentic local cultures are being crushed by capitalism and transnational companies. On the other hand proponents of the view that heterogeneity prevails or is even increasing (such as Hannerz, 1987; Kraidy, 2005; Pieterse, 1995; Stoddard and Cornwell, 1999) have their sympathy on the side of local people who are able to ingeniously turn foreign influences and conditions imposed on them into part of their cultural practices and identities.

To take an example, one of the most popular arguments by advocates of the homogenization thesis is that the media, especially television, eradicates differences and brings audiences around the world onto the same, universal plane of worldwide electronic media (e.g. Meyrowitz, 1986). The proponents of the hybridization thesis, on the other hand, point out that although the major foreign news events may be the same around the world, journalists tell them in ways that make them compatible for consumption by different national audiences (e.g. Gans, 1979; Gurevitch, Levy, and Roeh, 1991, p. 206; Liebes, 1992; Nossek, 2004). This finding has been celebrated as proof of the argument that globalization of news has not diminished the uniquely national character of news programs in different countries. Instead, Gurevitch et al. regard the tendency of news media to domesticate news stories as a "countervailing force to the pull of globalization" (p. 207).

Similar accounts of national differences in the face of global homogeneity can be found almost everywhere. However, we do not see these necessarily as evidence of "national differences" or even of hybrid solutions that somehow combine global and local impulses. Instead, the very construction of such distinctions, of national sovereignty and global impulses, is at stake. Michael Billig joins a tradition of constructionist research that touches on this topic precisely in the context of media to suggest that:

> The media of mass communication bring the flag across the contemporary hearth. Daily newspapers and logomanic politicians constantly flag the world of nations ... they address "us" as a national first person plural, and they situate "us" in the homeland within a world of nations. Nationhood is the context which must be assumed to understand so many banal utterances. Cumulatively, such flaggings provide daily, unmindful reminders of nationhood ... It is no wonder, then, that a national identity is seldom forgotten.
>
> (Billig, 1995, p. 174)

Billig draws attention to the construction of a national "us," parallel to the flattening of a global media sphere in which news circulates virtually without obstacles. By taking the analysis up a level of abstraction, Billig highlights the persistent, often only implicit, construction of the consciousness of national identity alongside the circulation of global news. This same trend can be seen in national policy-making. Just as domestic media houses report on global events while also "bringing the flag across," so national policy-makers draw on world-wide models and blueprints while reinforcing national identity. Policies are nowhere justified by arguing, "this is how *they* do it," but rather by constructing a national interest—and, therefore, national identity—from which a particular solution or eclectic mix of solutions is considered against its relevance for *us*.

In this light, the issue about explaining how interdependent national policy-making is conducted is not one of global homogeneity *versus* national differences, or of global enactment *versus* national solutions. Neoinstitutionalist principles allow us to question the very construction of these distinctions and to propose a formulation that can encompass both together. This brings us to the point that a fuller account of global isomorphism has to account for banal nationalism, or the sense that the specific policies developed are naturally "national."

From globalization to synchronization

In his wildly popular book on globalization—or, globalization 3.0 as he calls it—Thomas Friedman (2005) discusses the world's flatness as a shrinking of distances. "Individuals," he suggests, "must, and can, now ask: where do I fit into the global competition and opportunities of the day, and how can I, on my own, collaborate with others globally?" Friedman joins a body of literature celebrating the "flatness," as compression, of the world as bringing hitherto unimagined opportunities, particularly in business.

We agree with Friedman's and others' point that due to new information and communication technology and neoliberalization of the economy, distances and national boundaries have become less important in recent decades. There is however another sense in which the world has been flat for much longer. That is the point that there is no global hierarchical structure built above individual nation-states. As it is put in world polity theory, the world society is essentially stateless (Meyer, 2000). This means that there is no simple and straightforward explanation for global governance, or for the fact that there are global ideas and policy fashions that sweep throughout the world, often making the nation-states seem like a flock of birds. On the other hand the world polity theory tradition drawing on the diffusion research design is also unable to account for the turns that nation-states take. The global dynamics of constant changes and turns remain a lacuna.

As self-evident as the point about the world being flat may seem, mainstream research on global governance typically evades it, searching for ways to replace that image with assumptions about a hierarchical power structure operating overtly or covertly in the world system. Hence, scholarly books and articles dealing with global governance typically concentrate on the United Nations system and other international organizations as proxies for the missing world government (see e.g. Diehl and Frederking, 2010). Similarly, mainstream research in international studies stresses the role of powerful states or blocks that run the world. For instance, the Cold War world view perceived the world as consisting of two blocks, whereas a more recent discussion focused on the thesis of a clash of civilizations (Huntington, 1993, 1996). Dependency theory (Coram, 1994; Goldstone, 1998) and world systems theory (Wallerstein, 2004), on the other hand, have put forward the argument that dominance in the global system is all about economy and the capitalist system.

Although we share the view with these research traditions that international organizations, powerful states and global companies all play a role in the global system, we stress that reducing the question of power relations to who or what entity has "the power," makes us miss the fascinating way in which world society works. Following a constructionist perspective, we believe it is not very useful to adopt a base-superstructure model, and look for irreducible causal mechanisms, such as the capitalist economy, that operate behind the scenes at a somehow more "profound" level of reality. Rather, market mechanisms and the like are better seen as constructions used to justify policies that in fact draw on global ideas, as shown about the economy and associated business strategies by Kantola (Chapter 3) and Büttner (Chapter 5) in this book. This is also the case when considering "powerful" actors. As Michel Foucault once said, "In political thought and analysis, we still have not cut off the head of the king" (Foucault, 1980, pp. 88–89). By that he meant that we still tend to conceive of power in terms of a hierarchical structure with the king on top, although present-day society is a dislocated network of actors who attempt to govern by acting upon people's aspirations and beliefs. Foucault was talking about what he called elsewhere "governmentalization of the state" (Foucault, 2007, p. 109) by which he depicted the fact that in democracies governance works most effectively through guiding public opinion and mentalities.

The same applies to world society composed of separate states. The reason for states to adopt similar policies, hence synchronizing their movements, is not a hierarchical power structure in which a sovereign power center is able to determine what policies nation-states have to adopt (see Wilkinson, 1999). Although some nation-states certainly are weaker than others, they are allowed—or rather forced—to decide by themselves what decisions to take and to face the consequences. Hence power is based on what can be called *epistemic governance*, which means that different actors try to convince each other about what is rational, necessary, or the morally right thing to do. The outcome often is that national policy-makers view it as desirable to adopt similar ideas and strategies to those adopted by their counterparts in other states. In that sense the organization of the world society, composed of some 200 states, is lean.

The fact that nation-states often end up synchronizing their moves may create the impression that individual states' policy-makers are unthinking agents. They appear to be steered by genetic instincts like a shoal of fish, or by an independent mechanism such as technological or economic development. Similarly, world polity theory argues that they are mindlessly enacting world cultural scripts.

Although the outcome may create this impression, moves made by individual or collective actors are actually far from instinctual. In national or local governmental decision-making actors reflect on the different options available for each move and appeal to rational reasons and to the common good while also defending their stakeholder interests. Since cross-national comparisons and information about policies adopted in other countries are part of policy-making in all nation-states, the end result is that the entire system appears to be isomorphic. Yet the turns that single states or the world society as a whole takes are not predetermined or controlled by any single actor. Instead, this fascinating herd behavior resembles fashion: similar ideas circulate, amalgamating into ever-new combinations that are marketed and spread across the globe as new models. In that way these local processes, through which global trends are domesticated—interpreted locally to make them appear domestic—are a key engine of global social change.

National policy-making as domestication of global trends

References to global ideas and concepts and to what is going on elsewhere in the world are a regular aspect of politics in all nation-states, which form a densely networked world society. In that sense it is often difficult to say when a new idea arrives in a nation-state. For instance, when a domestic actor justifies a reform by a model or catchphrase put to practice in other countries, it is used as a justification precisely because the speaker in question trusts that compatriots are already familiar with it. Besides, the introduction of a specific model to national political discussion must not be seen as simple transfer of an idea from one country to another. Rather, local actors often play a crucial role in constructing, packaging and marketing the practices followed in another country as a clearly delineated "model," which may radically differ from the understanding of those policies in the "donor" country. As policy transfer researchers have also emphasized, local actors contest and socially construct the "success" and "appropriateness" of model policies (Acharya, 2004; Callon, 1986; Cortell and Davis, 2000; Dolowitz and Marsh, 1996). Thus, when we talk about domestication of global trends or ideas in this book, the concept of domestication is not a synonym for adoption, enactment or implementation of a particular model. Instead, it depicts a transformation in which a reform process initiated by references to exogenous models, ideas or catchwords results in people viewing the outcome as a unique domestic creation. In this respect the concept of domestication as it is defined here also differs from several other concepts that have been used in depicting the process. While concepts such as creolization (Hannerz, 1987), hybridization (Pieterse, 1995), localization (Acharya, 2004), translation (Czarniawska-Joerges and Sevón, 1996), and vernacularization (Levitt and Merry, 2009) conceptualize the difference between an "original" and a modified version, the concept of domestication calls attention to the conceptions of the actors. Our interest is in how policies are molded in such a way that, while drawing on identifiable global models, they are conceived as essentially domestic or natural: self-evident and universal. For instance, as the case of higher education reforms in Pakistan by Qadir (Chapter 9) shows, inter-textual references in policy documents often build a sense of 'national' history and a self-evident national trajectory.

This kind of process that leads to domestication of global ideas and trends does not deal with a specific, narrowly defined policy model, although a process may be triggered by the introduction of such a model. Rather, it is about a problem or a new item introduced to the national political agenda whose treatment in the domestic context means that the national discourse in the area is synchronized with those in other nation-states. In addition to routine appeals to world cultural principles, over the course of national policy-making knowledge about policies implemented in other countries may be brought up at several phases and many alternative policies may be suggested and examined (Greener, 2002).

Since there is constant exchange of information through innumerable links between actors in present-day networked world society, it is of course arbitrary to isolate a single process through which people get used to new trendy ideas and start to consider them as domestic or even part of national culture. At any moment in time, there are several such processes going on in different stages. On a global scale, these national processes can be seen as a constant cycle in which reforms made in some countries are constructed and marketed as new models in others, to be domesticated in different ways that give rise to yet another round of reforms. In that sense there is no natural starting point or end result in this cycle of global social change. However, for analytical purposes we suggest that in a single country such a process starts with the introduction of cross-national comparative data that results in a domestic field battle and eventually ends up in actors getting used to a new status quo as a natural and national state of affairs.

Cross-national comparisons

The synchronization of a national trajectory of changes with those having taken place elsewhere in the world occurs through the way in which a social problem and hence a need for reform is often defined and justified. In that sense, pointing out a problem is a starting point for a process of domestication. To quote Sahlin-Andersson (1996, p. 70), "local problems are constructed through comparing the local situation with that of other organizations." The same applies to nation-states. The case in this volume by Alasuutari (Chapter 2) examining justifications used by politicians in promoting or opposing new legislation in parliaments illustrates this herd-like behavior whereby nation-states keep an eye on prior moves of other nations in world society.

International comparisons have such effects in domestic contexts because of certain underlying world-cultural models such as the nation-state as a rational actor, as world polity theorists note (Meyer et al., 1997, p. 153). But another, often ignored, model is the idea that nation-states are engaged in competition with each other in the world economy and in other fields of struggle. Related to that, the use of comparisons draws on the banal nationalist idea that the domestic population forms a team in that competition, a community of citizens that share the interest of cherishing the competitiveness of the nation. This is most obvious in macroeconomic policy-making, and the case by Kantola here (Chapter 3) demonstrates how the very idea of competitiveness is brought into national policies in industrialized societies like Finland.

In addition, arguments in these discussions are typically premised on the tacit assumption that reforms made in different countries mark the path toward universal progress. Thus actors often appeal to what is happening elsewhere to advance reforms they would like to be made in a nation-state: for instance what the general trend is, how things are done in "leading" countries, or what are promoted as "best practices" by international governmental organizations. In such contexts international league tables are also commonly used to show how "we" are doing in comparison with others. Comparisons—either with international averages or against "best performers"—are often used in different ways to identify the "problem" and justify a particular reform (Tervonen-Goncalves, 2012).

Domestic field battles

Although reform processes are often started off by appeals to cross-national comparison, they end up enhancing rather than questioning the idea of a nation as an entity that follows its own trajectory, and that is particularly because the demand for a reform often triggers a battle on what we call the domestic political field. Drawing on new institutionalism (DiMaggio and Powell, 1983; Djelic and Sahlin-Andersson, 2006, pp. 18–24) and on Bourdieu's theory of fields (Bourdieu, 1991, 1993, 1996), by talking about national politics as a field we stress that actors' attempts to advance their goals cannot be understood in isolation from the institutionalized rules, practices and positions within which acts take place and are assigned meaning. To paraphrase DiMaggio and Powell's definition of an organizational field, by the political field of a nation-state we mean those actors and their mutual relations that, in the aggregate, constitute a recognized area of institutional life (DiMaggio and Powell, 1983, p. 148). To give a simple definition of a political field, it refers to the playing field in which domestic politics takes place and to the rules that constitute both all actors involved and what the game is all about.

The game comprises—and thus a field battle is premised on   two basic rules. On the one hand actors must justify their views and demands by appealing to the national interest, i.e. the common good of all the citizens. On the other hand participants share the assumption that the field is composed of different stakeholder groups and convictions and that knowingly or "instinctually" actors defend their group interests. Hence, the outcome of a demand for a reform depends on how convincingly the proponents of a reform argue that there is a problem and that the proposed solution is in the best interest of the nation. If the reform demand is convincing enough, it triggers a field battle in which different actors defend their positions by joining in the discussion about how the new idea or catchphrase should be turned into modified domestic practices.

Thus, in a sense policy-makers are most successful when they are able to depoliticize politics as a field in which different interests clash. That is why scientific research making claims about the most effective policies for a nation is so popular, which makes understandable the proliferation of information about other countries, their performance, and models adopted by them in different policy areas. As a plethora of case studies in different areas, for instance in education policy (Ertl, 2006; Grek, 2009; Rautalin and Alasuutari, 2007; Takayama, 2008), health and social policy (Greener, 2002; Schmid and Götze, 2009), or environmental policy (Beck, 2004; Pettenger, 2007) testifies, when suitable conditions are met, proposals or demands about reforms—backed up by international comparison or justified by an exogenous model—trigger a struggle among local actors.

Actors may also appeal to the opinions of a large group of citizens they claim to represent (Bourdieu, 1991) but even such an argument is defended by what is best for all or by a universal moral principle. Furthermore, besides using the international prestige or pressure associated with a transnational model as a form of capital (Bourdieu, 1977, 1984, 1995) in the domestic field, they may justify or oppose a reform by arguing how well or badly it is in concert with the national cultural and political tradition (Acharya, 2004).

Since the domestic field battle is of a rhetorical nature, in which actors try to convince others of their interpretation of facts and the proper conclusions to be drawn from them, it is not feasible to define objective conditions for the instigation of such a battle. When some actor or actors articulate the results of international comparison or other information about what is going on elsewhere as grounds for demands for reforms, they obviously assume that such reforms would be advantageous regarding their interests, convictions and position in the field. As a general rule it appears that a state's poor ranking in the international league tables is favorable for those who want reforms, whereas a good or fair ranking cannot be as easily capitalized as grounds for such demands. For instance, the OECD's PISA study aroused a panic particularly in Germany (Ertl, 2006; Ringarp and Rothland, 2010; Waldow, 2009) and Japan (Takayama, 2008), whereas good results in Finland attracted attention in the media but were not favorable for those who demanded reforms and increased resources for education (Grek, 2009; Rautalin and Alasuutari, 2007). Instead, as shown in this volume by Rautalin (Chapter 6), Finland's top ranking in PISA, celebrated in the national media, enabled the Ministry of Education to carry on its old development program without any resistance, although the program went against the prevailing wisdom of factors behind Finland's success. On the other hand, what is regarded as a "poor" ranking depends on the general expectations of a country's performance and to which reference group the performance is related. The moral panics aroused by the PISA in Germany and Japan are again good examples: those countries were far from the worst performers, but in both countries, expectations about their performance were much more ambitious.

Although in the domestic political field actors present their views as citizens, they typically represent collective actors such as different social classes, parties, professions, or branches of business, and those memberships are important for their constitution as agents and identities. In this respect, too, actors are motivated by transnational ideas and discourses, particularly because of international networks and associations established by such groups, whose local members introduce viewpoints and arguments to the domestic discussion.

A process of domestication may originate and take place in a number of fields. For instance, if the process leads to reform in the form of a new law, regulation or recommendation made at the national level, it typically passes through several organizational levels all the way to the everyday life of individual citizens, and in each context its implications are interpreted and negotiated. This means that the reform's eventual effects may turn into something other than what was originally planned, but it also means that the new ideas become familiar with the entire population and are integrated as part of the discourses by which practices related to the policy in question are conceived and debated (Alasuutari and Alasuutari, 2012). Second, the combination of comparison and competition and hence the idea of copying success, which leads to increased uniformity, may also originate at subnational levels, for instance among cities that adopt ideas from each other (Alasuutari, 2013).

Local actor roles may hence have or create a global dimension, so that even though decisions about reforms are made locally, the actor roles and their identities, such as political parties or professional associations, are the same in different domestic settings. The transformations of actors and fields caused by the domestication of global trends may mean that the new practices are established in a transnational context. Yet the nation-state framework remains central in these processes in several ways. Often these international activities are aimed at nation-states, for instance to establish agreements or to promote "best practices" for governments. If successful, they contribute to uniformity among nation-states, which means, however, not that their borders disappear or lose their meaning, but that they are strengthened by considerably affecting the conditions under which now transnational policies are to be realized. The case of the incorporation of a global model of human rights amid the drug wars of Colombia by Gallo-Cruz (Chapter 11) shows how these borders are strengthened despite the entry of international actors including non-governmental organizations (NGOs).

Naturalization as nationalization

After the turmoil and field battle triggered by the proposal of reforms to existing frameworks and practices, when a new status quo is achieved people quite soon get used to the way things are done; it is unnoticed, or considered as a natural and self-evident aspect of life. Although domestication means that exogenous models are introduced and that national frameworks and practices are synchronized with what is going on elsewhere, because the models in case have been domesticated into *their* daily lives, people tend to conceive of them as somehow inherently local. This is the case not only for policy models but also often for new catchwords that come to encompass all manners of existing activities, which evolve from something to think *about* into something to think *with* (Qadir and Alasuutari, 2013).

Some of the routinized practices, at some point created as an outcome of a process of domestication, may even be considered as characteristic features of the nation in question and emblems of a unique national culture. The notion of the 'German model' is a nice illustration of this. The re-democratization of West Germany after the Nazi regime took place under the guidance of the Allied countries, particularly the Americans: guidance that was later provided by the Marshall plan (Hogan, 1987; Junker, 2004). Yet, as soon as the German post-war economic miracle became world famous, the new social and economic order became known as the German model, and the credit for its formation was given to leading politicians, such as Ludwig Erhard, Germany's second chancellor. The German model also became a core foundational myth of the nation (Berndt, 2003). In other words, it was characterized as a unique configuration of international models, and hence attention to the international aspects and interaction was focused on the role of domestic actors and on the view of the German nation-state as a distinct entity. Hence local actors appeal to and construct a national trajectory of change so that while policies are synchronized with global trends, the idea of national uniqueness is cherished and reinforced.

The formation of public awareness of a genuinely national policy model may also be one upshot of international comparison. This is particularly the case when a nation-state is ranked high in international league tables. As was said above, in such cases the results of the comparison are not likely to result in public demands for reform, but instead they will attract public attention as a source of national pride and being a model country for the rest of the world. Obviously, what are believed to be the secrets behind the good results will be considered as principles that must also be honored in the future.

Domestication and global social change

This model of domestication by way of cross-national comparisons, domestic field battles and naturalization by nationalization, is of course simplified for the sake of clarity. We do not mean to suggest that we discard all assumptions about society as a system that is transformed by its inherent dynamism. Neither do we mean to argue that all change is brought about by international comparison and by policy changes made by governments. There certainly are mechanisms in the social fabric that make policy-makers look for solutions to problems, such as social unrest, that emerge from within a nation-state, just as mere diffusion can explain *some* trends in particular cases. We only argue that these explanations are far from comprehensive, and that public policy reforms are an important interface through which national paths are synchronized. Even if a problem is not constructed by comparing a nation-state to other states, solutions to emerging problems are often sought by studying how other countries have tackled similar problems.

The model of domestication entails the point that national policy-making synchronizes national trajectories, making nation-states adjust to ever new policy fashions. In this way it challenges previous world polity theory scholarship, which views interdependent decision-making as ever-growing isomorphism due to a saturation of the originally "Western" world culture of "modernity," as "world models" diffuse from centers to peripheries. We do not mean to entirely refute the historical story of globalization, but we stress that by virtue of the institutionalization of the nation-state system, world cultural values such as science, human rights, or national security have already spread throughout the world and guide national policy-making. However, at another level are the conceptual innovations that draw on these models, and these do indeed spread, mixing with each other and transforming into domesticated versions. These latter can be codified standards such as PISA or fashionable catchwords such as "economic competitiveness." They may emerge as supple, institutionally generated guidelines, such as formulations of a European social policy, discussed in Chapter 4, or organizational forms such as national bioethics committees. The circulation of these conceptual innovations, domesticated into local policies, make nation-states swim in formation and yet retain their notion of national uniqueness.

This approach to interdependent decision-making means that we do not see domestication as only "ritualized enactment" (Thomas, 2009) or "implementation" of global ideas by national polities. Rather, it is important to consider worldwide isomorphism as an ever-changing upshot of indeterminate national processes that continually also reinforce the sense of national ownership of policies.

Such a perspective necessarily challenges common scientific conceptions of power as not fully adequate to explain the current world society. In the view developed here, this world society consisting of nation-states is managed increasingly through epistemic governance, which works by making actors perceive the world and the current challenges similarly. In that sense, it is less important to look for power as a property of some "center" and more for power as a strategy, as "a network of relations, constantly in tension, in activity, rather than a privilege that one might possess" (Foucault, 1977, p. 26). Re-envisioning power in our perspective would thus highlight governance as ways by which actors work on people's wishes, aspirations and conceptions of reality, in order to affect their behavior. The nationalized constructions of conceptual innovations that in fact draw on globally present cultural models or assumptions, examined in this volume, illustrate the advantages of viewing governance in the stateless world society in this way.

Comparisons and domestic fields: contributions in this volume

The chapters in this book explore this framework of domestication with a variety of emphases. While all contributions are united by their bottom-up, national case perspective, and a broadly common methodology of discursive textual analysis, they represent the widest possible range of settings. They are grouped into two sections corresponding to the two overarching elements of domestication: cross-national comparisons and the entry of global ideas to the domestic field.

The chapters relating to cross-national comparisons all emphasize the point that domestic policy reforms are justified by what is going on in other nation-states, or how "our" nation is ranked in comparison with other countries. They underscore that nation-states are organized in the world polity as strategic actors that are socially constructed to look outward for "rational" and "competitive" policy development by way of comparisons. Each reform process is thus local but geared to producing synchronization with other states.

The chapters in the section on domestic field battles discuss what happens in the local field when a new policy model or idea is introduced. These chapters all highlight the paradoxical effect of a reform process: although it is often triggered by international comparison and justified by exogenous models, the focus on local politics makes it appear as entirely domestic event. The contributions have been expressly sought to highlight these aspects of domestication.

Cross-national comparisons

In Chapter 2, Pertti Alasuutari questions the myth of US exceptionalism by showing how it arises from a straightforward view of diffusion of policy models flowing from "centers" to "peripheries." By analyzing justifications of new legislation in parliamentary discussions in Argentina, Canada, Chile, Mexico, the UK, and the USA, Alasuutari points out the common rationales used to justify new legislation. The chapter illustrates not only implicit and explicit references to what is going on outside national borders being used as justifications, but also presents reasons for the differences between these countries in their reliance on such justifications.

Anu Kantola's contribution in Chapter 3 explores the domestication of the worldwide model of "global competitiveness" in national economies, focusing on Finland. Examining policy documents on national competitiveness, government manifestos from 1980 to 2011, and media reports, the chapter traces the importance of the very idea of comparisons and competition in national macroeconomic policy-making. Kantola underscores the national processes by which the global model of competitiveness has been used to gain political power within the nation-state, illustrating this in a multinational comparison. As above, the chapter illustrates the effectiveness of cross-national comparisons that rely on widely accepted models of economic policy, while at the same time building a national community in a state of economic competition with other nation-states.

In Chapter 4, Stefan Bernhard studies the Open Method of Coordination for social policy in the European Union, not with the common perspective that the alternative mechanism leads to policy-learning, but to show how it surrounds EU member states with a complex array of expectations that constitute a framework for legitimate action. Bernhard underlines the features of the mechanism that allow for nation-states to constantly develop in line with social expectations. The chapter stresses that the domestication of such global scripts for nation-state rationality in policy-making depends on the dynamic of power struggles in national fields that function as prisms for EU models, resulting in representational reconstructions in which national incumbents have the space to emphasize national idiosyncrasies as "comparative advantage." Bernhard's contribution highlights the utility of neoinstitutionalist perspectives in competitive comparisons when understanding social policy-making in Europe.

Remaining in the European Union, Sebastian Büttner discusses in Chapter 5 the emergence of new administrative regions in Poland to show that the "regional," far from being the site of original local culture and primary social integration, is already "global." Examining policy documents in Poland and the EU, Büttner demonstrates how Polish administrators rely on comparative information and external, professional consultants to institute regionalism as part of other worldwide models of economic competitiveness and "Europeanization." The chapter foregrounds the crucial role of "scientific expertise" in policy reforms, an expertise that almost invariably involves cross-national comparisons as justifications for the entirely national reform.

Ending the section, in Chapter 6 Marjaana Rautalin studies the paradoxical politics of Finnish curricular reform in the light of media publicity of the results of the PISA study, where the country ranked top. Unpacking media reports of the PISA results and of ongoing educational reforms in Finland, Rautalin shows how it is possible to follow through an educational reorganization that is entirely at odds with how national educational experts explain "success" in the international ranking. The contribution shows that favorable international ranking may, in fact, hurt reform-minded domestic actors, and that even contradictory reforms are possible in the face of cross-national comparisons as long as those actors maintain distinct fields on which to fight for their interests. Rautalin's contribution brings out the importance of the mediated public sphere for the domestication of global trends in modern societies where comparisons are utilized in national policy-making.

Domestic field battles and naturalization

The section on domestic field battles is opened in Chapter 7 with Daniel Maman and Zeev Rosenhek's discussion on the Central Bank of Israel's struggle for independence, which challenges mainstreams notions of this dominant global model being implemented as the straightforward result of forces operating at the global "level." Their detailed process-tracing analysis of the intensive intra-state struggle over the legal status of the Israeli Central Bank, which took place between the mid-1990s and 2010, underlines local political dynamics underpinning the processes of domestication of global institutional models. Maman and Rosenhek highlight the power relations between state agencies and the strategies that they deploy for advancing their interests, underlining that globalization does not function as a causal factor determining changes at the state level, but rather as a political resource mobilized by local actors to promote institutional transformations. Again, the contribution highlights the new insights that emerge from unpacking apparent global isomorphism from a bottom-up national perspective of synchronization.

In Chapter 8, Keita Takayama undertakes a genealogical study of the idea of *ikiru chikara* ("zest for living"), in educational policy reforms in Japan after the PISA "shock" in 2003. The chapter illustrates how disappointing comparative results are utilized by reform-minded political figures to manufacture a "crisis" and then to legitimize a set of contested reform plans against "global standards." By analyzing Japanese policy documents since the mid-1990s to trace the shifting articulations of one particular policy keyword, Takayama highlights the importance of the politics of ambiguity in keywords as central to domestic field battles, allowing governments to speak to competing political interests simultaneously. The contribution demonstrates the importance not only of catchwords but also of global benchmarking in a domestic policy field battle.

In Chapter 9 Ali Qadir discusses the relation between the hugely significant higher education reforms in Pakistan in 2002 and the recent global model put forward by UNESCO and the World Bank. By undertaking a detailed reading of the two reports, Qadir demonstrates how the Pakistani reform cannot be seen as a mere "enactment" of the global model, but rather a nationalized construct. The analysis foregrounds the importance of the weight of history, often by way of inter-textual references, and of conceptual abstractions—or "floating signifiers"—in the national processes of interpretation that justify the reform as entirely natural. The contribution underlines one way in which a national historical trajectory is constructed in national policy-making while taming foreign ideas.

Jukka Syvätera and Pertti Alasuutari, in Chapter 10, analyze the establishment of the National Advisory Board on Health Care Ethics in Finland as an example of the domestication of the transnational model of "ethical policy advice" in the form of national bioethics committees. The authors analyze policy documents and parliamentary discussions to highlight interest-based rationales in justifying such a body in the absence of any obvious functional need. Syvätera and Alasuutari's account foregrounds the local field battles that can shape the domestication process and help tame a foreign model, even though there is no immediate opposition to the idea itself.

Finally, in Chapter 11 Selina Gallo-Cruz documents the domestic development of institutionalized human rights in Colombia amid the "dirty war" of drugs and paramilitary forces. By providing a longitudinal overview of the process, Gallo-Cruz shows how an entirely global repertoire of human rights discourse becomes embedded in a complex national context by way of transnationally linked domestic actors with deep interests in the local field. The chapter underscores the importance of non-state actors in a wide-ranging account of the domestication process, against the overwhelming backdrop of violence and emergent democracy.

References

Acharya, A. (2004). How Ideas Spread: Whose Norms Matter? Norm Localization and Institutional Change in Asian Regionalism. *International Organization, 58*(2), 239–275.

Alasuutari, P. (2013). Spreading Global Models and Enhancing Banal Localism: The Case of Local Government Cultural Policy Development. *International Journal of Cultural Policy, 19*(1), 103–119.

Alasuutari, P. and Alasuutari, M. (2012). The Domestication of Early Childhood Education Plans in Finland. *Global Social Policy, 12*(2), 109–128.

Beck, S. (2004). Localising Global Change in Germany. In S. Jasanoff and M.L. Martello (eds), *Earthly Politics. Local And Global in Environmental Governance* (pp. 173–194). Cambridge, MA: MIT Press.

Beck, U. and Sznaider, N. (2006). Unpacking Cosmopolitanism for the Social Sciences: A Research Agenda. *British Journal of Sociology, 57*(1), 1–23.

Berndt, C. (2003). Territorialized Key Words and Methodological Nationalism. *European Urban and Regional Studies, 10*(4), 283–295.

Billig, M. (1995). *Banal Nationalism*. London: Sage.

Boli, J. (1987). World polity sources of expanding state authority and organizations, 1870–1970. In G.M. Thomas, J.W. Meyer, F.O. Ramirez, and J. Boli (eds), *Institutional Structure* (pp. 71–91). Beverley Hills, CA: Sage.

Boli, J. and Thomas, G.M. (eds) (1999). *Constructing World Culture: International Nongovernmental Organizations Since 1875*. Stanford, CA: Stanford University Press.

Bourdieu, P. (1977). *Outline of a Theory of Practice*. Cambridge: Cambridge University Press.

Bourdieu, P. (1984). *Distinction: A Social Critique of the Judgement of Taste*. London: Routledge and Kegan Paul.

Bourdieu, P. (1991). Political Representation: Elements for a theory of the Political Field. In J. B. Thompson (ed.), *Language and Symbolic Power* (pp. 171–202). Cambridge: Polity Press.

Bourdieu, P. (1993). *The Field of Cultural Production: Essays on Art and Literature*. New York: Columbia University Press.

Bourdieu, P. (1995). *The Logic of Practice*. Stanford, CA: Stanford University Press.

Bourdieu, P. (1996). *The Rules of Art: Genesis and Structure of the Literary Field*. Cambridge: Polity Press.

Bradley, K. and Ramirez, F.O. (1996). World Polity Promotion of Gender Parity: Women's Share of Higher Education, 1965–1985. *Research in Sociology of Education and Socialization, 11*, 63–91.

Callon, M. (1986). Some Elements of a Sociology of Translation: Domestication of the Scallops and the Fishermen of St Brieuc Bay. In J. Law (ed.), *Power, Action, and Belief: A New Sciology of Knowledge?* (pp. 196–223). London: Routledge & Kegan Paul

Chernilo, D. (2006). Social Theory's Methodological Nationalism: Myth and Reality. *European Journal of Social Theory, 9*(1), 5–22.

Coram, B.T. (1994). Structural Dependence: A Simple Marxian Analysis of the Limits to Redistribution with International Capital Transfers. *British Journal of Political Science, 24*(1), 139–148.

Cortell, A.P. and Davis, J.W., Jr (2000). Understanding the Domestic Impact of International Norms: A Research Agenda. *International Studies Review, 2*(1), 65–87.

Czarniawska-Joerges, B. and Sevón, G. (1996). *Translating Organizational Change.* Berlin: Walter de Gruyter.

Diehl, P.F. and Frederking, B. (2010). *The Politics of Global Governance: International Organizations in an Interdependent World* (4th ed.). Boulder, CO: Lynne Rienner Publishers.

DiMaggio, P.J. and Powell, W.W. (1983). The Iron Cage Revisited: Institutional Isomorphism and Collective Rationality in Organizational Fields. *American Sociological Review, 48*(2), 147–160.

Djelic, M.-L. and Sahlin-Andersson, K. (eds) (2006). *Transnational Governance: Institutional Dynamics of Regulation.* Cambridge: Cambridge University Press.

Dolowitz, D. and Marsh, D. (1996). Who Learns What From Whom: A Review of the Policy Transfer Literature. *Political Studies, 44*(2), 343–357.

Drori, G.S., Meyer, J.W., and Hwang, H. (2006). Introduction. In G. S. Drori, J. W. Meyer, and H. Hwang (eds), *Globalization and Organization* (pp. 1–22). Oxford: Oxford University Press.

Elliott, M.A. (2007). Human Rights and the Triumph of the Individual in World Culture. *Cultural Sociology, 1*(3), 343–363.

Ertl, H. (2006). Educational Standards and the Changing Discourse on Education: The Reception and Consequences of the PISA Study in Germany. *Oxford Review of Education, 32*(5), 619–634.

Foucault, M. (1977). *Discipline and Punish: The Birth of the Prison.* London: Penguin Books.

Foucault, M. (1980). *The History of Sexuality Vol. 1. An Introduction.* New York: Vintage Books.

Foucault, M. (2007). *Security, Territory, Population: Lectures at the College de France, 1977–78.* Basingstoke: Palgrave Macmillan.

Frank, D.J., Hironaka, A., and Schofer, E. (2000). The Nation-State and Natural Environment over the Twentieth Century. *American Sociological Review, 65*(1), 96–116.

Friedman, T.L. (2005). *The World is Flat: A Brief History of the Twenty-first Century.* New York: Farrar, Strauss and Giroux.

Gans, H.J. (1979). *Deciding What's News: A Study of CBS Evening News, NBC Nightly News, Newsweek, and Time* (1st edn). New York: Pantheon Books.

Goldstone, J.A. (1998). Initial Conditions, General Laws, Path Dependence, and Explanation in Historical Sociology. *American Journal of Sociology, 104*(3), 829–845.

Greener, I. (2002). Understanding NHS Reform: The Policy-Transfer, Social Learning, and Path-Dependency Perspectives. *Governance, 15*(2), 161.

Grek, S. (2009). Governing by Numbers: The PISA "Effect" in Europe. *Journal of Education Policy, 24*(1), 23–37.

Gurevitch, M., Levy, M.R., and Roeh, I. (1991). The Global Newsroom: Convergences and Diversities in the Globalisation of Television News. In P. Dahlgren and C. Sparks (eds), *Communications and Citizenship: Journalism and the Public Sphere in the New Media Age* (pp. 195–216). London: Routledge.

Hall, J. (1986). *Power and Liberties.* New York: Penguin.

Hannerz, U. (1987). The World in Creolization. *Africa, 57*(4), 546–559.

Harvey, D. (2005). *A Brief History of Neoliberalism.* Oxford, New York: Oxford University Press.

Hogan, M.J. (1987). *The Marshall Plan: America, Britain, and the Reconstruction of Western Europe, 1947–1952.* Cambridge: Cambridge University Press.

Huntington, S.P. (1993). The Clash of Civilizations? *Foreign Affairs, 72*(3), 22–49.

Huntington, S.P. (1996). *The Clash of Civilizations and the Remaking of World Order.* New York: Simon and Schuster.

Junker, D. (ed.). (2004). *The United States and Germany in the Era of the Cold War, 1945–1990: A Handbook.* New York: Cambridge University Press.

Kraidy, M. (2005). *Hybridity, Or the Cultural Logic of Globalization.* Philadelphia, PN: Temple University Press.

Levitt, P. and Merry, S. (2009). Vernacularization on the ground: local uses of global women's rights in Peru, China, India and the United States. *Global Networks, 9*(4), 441–461.

Liebes, T. (1992). Our War/Their War: Comparing the Intifadeh and the Gulf War on US and Israeli Television. *Critical Studies in Mass Communication, 9*(1), 44.

Meyer, J.W. (2000). Globalization: Sources and Effects on National States and Societies. *International Sociology, 15*(2), 233–248.

Meyer, J.W. (2004). The Nation as Babbitt: How Countries Conform. *Contexts, 3*(3), 42–47.

Meyer, J.W. (2007). Globalization: Theory and Trends. *International Journal of Comparative Sociology, 48*(4), 261–273.

Meyer, J.W. (2010). World Society, Institutional Theories, and the Actor. *Annual Review of Sociology, 36*, 1–20.

Meyer, J.W., Boli, J., Thomas, G.M., and Ramirez, F.O. (1997). World Society and the Nation-State. *American Journal of Sociology, 103*(1), 144–181.

Meyer, J.W., Ramirez, F.O., and Soysal, Y. (1992). World Expansion of Mass Education. *Sociology of Education, 65*(2), 128–149.

Meyrowitz, J. (1986). *No Sense of Place: The Impact of Electronic Media on Social Behavior.* New York: Oxford University Press.

Nossek, H. (2004). Our News and Their News. *Journalism, 5*(3), 343–368.

Pettenger, M.E. (2007). The Netherlands' Climate Change Policy: Constructing Themselves/Constructiong Climate Change. In M.E. Pettenger (ed.), *The Social Construction of Climate Change* (pp. 51–74). Farnham: Ashgate.

Pieterse, J.N. (1995). Globalization as Hybridization. In M. Featherstone, S. Lash, and R. Robertson (eds), *Global Modernities* (pp. 45–68). London: Sage.

Powell, W.W. and DiMaggio, P.J. (eds) (1991). *The New Institutionalism in Organizational Analysis.* Chicago, IL: University of Chicago Press.

Qadir, A. and Alasuutari, P. (2013). Taming terror: Domestication of the war on terror in the Pakistan media. *Asian Journal of Communication, Online first.* doi:10.1080/012929 86.2013.764905.

Ramirez, F.O. and Weiss, J. (1979). The political incorporation of women. In J. W. Meyer and M. T. Hannan (eds), *National Development and the World System* (pp. 238–249). Chicago, IL: University of Chicago Press.

Rautalin, M. and Alasuutari, P. (2007). The Curse of Success: The Impact of the OECD PISA Study on the Discourses of the Teaching Profession in Finland. *European Educational Research Journal, 7*(4), 349–364.

Ringarp, J. and Rothland, M. (2010). Is the Grass Always Greener? The Effect of the PISA Results on Education Debates in Sweden and Germany. *European Educational Research Journal, 9*(3), 422–430.

Ritzer, G. (1996). *The McDonaldization of Society: An Investigation into the Changing Character of Contemporary Social Life* (Rev. edn). Thousand Oaks, CA: Pine Forge Press.

Ritzer, G. (2004). *The Globalization of Nothing.* Thousand Oaks, CA: Pine Forge Press.

Sahlin-Andersson, K. (1996). Imitating by Editing Success: The Construction of Organ-ization Fields. In B. Czarniawska-Joerges and G. Sevón (eds), *Translating Organizational Change* (pp. 69–92). Berlin: Walter de Gruyter.

Schmid, A. and Götze, R. (2009). Cross-national policy learning in health system reform: The case of Diagnosis Related Groups. *International Social Security Review, 62*(4), 21–40.

Schofer, E. and Meyer, J.W. (2005). Worldwide Expansion of Higher Education in the 20th Century. *American Sociological Review, 70*, 898–920.

Simmons, B.A., Dobbin, F., and Garrett, G. (eds) (2008). *The Global Diffusion of Markets and Democracy*. Cambridge: Cambridge University Press.

Stoddard, E. and Cornwell, G.H. (1999). Cosmopolitan or Mongrel? Creolite, Hybridity and "Douglarisation" in Trinidad. *European Journal of Cultural Studies, 2*(3), 331–353.

Takayama, K. (2008). The Politics of International League Tables: PISA in Japan's Achievement Crisis Debate. *Comparative Education, 44*(4), 387–407.

Tervonen-Goncalves, L. (2012). From Averages To Best Performers: Use of Comparisons in Identity Formation. *Critical Polity Studies, 6*(3), 304–323. doi:10.1080/194601 71.2012.717784.

Thomas, G.M. (2009). World Polity, World Culture, World Society. *International Political Sociology, 3*(1), 115–119.

Waldow, F. (2009). What PISA Did and Did Not Do: Germany after the "PISA-shock." *European Educational Research Journal, 8*(3), 476–483.

Wallerstein, I.M. (2004). *World-Systems Analysis: An Introduction*. Durham, NC: Duke University Press.

Wilkinson, D. (1999). Unipolarity Without Hegemony. *International Studies Review, 1*(2), 141–172.

Part I
Cross-national comparisons

2 Interdependent decision-making in practice

Justification of new legislation in six nation-states[1]

Pertti Alasuutari

Introduction

Although it is quite obvious that national governments' decision-making is interdependent—i.e. that "policy decisions in a given country are systematically conditioned by prior policy choices made in other countries" (Simmons, Dobbin, and Garrett, 2008, p. 7), there is lack of research on how this actually takes place. We need to know better how it is that information about the acts of other national governments, the views held within the international community on rational and acceptable policies and about the global context as a whole, become part of the domestic setting in which policy decisions are made. The scarcity of research on this question is quite peculiar when viewed against the fact that in many nation-states the records that document the law-making process are readily available. For instance the data analyzed in this chapter—the minutes of the parliamentary debates through which new legislation passes—are public documents in practically all nation-states. Yet only a few researchers have studied these materials in order to study the rationales used in debating new legislation.

The dearth of previous research in this area does not mean that there is lack of interest in how governments are affected in their policy-making by their counterparts in other countries. It is only that this phenomenon has normally been operationalized as an object of research by studying the diffusion of policies across national borders. As part of the proliferation of research and theorizing on globalization, defined as growth of cross-border flows of capital, goods, people, and ideas (Foster, 1991; Iwabuchi, 2008; McGrew, 1998), the origins and directions of the flow of models have become an increasingly popular object of research in recent decades. For instance, Ritzer (1996, 1998) has discussed the spread of the chain of McDonald's restaurants as an example of standards and management ideas originating in the USA. The typical picture emerging from empirical studies in this research tradition is that developing or "third world" states conform to models flowing from the "West" (see e.g. Bradley and Ramirez, 1996; Meyer, Ramirez, and Soysal, 1992; Shandra, 2007; Tsutsui and Wotipka, 2004).

As to why ideas spread, four different causal mechanisms have been identified: coercion, competition, learning, and emulation (Dobbin, Simmons, and Garrett, 2007; Simmons et al., 2008). Evidence on these reasons is however

based on cross-national comparative statistical analysis, which is why it is operationalized in particular ways. For instance, to support the hypothesis that competition accounts for policy diffusion, "a policy innovation would have to be
shown to be conditioned by the policies of competitors for the resources in play"
(Simmons et al., 2008, p. 24). In other words, although the researchers talk about
nation-states' interdependent decision-making, the rationales through which
policy-makers have arrived at their decisions are not studied. The assumptions
about these four causal factors are based on circumstantial evidence, and how
actors actually arrive at their decisions remains a black box.

Policy transfer research has shed some light on this darkness. The studies
have shown that transferring policies or norms from donors to recipients is far
from a simple event. To succeed, "norm-takers" need to be able to build congru-
ence between transnational norms and local beliefs and practices (Acharya,
2004), and to construct the proposed policy as a great success, and suitable to the
recipient's institutional context (Cook, 2008; Dolowitz and Marsh, 1996; Evans
and Davies, 1999). Policy transfer research has also paid attention to international governmental organizations such as the Organisation for Co-operation
and Development (OECD) and the World Bank, and non-governmental organizations such as Transparency International and Freedom House as cultural inter-
mediaries, consultants of national governments, and agents in global governance
(Cerny, 2012; Lowenheim, 2007; Mahon, 2009, 2010; Mahon and McBride,
2008; Woodward, 2009). In addition to promoting "best practices" and giving
recommendations, they measure and track the quality of governance among
states by "governance indicators" (Buduru and Pal, 2010). Yet the focus of these
studies on the transfer of particular policies and on the actors that act as mediators in transmitting policies between states has meant that the way interdependent decision-making actually takes place has been neglected.

This chapter aims to fill out that gap by studying nation-states' decision-making
in practice. The object of research is not the diffusion of particular models or the
factors that affect it but rather how national parliaments negotiate new legislation
and how the actions of other countries are part of those debates. Since it is obvious
that nation-states take other states' policies in consideration when making national
decisions, this chapter highlights how it works by analyzing the rationales used in
proposing reforms and debating them. How are prior policy decisions of other
countries brought to the attention of policy-makers? What is the role of such
information in motivating and justifying reforms and new legislation? Are there
big differences between nation-states in this respect; for instance, are policy-makers
in dominant countries more reluctant to propose adopting ideas from others? These
are the questions addressed by analyzing argumentation in policy making in six
nation-states: Argentina, Canada, Chile, Mexico, the UK, and the USA.

By studying how reforms are debated, this chapter also sheds light on the
domestication of global trends—that is, the ways in which policy-making is made
to seem uniquely national although new laws contribute to synchronizing national
paths with each other. As the analysis will show, evoking the national interest and
the nation as the self-evident object of identification is key to this magic.

The chapter is organized as follows. After discussing what it entails to study interdependent decision-making from the viewpoint of argumentation, I introduce the data and methodology. The empirical section shows how reforms are promoted and in what ways references to other countries are used as justification in the parliaments of the six countries studied here. On the basis of a typology created, I discuss statistical differences between the six countries.

Interdependent decision-making as argumentation

Viewed from the perspective of policy diffusion research, studying the political debates in which national policies are decided may seem pointless. If the actual behavior of a nation-state is considered as proof of a "causal mechanism" such as coercion, it seems irrelevant what the actors think or how decisions are justified. This is indeed the stance taken toward actorhood in the policy diffusion tradition. For instance, the neoinstitutionalist world polity theory emphasizes that individual and institutional actors and their identities are constituted by world culture, which is why actors unthinkingly enact global models and scripts. Such models comprise world culture, the spread of which is considered as the reason for the remarkable isomorphism found in the modern world (Meyer, Boli, Thomas, and Ramirez, 1997; Meyer, Krücken, and Drori, 2009). According to world polity scholars, these models are rooted in nineteenth-century Western culture but since globalized, carried by the infrastructure of world society, and expressed in the multiple ways particular groups relate to universal ideals (Lechner and Boli, 2005, p. 6).

Local politics is however interesting and important from the domestication perspective, which regards global changes as outcomes of contingent historical processes. Instead of considering world culture as some kind of gyroscope that pervades the world and makes actors and organizations increasingly isomorphic, the domestication framework stresses that the turns individual actors and states and the world society as a whole take are not dictated by ready-made scripts. Rather, it is important to make a distinction between the already globalized basic world cultural values and principles (such as science, equality or the national interest), institutionalized in the nation-state system, and the global spread of ever-new fashions, standards, and catchwords to which nation-states adapt in their policy-making. The domestication of such conceptual innovations does not mean that nation-states become increasingly similar, but makes national decision-making interdependent so that national paths are synchronized with each other.

This perspective makes a corrective to the underdeveloped notion of agency and the rudimentary concept of culture within world polity theory. Since the some 200 nation-states are institutionally more or less copies of each other with a government, ministries and many other private and public institutions, it is obvious that they comprise a cultural system. However, contrary to assumptions in many texts representing world polity theory, it does not mean that world culture is a unified set of values, and scripts deduced from them. Rather, as a detailed treatment of the ideals, principles, and underlying premises used in argumentation will show, people's shared values are mutually contradictory so that moral dilemmas are the rule rather than an exception (MacIntyre, 1981). Even if participants reach an agreement about the stress laid on potentially conflicting values such as individual freedom and equality, they may well disagree on how to translate the principles into practice.

It is also important to stress that studying justifications used in decision-making does not equate to scrutinizing people's motives. Since political decisions are made in public forums, with the parliament as the final and most important one, justifications tell us what is politically correct or morally appropriate. From the constructionist and neoinstitutionalist perspective employed here, the fact that we have no access to the ultimate reasons or innermost motives of decision-makers is not a problem but rather an important starting point. Public justifications are interesting precisely because they reflect the culture of world polity. We may well speculate on the politicians' real motives and underlying interests, but the public justifications are considered as rational and appropriate, in concert with the virtues that the world cultural system honors.

Besides, world culture should not be conceived as containing only generally honored values and principles. It also comprises shared knowledge about less virtuous motives such as individual gains or narrow group interests, the expression of which is not considered appropriate or a successful strategy by those who promote a new policy. Hence policy-makers need to appear sincere in defending appropriate values and motives against others' healthy suspicions.

As world polity theory stresses, in that sense world culture constitutes actors (Meyer, 2010), but yet it leaves a lot of latitude for local differences. Therefore it is even more fascinating that nation-states end up synchronizing national trajectories with those of other countries. This is not only because world culture permeates local realities; it is also because states and individual actors keep a keen eye on what is taking place in other states and react to them in their policies.

This perspective on the synchronization of national trajectories puts world-wide models in a new light. While the mainstream policy diffusion research treats policy models as objective givens, the spread of which to different countries constitutes the default research design, this perspective emphasizes that local "policy entrepreneurs" (Béland, 2005; Dolowitz and Marsh, 2000; Hulme, 2006), rather than exogenous models, are the primary actors through which national trajectories are synchronized. From this perspective, domestic actors do not just passively react to exogenous models or pressures, but rather advance their own views and interests by directing their compatriots' attention to what is going on elsewhere, constructing policies adopted in other countries as a distinct model and presenting evidence of their success (Acharya, 2004; Alasuutari, 2013; Callon, 1986; Cook, 2008; Cortell and Davis, 2000; Dolowitz and Marsh, 1996; Evans and Davies, 1999), hence translating global ideas to local contexts (Czarniawska-Joerges and Sevón, 1996, 2005). Furthermore, when the domestic debates related to new legislation are studied as an interface through which changes taking place in different nation-states may be synchronized, it becomes clear that these debates are seldom about enacting a particular, narrowly defined policy or model. Rather, they are about a problem or a new item introduced to the national political agenda; a problem whose treatment in the domestic context means that the national agenda and discourse in the area are synchronized with those in other nation-states.

The world cultural system thus comprises two basic aspects. On the one hand world culture consists of shared assumptions, values and principles, stemming from and guiding the institutional order of world polity. They are used as premises in justifying policies in different organizational contexts, for instance in national parliaments. On the other hand there are new ideas and models circulating throughout the globe, the construction and promotion of which also appeal to the shared premises.

Although permeated by the same world culture, there seem to be differences in the way in which national trajectories are synchronized with those of other countries. It could be hypothesized that in some countries it is commonplace to appeal to the models adopted in other countries or to the ranking of the country in international comparison as justification for a reform, whereas in others such references are rare. This means that reforms are justified by other means, for instance by referring to an alarming development or to statistical data about inequality in the country in question. It does not necessarily mean that such nation-states pay no attention to international developments; it only means that such comparisons are not actively used as grounds for reforms in public discussion. We could talk about differing "political cultures"—that is, local sets of default expectations about valid and acceptable modes of argumentation.

For instance, the US political culture seems to be less sympathetic to justifications appealing to what is taking place in other countries. Such reluctance to learn from the experience of others could be attributed to the paradigm of US exceptionalism,[2] according to which the USA is so different from other countries that models adopted by other countries are hardly applicable to it. As expert interviewees in Martens and Dobbins' (2010) study of American education policy say, the image predominates that the USA is somehow different from the rest of the world and that is why it is not fair or reasonable to compare it to other countries or to expect it to learn from other systems. Furthermore, it could be hypothesized that US political culture is less approving of references to other countries because in the USA it is commonly assumed that it is the leading country. Therefore, the fact that a policy has originated elsewhere may not be considered as a strong justification for adopting the same model because there is a conviction that the US model is more rational and efficient.

Although the paradigm of American exceptionalism is an old one, thus far it has not been tested empirically. This makes the current study particularly important because the data allow us to analyze the differences and similarities in the ways in which new legislation in justified in the six countries compared. More generally, since these six countries represent two language areas and differ in their affluence and in their economic and cultural integration with the rest of the world (see Table 2.1), it is interesting to see whether those differences seem to have a bearing on justifications used in political decision-making.

Table 2.1 GDP per capita and share of international trade of the countries compared

Country	GDP per capita (US$)[1]	Share of international trade in GDP (%)[2]
Argentina	10,942	n.a.
Canada	50,345	34.3
Chile	14,394	n.a.
Mexico	10,047	29.4
UK	39,038	30.4
USA	48,112	15.2

Sources
1 World Bank, 2011.
2 Organisation for Economic Co-operation and Development, 2011.

Data and methodology

Basically the way in which new legislation is debated and created in so-called Western democracies is quite uniform. That is because parliamentary democracy is part of world culture, the culture of world polity institutionalized in world cultural models: the parliament, government and democratic process of political decision-making being an essential part of them. However, there are slightly different versions of the way in which the passing of laws takes place. Comparing Canada and the UK is quite easy because of the long colonial link between these countries, which is why both countries represent the so-called Westminster system. The US parliamentary system also has a historic link to the UK, but as a federal state applying a bicameral presidential system it has its own features. In that respect the US system is closer to Argentina, Chile, and Mexico, which also apply a presidential system in which the president is the leader of the cabinet of ministers. However, despite these differences in all the six countries compared, a floor debate on a bill, often called the second reading, is a common feature. That is why parliamentary debates are an apparent object of analysis when comparing argumentation in law-making.

The data analyzed here comprise parliamentary debates of government bills from the six countries compared during the period 2001–2012. From each country, a sample of bills was collected: 61 debates from Argentina, 61 from Canada, 68 from Chile, 65 from Mexico, 84 from the UK, and 63 from the USA. The total amount of bills analyzed is 402. The sampling method could be characterized as stratified purposive random sampling. The objective in picking out the cases was to spread the roughly 60 debates chosen from each country as evenly as possible through the period. The second objective was to pick debates from different policy areas to maximize the range of arguments used and also to enable studying cross-sectoral differences in the justifications. On the other hand, due to institutional differences there is no self-evident, uniform division into different policy areas that could be used in deciding which sectors to choose. Instead, the breakdown of the cases into ten policy areas presented in Table 2.2 is in itself an interpretation and approximation. Furthermore, we avoided choosing debates on government bills that were only technical amendments to an existing law, in which case discussions were often very brief. There are also significant differences in the way parliamentary documents are archived and in how well the search functions work, which all had a bearing on how easy it was to see the pool of debates from which to choose the cases. Because of the sampling criteria and technical conditions, the selection of cases could not be conducted blindly, but sampling was random in the sense that there were no additional criteria guiding the choice of cases. The breakdown of the debates to different policy areas and years is presented in Tables 2.2 and 2.3.

As a text corpus the research material is extensive, running to thousands of pages, all of which are available online on the web pages of the national parliaments in question. In the data analysis, the interest has been on different modes of justification for or against the legislation in question. The different forms of justification found in the data were arrived at inductively through a qualitative approach that makes use of rhetorical analysis (Perelman, 1982). In other words, the analysis is not guided by any predefined theory about the ways in which new legislation is—or should be—justified in national parliaments. Following another fundamental principle of qualitative research (see for example Alasuutari, Bickman and Brannen, 2008), the objective was to create a categorization that applies to all cases. In selecting examples about these modes of justification in the next section, the idea is not to present "typical" cases or those that fit well into the categorization, but rather to deal with and discuss the internal variation within each category.

Considering the way in which the data sampling was conducted, it is obvious that the interpretations cannot rely on minor statistical differences between variables or on multivariate analysis, which aims to detect complex causal paths allegedly responsible for national or other differences in the data. On the other hand, there is no reason to assume that the rough differences found between the countries in the frequency of different modes of justification could be due to skewed sampling.

Debating reforms in the transnational framework

When we look at the parliamentary debates in the countries studied here, on closer scrutiny they are much alike regardless of the nation-state in question. The modes of justification and figures of speech are very similar, with slight variations in rhetorical style and emphasis due to differences in the domestic configuration of the field of parties, the degree of independence of different parts of the country, and the way in which parliamentary work is organized. In this sense we are at the very core of world culture, institutionalized in the system of regional states, each of which contains the same basic institutions and in which argumentation on policy-making is pretty similar.

There are three main elements or groups of arguments in the justification, reflecting the basic premises that stem from the institutional conditions of the work of national parliaments. The first one is the underlining assumption that the proposed measures serve the interests of the nation. The second group of arguments

Table 2.2 The breakdown of debates into different policy areas (%)

Policy area	Canada		UK		USA		Argentina		Chile		Mexico		Total	
Civic	5	8.2	13	15.5	2	3.2	13	21.3	12	17.6	9	13.8	54	13.4
Consumption	6	9.8	15	17.9	5	7.9	2	3.3	6	8.8	9	13.8	43	10.7
Crime	2	3.3	11	13.1	0	0.0	7	11.5	15	22.11	11	16.9	46	11.4
Education	0	0.0	5	6.0	6	9.5	0	0.0	3	4.4	1	1.5	15	3.7
Employment	0	0.0	3	3.6	6	9.5	1	1.6	2	2.9	0	0.0	12	3.0
Environment	7	11.5	10	11.9	7	11.1	1	1.6	3	4.4	6	9.2	34	8.5
Fiscal	9	14.8	4	4.8	5	7.9	22	36.1	10	14.7	17	26.2	67	16.7
Foreign and security	5	8.2	4	4.8	10	15.9	8	13.1	7	10.3	9	13.8	43	10.7
Health	8	13.1	4	4.8	4	6.3	0	0.0	0	0.0	0	0.0	16	4.0
Science and technology	9	14.8	0	0.0	2	3.2	3	4.9	1	1.5	0	0.0	15	3.7
Social	10	16.4	15	17.9	16	25.4	4	6.6	9	13.2	3	4.6	57	14.2
Total	61	100.0	84	100.0	63	100.0	61	100.0	68	100.0	65	100.0	402	100.0

Table 2.3 The breakdown of debates into different years (%)

Year		Country						
		Canada	UK	USA	Argentina	Chile	Mexico	Total
2001		5	10	5	5	10	10	45
		8.2	11.9	7.9	8.2	14.7	15.4	11.2
2002		1	7	8	8	9	5	38
		1.6	8.3	12.7	13.1	13.2	7.7	9.5
2003		5	8	8	9	10	8	48
		8.2	9.5	12.7	14.8	14.7	12.3	11.9
2004		7	10	9	6	6	5	43
		11.5	11.9	14.3	9.8	8.8	7.7	10.7
2005		5	11	6	2	5	3	32
		8.2	13.1	9.5	3.3	7.4	4.6	8.0
2006		4	0	4	7	3	5	23
		6.6	0.0	6.3	11.5	4.4	7.7	5.7
2007		3	8	5	5	5	3	29
		4.9	9.5	7.9	8.2	7.4	4.6	7.2
2008		3	7	6	7	4	7	34
		4.9	8.3	9.5	11.5	5.9	10.8	8.5
2009		14	4	5	3	4	3	33
		23.0	4.8	7.9	4.9	5.9	4.6	8.2
2010		13	8	2	6	4	5	38
		21.3	9.5	3.2	9.8	5.9	7.7	9.5
2011		1	10	4	3	4	4	26
		1.6	11.9	6.3	4.9	5.9	6.2	6.5
2012		0	1	1	0	4	7	13
		0.0	1.2	1.6	0.0	5.9	10.8	3.2
Total		61	84	63	61	68	65	402
		100.0	100.0	100.0	100.0	100.0	100.0	100.0

comprises justifications that aim to convince the audience of the existence, scope and gravity of a problem or a need for change. The third comprises argumentation on the rationality, efficiency and morality of the proposed solution.

In all these instances, speakers may evoke the international community within which national decision-making takes place. They may appeal to the same principles of rationality, to rules of and commitments toward the international community, to assumptions about general laws of development, to international comparisons, and to experiences from other countries.

Evoking the international community and hence the global culture of world society is not always conscious and explicit, but open references to what is going on outside the national borders are common. To simplify, I suggest we can identify five different ways in which references to other countries are an explicit mode of justification. These are international comparisons, international treaties or norms, exogenous policy models, models considered as something that other countries should adopt, and the nation's reputation.

International comparisons are typically used as justification by pointing out that the nation is not doing well enough in comparison with other countries or with its proper reference group. Invoking the international comparative perspective on a policy area can be quite blunt, clearly meant to show that reforms are needed. Below is an example from the UK:

> The second function of the NHS is that of the delivery of health care, which is where the NHS falls down. Its delivery is poor. Our outcomes are unacceptable. The chance of surviving stomach cancer in the United Kingdom for five years is only about a quarter of the chance in Germany and the chance of surviving lung cancer for five years in the United Kingdom is half of the chance in Germany. Life expectancy in this country—the world's fourth biggest economy—is 19th in the world, similar to that in Turkey.
>
> (Parliament of UK, 2001)

International treaties or norms may appear as part of a debate on a reform in a number of ways. First, keeping the commitments the country has made may be presented as a matter of honor and correspondingly, a country that fails to keep its promises may be criticized. Second, the fact that a principle has been given the status of an international norm can be used as grounds for arguing that it is a value that the nation needs to respect. Therefore, removing a contradiction between national legislation and the international convention can be presented as a strong argument:

> Conscientious objection exists in 42 countries with conscription armies. This mode is in the United Nations resolution on military service, in international agreements and legislations of Argentina, Paraguay, Peru, Italy, France, England, and so on ... Therefore, I appeal to approve the project ... for indeed it helps to modernize the military service in our country.
>
> (Parliament of Chile, 2004)

The third type of reference to the world outside the nation-state in question is a reference to a model adopted elsewhere. Speakers may refer to its success in other countries, or they may compare the ways in which a similar reform has been done in different countries and suggest a solution that makes use of "best practices," the evidence of which may stem from other countries directly or from a report in which different national policies are reviewed:

> That experience of a coalition government, unprecedented in Argentina, did not work as in the brother country of Chile. In that country, it has been the instrument of democracy because it allowed its consolidation. The Chilean coalition was a good example of governing in alliance. But in Argentina, after fifteen months, the experience is frustrating.
>
> (Parliament of Argentina, 2001)

Fourth, speakers may defend a model by saying that the nation provides an exemplar for other countries to follow. For instance, in discussing the National Insurance Contributions Bill in the UK, the Chief Secretary to the Treasury, Mr Andrew Smith, said: "It is also significant that this is not just about a system of health care in the United Kingdom. If we get this right, it will be a model for other countries" (Parliament of UK, 2002). Such an argument obviously appeals to the national pride of compatriots. Economic motives may also be associated with such an argument: a good model to be marketed elsewhere could serve as a foundation for consulting business. It may also be motivated by general goodwill, i.e. the will and duty of national policy-makers not only to make things right in their home country but also provide a good model for others to follow. Referring to the international community in this way is, however, quite rare. In the data, there are altogether twelve such mentions: six in Canada, four in Argentina, and two in the UK, which is why it is not included in the comparative analysis discussed in the next section.

Finally, reforms may be promoted or criticized by appealing to the nation's international reputation. Failure to behave in a manner that is considered acceptable by the international community is in other words considered harmful for the country. It is assumed to be something that undermines the respect of and goodwill toward the nation. On the other hand, a well-functioning policy model may also be promoted as something that adds to the country's international image:

> I have already mentioned the failure of Sheila Copps' national action program on climate change in 1995. It is just one of many examples where we have failed. Canada is now approximately 28% above, not below, 1990 levels. To be blunt, Canada is an embarrassment on the world stage. We have retreated from recent world meetings in Bali and Poznan with a folder of fossil-of-the-day awards.
>
> (Parliament of Canada, 2009)

National differences

As has become evident in previous sections, the ways in which new legislation is justified is quite uniform in the six countries studied here. Regarding the prevalence of the ways in which speakers refer to the international community there are, however, differences between the six countries. They are presented in Figure 2.1.

To start with, it appears that on the whole, it is common in the most affluent countries, such as Canada and the UK, to make use of cross-national comparison and international norms or recommendations when debating new legislation. In that respect the USA is an exceptional case. Although it is a core country in the international system with a high gross domestic product (GDP) per capita (see Table 2.1), new legislation is considered in an international framework more seldom than in Argentina, Canada, or the UK. The difference in political cultures is even clearer when we consider references to international norms or standards related to the issue debated. While in Canada and the UK international norms are referred to in more than 40 percent of cases, in the USA such a reference can be found only in 3 percent of them. A similar difference can be found in references to models used elsewhere in dealing with a problem. In the USA the percentage of such references is lowest of all the countries compared.

Although Canada and the UK appear to be quite similar in some respects, the data also show an interesting difference between them, and that has to do with the general attitude toward international policy learning. Even though debates in the UK parliament contain references to international conventions or treaties, including EU laws that bind its member states, they are commonly treated as obligations or limitations rather than as facts that support the importance of the principle behind the convention. Similarly, although models or schemes that are adopted elsewhere are commonly mentioned, they are seldom suggested as

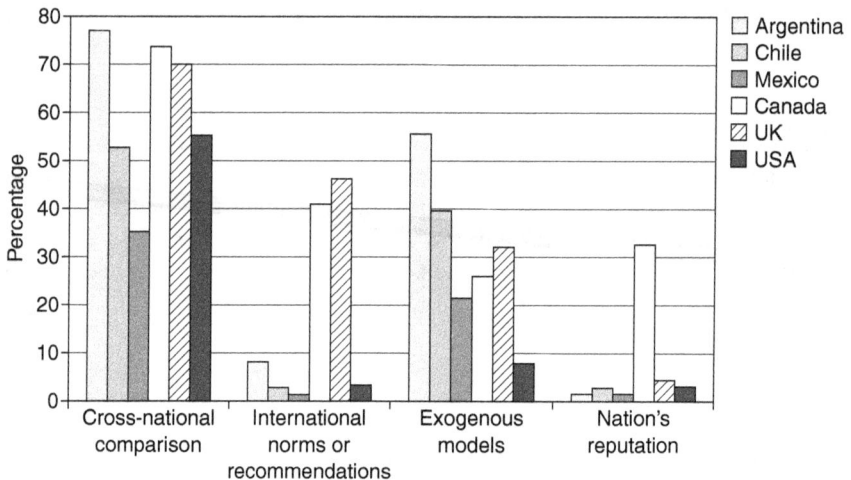

Figure 2.1 Frequency of references to other countries in parliamentary debates in the countries compared (%).

something to learn from. The Canadians' inclination to deliberate on national policies in a global framework is evident, too, in the opposite way: as mentioned in the section that discusses debating reforms in the transnational framework, raising a domestic solution as an exportable standard for other countries to follow is also most common in Canadian debates. Furthermore, in one-third of the debates, the acts of Canada are assessed from the viewpoint of the country's international reputation—a discourse that is quite rare in all other countries compared.

In this general attitude toward opinions and policies assumed elsewhere in the world, the USA is clearly the most insular of these six countries compared. Although there are cases in the data in which a domestic scheme is acclaimed as a model for others, they are occasions in which speakers hope that a program which the federal government supports will be enacted in different institutions by different US states. Overall, the US political culture does not seem to favor arguments that justify a policy by referring to its success in other countries. In that sense the assumption of US exceptionalism is supported by empirical evidence.

The fact that there are so few references in the US debates to international comparisons or to policy solutions adopted elsewhere is even more striking when we bear in mind the general pattern, which seems to suggest that the more a nation-state is economically and culturally integrated with the rest of the world, the more common it is to justify or criticize policy proposals by the international context. In line with this pattern, of the Latin American countries' references to cross-national comparisons, international norms, and exogenous models are least frequent in Mexico, which has the lowest GDP per capita. Furthermore, references to international norms and recommendations also seem to be much less common in the Latin American countries than in Canada and the UK. Possessing a political culture that does not favor references to the international context in its decision-making, with its GDP per capita on a par with Canada, the USA is a clear exception to the overall pattern. Instead, in many respects it resembles Mexico, which has the lowest GDP per capita of all the six countries compared.

Since other nation-states' policies are less frequently used as part of the argumentation on national decision-making in Mexico and the USA, it is interesting to see what rationales are commonly used in these countries. To pursue this question, let us also compare the frequency with which some other common justifications are employed in the six countries. The justifications compared are efficiency, scientific evidence, economic growth, and national security (see Figure 2.2).

As Figure 2.2 shows, there is no single mode of argumentation that would explain the scarce references to international comparison, international norms, or exogenous models as justification in Mexico and USA. One could for instance expect that the efficiency of a proposed or criticized policy and scientific evidence to support it—or proving the gravity of a problem—would be used more frequently, but there is no clear pattern in this respect. Scientific evidence is used as justification in Mexico more frequently than in the other two Latin American countries, but on the other hand the UK is the topmost country in this respect.

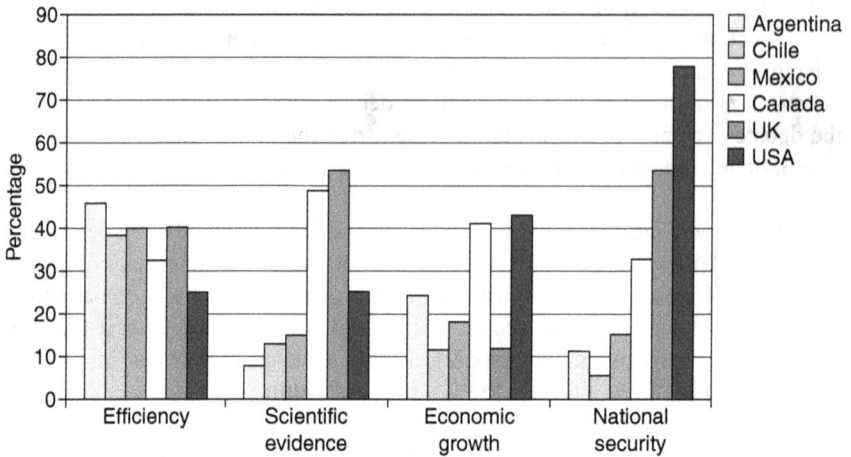

Figure 2.2 Frequency of justifications used in parliamentary debates in the countries compared (%).

Most interestingly, economic growth and national security are used most frequently in the USA, which implies that the bearing of the international community on US policy-making is particularly filtered through these two discursive realms.

In that way the international context in which policy decisions are made in a powerful country such as the USA is built into the domestic reality. In the economy, foreign trade is less an issue for the USA because the domestic market is so big, as can be seen from Table 2.1. Foreign trade is only 15 percent of GDP in the USA, while the same figure is twice as high in Canada, Mexico, and the UK (i.e. 30 percent of GDP). Of course global economic trends have an effect on the domestic market and on economic growth, but in the USA they are viewed as some kind of human-made international weather front and in that sense as external conditions for domestic actors. A policy can be justified by the argument that it increases economic growth without mentioning whether other countries have also adopted it or whether it is a global model, because beliefs about rational and efficient solutions are considered as universal knowledge about the economy and society. In a similar vein national security is a self-evident premise for new legislation, and even though the threat is often considered to be external, the measures taken are not necessarily justified by what is going on in other countries.

Discussion

In this chapter I set out to ask how global models and other countries' behavior are adopted when policy-makers debate domestic decisions, thus contributing to the synchronization of national policies. The general objective of this bottom-up approach to interdependent decision-making was to shed more light on how, permeated by world culture and composed of some 200 formally independent states, the world polity functions as an unexpectedly isomorphic system, in which national governments often seem to adopt similar policies.

The analysis of the ways in which policies are justified or criticized in national parliamentary debates in Argentina, Canada, Chile, Mexico, the UK, and the USA showed that acts of governments and other agents in the global system are an essential part of the factors to which actors refer in their argumentation, which is composed of three main premises. First, all proposed measures are presented in the interest of the nation. Second, the speakers argue about the existence and seriousness of the problem. Third, the argumentation concerns the rationality, efficiency, and morality of the proposed solutions. In all of these points speakers may substantiate their arguments with cross-national comparisons and facts concerning the experience or behavior of other nation-states. In that sense decision-making in nation-states, which are institutionally replicas of each other, is clearly interdependent.

Yet in light of the data from the six countries studied here, the image created by policy diffusion research of interdependent decision-making as a constant flow of worldwide models enacted by national parliaments is biased. New legislation is seldom promoted by appealing to a single model implemented by other countries. Rather, the global system could be characterized by a world culture in which the infrastructures of nation-states and basic premises used in argumentation are the same, and actors also share a number of trendy ideas and concepts. Consequently, as upshots of domestic debates in which actors utilize these same elements, countries make similar decisions. This description of the system may sound similar to saying that the same models are spread throughout the world, but the point is that the decisions are seldom based on an entirely new idea. Rather, actors appeal to the same repertoire of premises, ideas, and principles to promote decisions that contribute to synchronizing the government's moves with those of others. Yet in national contexts, because the national first person plural "us" is a self-evident perspective from which cross-national comparisons and internationally recommendable policies are viewed, the synchronizing effect of national policy-making goes largely unnoticed, and global trends are domesticated: the polies devised are experienced as "our" strategies.

In policy diffusion research it has been pointed out that interdependent decision-making is the result of four causal mechanisms: coercion, competition, learning, and emulation (Simmons et al., 2008). Viewed from the perspective of actual decision-making situations, it is not possible to identify such mechanisms at play. Perhaps with the exception of coercion, which is seldom if ever considered as an honorable motive for action by a sovereign state, speakers may appeal to any of these reasons in promoting new legislation because they are widely shared cultural models. However, rather than attributing the synchronization of national policies to distinct causal mechanisms it is better to think of it as a systemic feature of the parcelized world polity.

The analysis also showed that there are national differences in the ways government bills are debated. On the whole, the statistical analysis of the frequencies by which speakers appeal to different rationales in justifying or criticizing national policies suggests that the more firmly a nation-state is economically, politically, and culturally integrated with other nation-states, the more frequently national policies are justified by cross-national comparisons, international norms, and models adopted elsewhere. Accordingly, these legitimations are most commonly used in Canada and the UK, whereas in Mexico, with its lowest GDP per capita of the six countries compared, references to cross-national comparisons and international norms are least common.

In this respect the USA is clearly an exception. Although it is a core country, references to international norms and models adopted in other countries particularly are much less common in its parliamentary debates than in Canada and the UK, which are its closest counterparts. Instead, in some respects the statistical profile of arguments used in US parliamentary discourse resembles that of Mexico. In the USA policies are justified by common goals and by national interests such as economic growth or national security, not by international norms or by the nation's reputation in the world. This does not mean that in these countries national policy-making is uninfluenced by what is going on elsewhere. It is only that, in the USA, the rest of the world is primarily represented as the environment that affects the conditions under which decisions are made, rather than as an international community of peers.

Given the nature of the sample of parliamentary debates on which these inferences are based, the results of this analysis must be considered only as initial hypotheses. More research will be needed for instance to see how much arguments used in the debates depend on the policy area in question. Yet the general pattern emerging from this study seems obvious. According to it, references to policies, the successes and failures of other countries, are most common in affluent countries, which are also most interdependent and intertwined with each other in a number of ways. The same pattern can in fact be detected from policy diffusion research, which shows that new models first spread to the affluent countries, from where they gradually trickle down to less prosperous nation-states and finally, often with special support and promotion provided by the UN and its specialized agencies, such as the International Labour Organization (ILO) and the Food and Agriculture Organization (FAO), they also spread to the developing countries.

However, when in this study this pattern has been viewed from the perspective of the discourses within which national decisions are made, it shows the phenomenon in a different light. While the prevalent conception creates the image that the less affluent and developing countries are at the receiving end, following the suit of "leading" powerful or otherwise influential countries (see e.g. Kelemen and Sibbitt, 2002; Ritzer, 1996), this study suggests an opposite image. If we try to picture in mind a stereotypical country in which policies are created and decided independently from exogenous models, justifying them only by reasoning about what would best suit the situation, such a nation-state would most likely be a developing country. Correspondingly, if we imagine a classic case of a parliamentary or public discussion in which a policy is promoted by referring to reforms made in other countries, the case in point would most likely take place in an affluent liberal democracy. In other words, stereotypical national sovereignty assumed in the dominant paradigm of independent decision-making is closest to reality in the case of developing countries.

Yet this does not mean that governments either in the "center" or in the "periphery" follow fashions by adopting policies invented in another country. It is more accurate to conceive of the synchronization of national paths and policies by saying that there is constant circulation of information and ideas across borders. Named and identifiable models are not the starting point of or reason for, but rather a product of, global isomorphism and interdependent policy-making. That is, actors such as policy experts or policy-makers construct, package, and name practices that they promote or oppose as models, which are then used as raw material in debating a policy in another country. Such debate often results in a policy that is yet another mixture of the same basic ideas and assumptions circulating on the globe.

Notes

1 I am deeply grateful for Oscar-Mario Miranda from Tecnológico de Monterrey, Mexico, for his help in collecting and coding the data used in this study, and particularly in collecting and coding the data from Latin American countries on his own initiative. Without his help it would not have been possible to conduct this study.
2 The idea of the USA as an exception was first formulated by Alexis de Tocqueville (1840, pp. 36–37).

References

Acharya, A. (2004). How Ideas Spread: Whose Norms Matter? Norm Localization and Institutional Change in Asian Regionalism. *International Organization, 58*(2), 239–275.

Alasuutari, P. (2013). Spreading Global Models and Enhancing Banal Localism: The Case of Local Government Cultural Policy Development. *International Journal of Cultural Policy, 19*(1), 103–119.

Alasuutari, P., Bickman, L., and Brannen, J. (eds) (2008). *The SAGE Handbook of Social Research Methods*. London: Sage.

Béland, D. (2005). Ideas and Social Policy: An Institutionalist Perspective. *Social Policy & Administration, 39*(1), 1–18.

Bradley, K. and Ramirez, F. (1996). World Polity Promotion of Gender Parity: Women's Share of Higher Education, 1965–85. *Research in Sociology of Education and Socialization, 11*, 63–91.

Buduru, B. and Pal, L.A. (2010). The Globalized State: Measuring and Monitoring Governance. *European Journal of Cultural Studies, 13*(4), 511–530. doi:10.1177/1367549410377144.

Callon, M. (1986). Some Elements of a Sociology of Translation: Domestication of the Scallops and the Fishermen of St Brieuc Bay. In J. Law (ed.), *Power, Action, and Belief: A New Sciology of Knowledge?* (pp. 196–223). London: Routledge & Kegan Paul.

Cerny, P.G. (2012). Globalization and the Transformation of Power. In M. Haugaard and K. Ryan (eds), *Political Power: The Development of the Field* (pp. 185–213). Opladen, Germany: Barbara Budrich Publishers.

Cook, I.R. (2008). Mobilising Urban Policies: The Policy Transfer of US Business Improvement Districts to England and Wales. *Urban Studies, 45*(4), 773–795. doi:10.1177/0042098007088468.

Cortell, A.P. and Davis, J.W., Jr (2000). Understanding the Domestic Impact of International Norms: A Research Agenda. *International Studies Review, 2*(1), 65–87.

Czarniawska-Joerges, B. and Sevón, G. (1996). Introduction. In B. Czarniawska-Joerges and G. Sevón (eds), *Translating Organizational Change* (pp. 1–12). Berlin: Walter de Gruyer.

Czarniawska-Joerges, B. and Sevón, G. (2005). *Global Ideas: How Ideas, Objects and Practices Travel in the Global Economy*. Malmö: Liber and Copenhagen Business School Press.

de Tocqueville, A. (1840). *Democracy in America: Part the Second; the Social Influence of Democracy*. New York: J. & H.G. Langley.

Dobbin, F., Simmons, B., and Garrett, G. (2007). The Global Diffusion of Public Policies: Social Construction, Coercion, Competition, or Learning? *Annual Review of Sociology, 33*(1), 449–472. doi:10.1146/annurev.soc.33.090106.142507.

Dolowitz, D. and Marsh, D. (1996). Who Learns What From Whom: A Review of the Policy Transfer Literature. *Political Studies, 44*(2), 343–357.

Dolowitz, D. and Marsh, D. (2000). Learning from Abroad: The Role of Policy Transfer in Contemporary Policy-Making. *Governance, 13*(1), 5–23.

Evans, M. and Davies, J. (1999). Understanding Policy Transfer: A Multi-Level, Multi-Disciplinary Perspective. *Public Administration, 77*(2), 361–385.

Foster, R.J. (1991). Making National Cultures in the Global Ecumene. *Annual Review of Anthropology, 20*, 235–260.

Hulme, R. (2006). The Role of Policy Transfer in Assessing the Impact of American Ideas on British Social Policy. *Global Social Policy, 6*(2), 173–195. doi:10.1177/1468018106065365.

Iwabuchi, K. (2008). Lost in TransNation: Tokyo and the Urban Imaginary in the Era of Globalization. *Inter-Asia Cultural Studies, 9*(4), 543–556.

Kelemen, R.D. and Sibbitt, E.C. (2002). The Americanization of Japanese Law. *Journal of International Economic Law, 23*(2), 269–323.

Lechner, F.J. and Boli, J. (2005). *World Culture: Origins and Consequences*. Malden: Blackwell.

Lowenheim, O. (2007). Examination Period: The Rise of Rating and Ranking in International Politics. *Conference Papers—International Studies Association*, 1.

MacIntyre, A.C. (1981). *After Virtue: A Study in Moral Theory*. Notre Dame, IN: University of Notre Dame Press.

Mahon, R. (2009). The OECD's Discourse on the Reconciliation of Work and Family Life. *Global Social Policy, 9*(2), 183–204. doi:10.1177/1468018109104625.

Mahon, R. (2010). After Neo-Liberalism? The OECD, the World Bank and the Child. *Global Social Policy, 10*(2), 172–192.

Mahon, R. and McBride, S. (eds) (2008). *The OECD and Transnational Governance*. Vancouver, BC: University of British Columbia Press.

Martens, K. and Dobbins, M. (2010). A Contrasting Case—the USA. and Its Weak Response to Internationalization Processes in Education Policy. In K. Martens, A.-K. Nagel, M. Windzio, and A. Weymann (eds), *Transformation of Education Policy* (pp. 179–195). London: Palgrave.

McGrew, A.G. (1998). The Globalisation Debate: Putting the Advanced Capitalist State in its Place. *Global Society: Journal of Interdisciplinary International Relations, 12*(3), 299.

Meyer, J.W. (2010). World Society, Institutional Theories, and the Actor. *Annual Review of Sociology, 36*, 1–20.

Meyer, J.W., Boli, J., Thomas, G.M., and Ramirez, F.O. (1997). World Society and the Nation-State. *American Journal of Sociology, 103*(1), 144–181.

Meyer, J.W., Krücken, G., and Drori, G.S. (eds) (2009). *World Society: The Writings of John W. Meyer*. Oxford: Oxford University Press.

Meyer, J.W., Ramirez, F.O., and Soysal, Y. (1992). World Expansion of Mass Education, 1870–1980. *Sociology of Education, 65*(2), 128–149.

Organisation for Economic Co-operation and Development (2011). OECD Factbook 2010: Economic, Environmental and Social Statistics.

Parliament of Argentina (2001, 26 March). *Debate on Authority Delegation of the Executive Power*. Chamber of Deputies Debates, 6th Reunion, 3rd Session. Retrieved 6 August 2013 from: http://www1.hcdn.gov.ar/sesionesxml/reunion.asp?p=119&r=6.

Parliament of Canada (2009, 4 March). *Debate on Climate Change Accountability Act*. House of Commons Debates, 40th Parliament, 2nd Session, vol 144, number 23. Retrieved 6 August 2013 from: www.parl.gc.ca/HousePublications/Publication.aspx?Pub=Hansard&Doc=23&Parl=40&Ses=2&Language=E&Mode=1#OOB-2636465.

Parliament of Chile (2004, 13 July). *Debate on Modernization of Conscription*. Chamber of Deputies Debates, 351st Legislature, 14th Session. Retrieved 6 August 2013 from: www.camara.cl/trabajamos/sala_documentos.aspx?prmTIPO=BOLETIN.

Parliament of UK (2001, 10 January). *Debate on Health and Social Care Bill*. HC Debate, vol. 360, cc. 1080–1125. Retrieved 4 August 2013 from: http://hansard.millbanksystems.com/commons/2001/jan/10/health-and-social-care-bill.

Parliament of UK (2002, 13 May). *Debate on National Insurance Contributions Bill*. HC Debate, vol. 385, cc. 534–612. Retrieved 6 August 2013 from: http://hansard.millbanksystems.com/commons/2002/may/13/national-insurance-contributions-bill#column_534.

Perelman, C. (1982). *The Realm of Rhetoric*. Notre Dame, IN: University of Notre Dame Press.

Ritzer, G. (1996). *The McDonaldization of Society: An Investigation into the Changing Character of Contemporary Social Life* (Rev. edn). Thousand Oaks, CA: Pine Forge Press.

Ritzer, G. (1998). *The McDonaldization Thesis: Explorations and Extensions*. Thousand Oaks, CA: Sage Publications.

Shandra, J.M. (2007). The World Polity and Deforestation. *International Journal of Comparative Sociology, 48*(1), 5–27.

Simmons, B.A., Dobbin, F., and Garrett, G. (2008). Introduction: The Diffusion of Liberalization. In B.A. Simmons, F. Dobbin, and G. Garrett (eds), *The Global Diffusion of Markets and Democracy* (pp. 1–63). Cambridge: Cambridge University Press.

Tsutsui, K. and Wotipka, C.M. (2004). Global Civil Society and the International Human Rights Movement: Citizen Participation in Human Rights International Nongovernmental Organizations. *Social Forces, 83*(2), 587–620.

Woodward, R. (2009). *The Organisation for Economic Co-operation and Development (OECD)*. Milton Park: Routledge.

World Bank (2011). GDP per capita. Retrieved 5 April 2013 from http://data.worldbank.org/indicator/NY.GDP.PCAP.CD.

3 Unholy alliances

Competitiveness as a domestic power strategy

Anu Kantola

National competitiveness has become a central political target for many governments around the world. It is an idea, however, that is hard to place in the traditional political spectrum. Ronald Reagan and Tony Blair treasured it; Margaret Thatcher overtly disliked it. In this chapter I suggest that the domestication of national competitiveness in national politics has been conditioned by its usability in the exercise of political power.

John Meyer's (2004) idea of the nation-state as Babbitt, the character from the novel of the same name by Sinclair Lewis, suits the adoption of national competitiveness as a national policy choice. Many nations have implemented such policies in order to appear credible in the eyes of the global society. The widespread adoption of competitiveness policies has undoubtedly been facilitated by the ethos of modernization and the will to modernize, and in this will, reforms made elsewhere are naturalized as part of the trajectory for a better future (Alasuutari, 2011; Lodge, 2007; Reubi, 2010). With regard to national competitiveness, policies are based on the idea of social engineering with transnational experts and indicators providing guidelines for high-modernist, rationally planned development (Kantola and Seeck, 2010). However, when we study how new policies are actually adopted within a nation-state, the picture is more complicated. From the outset the nation state can be conceived as a single actor, but in fact policies are outcomes of domestic field battles (Alasuutari, 2013; Alasuutari and Qadir, introduction to this volume), in which different actors and stakeholders justify or oppose reforms with reference to the national interest, for instance by appealing to successes or failures of policies adopted elsewhere (Meyer, Boli, Thomas, and Ramirez, 1997, p. 161). These claims also work as a strategy for stakeholders to defend their own positions in the domestic political field. In this chapter, I show how the idea of national competitiveness is used in national politics as different political actors try to gain power.

Theoretically, I use Foucauldian studies on governmentality, which suggest that consent is often at the heart of political power. The policy practices of national competitiveness have been formulated in a transnational regime of expertise, which has been domesticated by nation states. Below, I describe the formation of the world model of competitiveness: how a new international body of knowledge developed and provided a problem, an analysis and solutions.

Second, I focus on the "real" uses of power: how the concept was used to gain power in politics in Finland, a country often cited as a model of competitiveness. I analyze policy documents on national competitiveness, government manifestos from 1980 to 2011 and the archives of *Helsingin Sanomat*, the largest daily newspaper in Finland, using the keyword "competitiveness." I describe how in Finland, as in many other countries, competitiveness has been used to gain political power within the nation state. Finally, I discuss the case of Finland in a comparative international context.

Productive power

The exercise of power has classically been understood as a coercive undertaking: the ability to impose one's will over others, despite resistance. This notion of coercive power, however, does not include the productive elements of power. To be effective, power often needs to build up consent and coalitions rather than to coerce and restrict by force. In this sense Michel Foucault's work offers a way of seeing power as a productive and positive undertaking. The notion of governmentality (Foucault, 2004a, 2004b) particularly emphasizes the productivity of power. In contrast to discipline, governmentality strives to produce and maximize the life of a population with knowledge-based techniques and power tactics (Foucault, 2004b, pp. 109–113). As Barry Hindess (1996, pp. 114–145) has observed, Foucault placed consent at the center of power. Modern governance strives to produce systems that foster the general good. The exercise of power is a productive undertaking, which constructs identities, creates meaning, calls for allies and builds coalitions. Power also needs to present issues, problems, and solutions in ways that attract, entice, and persuade its subjects (Seeck and Kantola, 2009).

The exercise of power does not take place through the will of sovereign rulers, but rather through regimes of practices, routine ways of doing things that pertain to certain times and places and that have particular rationales, strategies and techniques (Dean, 1999, pp. 21–23). These regimes clearly build on specific forms of expertise and knowledge production. Economics especially has developed into a specific domain of knowledge that is used to maximize the productivity of populations (Foucault, 2004a, pp. 247–252; 2004b, pp. 76–77, 106–108; Rose, 1999, pp. 24–40).

Moreover, Foucault (2004b, pp. 121–122) maintained that one should analyze global projects of governmentality, such as public hygiene, or competitiveness, which develop a battery of techniques. Such projects construct global orders and technologies of power that work outside institutions. Thus, the genealogy of these projects needs to be analyzed: to step outside the institution and examine the network of alliances, communication, and points of support (Foucault, 2004b, pp. 120–122).

National competitiveness fits Foucault's idea of a global project. It is based on theories of political economy, which have turned into global indicators and expertise. Moreover, national competitiveness has been utilized as a power tactic as states try to govern their populations and maximize their productivity by for-mulating policies and strategies of competitiveness. Below, I show how national competitiveness has been constructed as a global regime of knowledge-based practices and expertise and how it has been domesticated locally within the nation state of Finland.

Nations in competition: the making of the global project

The problem of national competitiveness dates back to the beginnings of the modern state. Foucault (2004b, pp. 292–295) suggested that the notion of states in competition with each other emerged in the sixteenth and seventeenth centur-ies when dynastic rivalries between princes were transformed into competition among states. Throughout history national competitiveness has been closely tied to varying forms of knowledge production, which have deciphered the problem, measured it, and helped to formulate policy imperatives. The rapid rise and sub-sequent demise of Spain as an imperial power in the sixteenth and seventeenth centuries was a paradigmatic "case study" of competitiveness for the whole of Europe. Chroniclers, historians, and economists reflected the sudden rise and demise of the country and worked out a new *raison d'État* that combined the state with economic competition. For Foucault, this shift—a transition from the rivalry of princes to the competition of states—was one of the most fundamental mutations in Western political life and culture (2004b, p. 294).

The rise of the competitive state was also part of a wider development. Since the middle of the sixteenth century, the art of government was concerned increasingly with how to introduce economy into political practice (Foucault, 2000, p. 207). Consequently, political economy gained a prominent role in for-mulating state reason. Adam Smith imagined society as an economic apparatus, and David Ricardo's theory on comparative advantage conceptualized the rela-tions between states in economic terms (Hindess, 1998, pp. 213–223; Rose, 1999, pp. 33–39).

In the twentieth century Ricardo's theory of competitive advantage was the best-known explanation of national competitiveness, as imperial powers con-cerned themselves with competitiveness. For instance, the Great Exhibition of 1851 in London's Crystal Palace was Prince Albert's attempt to demonstrate the growing strength of German industry and the competitive challenge from over-seas. At the same time a polemic entitled *Made in Germany* described the new German products and the danger they posed to the British Empire and its indus-tries in the nineteenth century (Francis, 1992, p. 63).

Political concerns over competitiveness mounted after the Second World War (1939–1945). Economists assessed nations' international competitiveness by using the price indices of internationally traded goods (e.g. Kravis and Lipsey, 1967, 1971; Richardson, 1972). In many countries price competitiveness became a major national issue. The Western powers especially became anxious about their performance in the world economy. In the late 1950s Britain became con-cerned with its economic decline; France launched a campaign against foreign investments; and the USA was concerned over its balance of payments (Godin, 2004, pp. 1217–1219).

In the 1970s, however, the nation states entered a new political environment. A strong deregulatory trend increased the fluidity of capital, goods, and services. Increasingly, the nation state faced harsh competition in financial capital, company headquarters and industrial sites, as well as through the increasing power of multinational corporations (Schmidt, 1995; Sklair, 2002; Strange, 1996; Warf, 1999). With these developments, price competitiveness gradually began losing its importance, replaced by a new technology-orientated understanding of national competitiveness.

This new understanding had originated in the Austrian economics schools of the early twentieth century, where it was believed that discovery was the way to survive competition (Kirzner, 1997). Josef Schumpeter, an Austrian political economist, suggested that technological advances and entrepreneurship were important if one intended to survive the change (Schumpeter, 1992[1943], pp. 84, 132). In the first half of the twentieth century Schumpeter was almost alone in his emphasis on innovation in competition. However, in the 1970s his ideas started to gain momentum, thanks to the oil crisis and the emergence of the new information technologies. By the 1980s new theories of innovation and the dynamics of economic development became prominent in economics (Freeman, 1984, 1990; Freeman and Soete, 1987; OECD, 1997; Perez, 1983; Stoneman, 1995). Trade theories also showed the Schumpeterian impact: Technology-related factors became central to a country's trade performance, and national competitiveness became closely associated with technology and innovation (De la Mothe and Dufour, 1995, p. 219; Fagerberg, 1988, pp. 361–371; Hämäläinen, 2003, pp. 35–53, 104–112; Krugman, 1995; Sharp, 1997; Starr and Ullmann, 1988; Stoneman, 1995).

In politics, government policies focused increasingly on science and technology. The boundaries between science and technology policy and the more traditional economic, industrial, trade, and foreign policies shifted. High-tech policies represented a new form of government intervention as countries began to assess their technological profiles and reform their societies with an eye on the dynamics of innovativeness (De la Mothe and Dufour, 1995).

The growing emphasis on technology was also reflected in international economic indicators. The research and development indicators became crucial with regard to the rhetoric of competitiveness. The OECD also played a central role: It classified research-intensive industries, evaluated their competitive role in the international position of countries, and set up policy processes (Godin, 2004, pp. 1220–1225).

The business sector meanwhile developed its own indicators. The first competitiveness indicator was established by the European Management Forum, the forerunner of the World Economic Forum (WEF). The first competitiveness evaluation in 1979 included 16 European countries, but gradually the assessment extended to more than 100 countries. In the mid-1990s the World Competitiveness Center of the Institute for Management Development, a Swiss-based management school, developed its own indicator. Currently, the Center publishes the *World Competitiveness Yearbook*, which rates 60 countries using over 300 criteria. These two well-known indicators have been followed by various consulting efforts and measures that benchmark regions worldwide. The importance of the indicators has been considerable in bringing competitiveness onto the political agenda. Indicators result in lists of countries and generate political discussions about a given country's ranking in the indicator following publication of the ratings.

Moreover, a growing number of organizational management scholars and business practitioners have become interested in competitiveness and are creating consulting practices based on it (Hämäläinen, 2003, p. 3). The best-known consultant was Harvard professor Michael Porter, who used Schumpeterian theories to develop a state-of-the-art theory of a nation's competitiveness (Porter, 1990, pp. 13–20, 70). His "Diamond model" was circulated around the world as part of a package of his theories in easy-to-use political toolkits, which have subsequently guided national policies worldwide (Kantola and Seeck, 2010).

Schumpeterian theories of national competitiveness were gradually modified to a world model (Meyer et al., 1997), which filtered into national politics. At the core of the model are expertise and know-how. The assessments of competitiveness map out resources and dynamics. For instance, in Porter's model a nation's resources are charted in a seemingly clear and unquestionable way. However, the domestication of competitiveness has not been as easy and fluent as the models and indicators often suggest. In order to understand the dynamics of domestication one needs to look at local relations of power, in this case, in Finland.

Finland: power and competitiveness

In the first four decades after the Second World War, price competitiveness formed a central political imperative in Finland. Economic growth and the competitiveness of export industries were central aims in politics. In the strongly regulated national economy, recurring devaluations improved the price competitiveness of main exports and national industries (Kananen, 2011, pp. 136–144). Because faith in export industries was important for trade unions and for farmers who owned forests, a trilateral system of negotiations was devised to guarantee competitive wage levels and assess the need for devaluations. As the price competitiveness of export industries weakened, devaluations were carried out in conjunction with governmental policies, alleviating the impact of inflation on labor.

With financial liberalization in the 1980s and with the fall of the Soviet Union, these policies started to change. In 1987 Finland's right-wing Government adopted a monetarist policy of maintaining a stable currency and, when Finland joined the European Monetary Union (EMU) in the 1990s, devaluation became impossible (Kantola, 2002, pp. 107–144, 267–276). Price competitiveness was no longer a meaningful political idea.

Schumpeterian ideas about the importance of technology had been circulated in Finland since the 1960s, especially via Sweden and by the OECD. Since the

1960s, the Ministry of Trade and Industry had used Schumpeterian competitiveness to formulate new policies. New institutions such as Sitra (the Finnish Innovation Fund and business and technology-orientated think tank) were founded, and the Government started new programs for advancing technology. Schumpeterian policies entered Finland in full force in the early 1990s when Finland experienced a severe financial crisis in the aftermath of financial liberalization, followed by an economic boom.

In 1992, in the midst of the financial crisis, Sitra and the research institute for the business sector, ETLA (*Elinkeinoelämän tutkimuslaitos*: Research Institute of the Finnish Economy), kicked off a research project to assess Finnish competitiveness. The analytical framework was borrowed from the Diamond model of Michael Porter, who also visited the country in the early 1990s. The project's initiators were close to the business sector. Yet in order to become influential in Finnish politics, it was necessary to build a wider coalition. Thus, other research institutes and interest groups were gradually recruited to the project, which evolved into a major undertaking. Several universities, as well as economic research institutes which were close to the major parties, the Social Democrats and the Centre Party, joined in. Various ministries as well as companies and business organizations funded the process.

All of the actors involved came to share a common understanding of Finnish society based on economic expertise. The emerging coalition endorsed the Schumpeterian notion of competitiveness, which was introduced through an extensive analysis of the strengths and weaknesses of Finland's competitiveness. The project published a report on the national industrial strategy, which emphasized the need for a new industrial policy that would allocate public funds for research and development activities (Hernesniemi, Lammi, and Ylä-Anttila, 1995).

The report proved to be influential, as it formulated a joint knowledge basis for consensual politics and a national rationale that overcame political differences. First and foremost, the new industrial policy was used mainly by the corporate and business sector to gain public funding. More public funds were allocated to research and development by different means. The industries, following Porter's cluster theory, organized into clusters, which then worked as vehicles for obtaining funding. Clusters applied for and received European Union (EU) and government funding for their research and development activities. In terms of public funding, the results were impressive. In the 1980s public money for research and innovation increased approximately 10 percent every year, a record in OECD countries. By 2006 Finland was devoting 3.4 percent of its GDP to research and innovation, a world record. Along with Sweden, Finland was the only EU country to surpass the 3 percent limit established in the EU's Lisbon strategy (VNK, 2005b, p. 38; 2007, pp. 10–11).

Public sector financial cutbacks were the other cornerstone of the competitiveness policies: The size of the public sector was supposed to be reduced and efficiency increased (Kantola and Kananen, 2013; Määttä, 2005, pp. 240–247). The most prominent actor in these policies was the powerful Ministry of

Finance, which in the midst of the 1990s recession devised a strategy for Finland in the name of national competitiveness. The strategy included a range of related policies such as significant tax cuts (VNK, 2007, p. 66), and a quick reduction of public debt (VNK, 2007, pp. 10, 65), as well as efficiency policies in the public sector (VNK, 2007, p. 64). As a result the Finnish public sector employs 4 to 7 percent fewer people than other Nordic countries with similar welfare models (VNK, 2005a, p. 99; 2005b, pp. 22, 34).

These reallocations reflected underlying power struggles. As Bengt Flyvbjerg (1998, pp. 39–42) noted, political power struggles are most clearly reflected in the reallocation of public funds. The new competitiveness policy was used to allocate public funding for export industries and their research activities, while at the same time public sector and welfare services were cut back. Using Schumpeterian analysis, the private sector was able to find allies in policy-makers and create a coalition that devised a strategy in which the "real competitiveness" of the export industries (Lemola, 2001, p. 29) was placed at the heart of Finnish success, with other sectors expected to lend support.

However, in this process other political actors realized the value of competitiveness, which gradually became a key idea in framing and legitimizing policies in a variety of sectors. If a policy sector wanted to appear credible in national politics, it needed to justify its aims by appealing to competitiveness. The change can be seen clearly in government programs—the policy manifestos, which Finnish governments give out at the beginning of their terms of office. In the 1980s "competitiveness" was used sparingly in the programs and mentioned only a few times in each of them. The concept started to gain importance in the 1990s. The right-wing coalition government of the agrarian Centre Party and the Conservatives used it nine times, and the wide consensual "Rainbow" coalition governments, led by Social Democrats and Conservatives, subsequently invoked it 12 and 16 times respectively. The uses of competitiveness proliferated and were circulated in different policy areas. The notion was first used in discussions about the competitiveness of Finnish export industries, meaning, for instance, low rates of inflation and taxation to encourage employment. However, other policy areas were also gradually framed in the name of competitiveness. Agricultural policies needed to guarantee the competitiveness of Finnish agriculture. Road and traffic policies needed to enhance the competitiveness of the business sector. Education, science, and research policies were upgraded in order to enhance national competitiveness. Environmental and energy policies needed to take into account the national competitiveness. After the year 2000, competitiveness became a cornerstone of Finnish policy-making. In 2003 it was mentioned in the government programs 31 times; in 2007, 38 times; and in 2011, 49 times.

This turn was clearly apparent in public discussions as well. Originally, it was the business and industry sectors that used competitiveness as a political argument to back their political aims. Thus, in the 1990s, when Finland was not particularly good in international ratings, the corporate sector wanted to break down national regulation, open up the economy, and put an end to the frequent strikes

(*Helsingin Sanomat*, 23 September 1990). Typically, Finnish industrialists also criticised high taxation and the large public sector in the name of national competitiveness. This line of reasoning has continued since 2000 as business leaders routinely come out in favor of competitiveness by demanding lower wages or less environmental regulation (*Helsingin Sanomat*, 30 September 2012; *Helsingin Sanomat*, 14 October 2012).

However, in the late 1990s, Finland began showing very good results in international competitiveness rankings. Some of the rankings, for instance, the WEF and International Monetary Fund (IMF) indexes, widened their scope of variables and viewed the public sector as a positive resource for national competitiveness. Finland, described as "the most competitive country in the world," started to become a model of competitiveness, thanks to its economic policies and societal models, which were perceived as exceptionally successful (Kantola, 2010; Kantola and Seeck, 2010). At this point, the traditional defenders of competitiveness, namely the business sector, distanced themselves from the concept. Finnish organizations of industrialists, as well as researchers close to the business sector, began to criticize Finland's success in the rankings and became skeptical of the indicators and their reliability (*Helsingin Sanomat*, 25 February 1998; *Helsingin Sanomat*, 21 April 1999; *Helsingin Sanomat*, 19 October 2001; *Helsingin Sanomat*, 16 October 2004).

At the same time competitiveness was taken up by their political opponents. For instance, the Ministry of the Environment used national competitiveness and Porter's work to back up the need for reduction of greenhouse gases (*Helsingin Sanomat*, 19 April 2001). The Minister of Finance, Eero Heinäluoma, defended publicly financed daycare for children, stating that Porter's work showed how the basis of society must be in order, meaning that public daycare is also important for the export industries (*Helsingin Sanomat*, 10 September 2005). The largest Finnish trade union, SAK (Suomen Ammattiliittojen Keskusjärjestö, the Central Organization of Finnish Trade Unions), suggested that the deteriorating meaningfulness of work hampers Finland's competitiveness (*Helsingin Sanomat*, 3 November 2012).

All of this signaled power struggles that were taking place with regard to public funds and policies. In the 1990s the Schumpeterian notion was used to cut funding to the public sector and allocate funds to research and development in industry. The power of the export industries was enhanced at the expense of the public sector workers. The export industries and their political allies also used national competitiveness as a standard argument to gain more public funds for the business sector and promote business-friendly tax and employment policies. Since 2000, competitiveness has become a central rationale of power for the Finnish broadly-based coalition governments. All those who see themselves as contributing to the nation's competitiveness could join in the coalition, and all who wanted to join the government defined their actions in the name of competitiveness. This broad new framework, however, was so general that it could also be taken up by those who wanted to defend public sector activities, thereby multiplying the uses of competitiveness.

With regard to the adoption of Schumpeterian competitiveness, Finns were certainly Babbitts, a "wannabe" nation of modernization, who would like to succeed in the eyes of the world. In particular, success in the competitiveness indicators became of part of a shift whereby, with the fall of the Soviet Union, Finland allied with Western Europe politically and economically, and gained credibility as a successful market economy. This urge to Westernize has been the more pressing as the country's international image has been shadowed by Russian and Soviet influence (Kantola, 2010), and Finns have felt a strong need to appear Western. In this respect Finns are not alone; the urge to Westernize has been an important theme in the narrative of modernization. The West has been regarded as the future, and the East as the primordial past.

At the same time, competitiveness became a central concept related to power. Finland's governments are often broad-based coalitions, which need to find a common rationale. In the 1990s the rise of national competitiveness took place in the Rainbow Coalition, which included all the major parties from the left and the right, excluding only the Centre Party. Moreover, the agrarian Centre Party and the Social Democratic Party especially have been hampered by the diminishing size of their original class base; increasingly, they are giving up their class-based ideologies and endorsing ideas that strive to adopt the ideals of the growing middle-class population. National competitiveness suits these needs. It is a flexible concept by which different parties can merge their interests and form a working coalition for the exercise of power in government. It also provides a politically neutral centrist concept that does not rule out any voters.

The Schumpeterian theory of competitiveness, the Porterian model and international rankings have all played a role in legitimating the government in power and granting it an air of credibility. The Porterian framework especially has provided a transnational knowledge brand (Sum, 2010) that could be utilized when Finnish industries and their think tanks organized a coalition that reformulated the task of national politics. The governments seemed actively to foster a Finnish society facing the perils of globalization and the rationale of competitiveness became a call for power, whereby political actors began defining themselves in the name of competitiveness as they struggled to gain power over public funds. This power struggle did not take place between different concepts; rather it was a battle over the content of one rationale. The battle for power thus became a battle for truth and knowledge (Flyvbjerg, 1998, pp. 25–38; Foucault, 2000, pp. 199–233; Rose, 1999, pp. 28–30).

Discussion

The case of Finland discussed in this chapter shows well how the idea of national competitiveness was used to create a legitimizing rationale for consensual governments. But Finland is not an isolated or exceptional case. Rather, national competitiveness is a world model that has been employed in several countries in a similar vein.

For instance, in 1983 the Reagan administration set up the Commission on Industrial Competitiveness, which was succeeded by the Council on Competitiveness. Both consisted of industrial, labor and university leaders whose charge was "to elevate national competitiveness to the forefront of national consciousness" (Godin, 2004, pp. 1221–1222). Competitiveness policies were also used as an overtly national concept in the UK (Keep and Mayhew, 1999, p. 2; Oughton, 1997, p. 1487), in the German-speaking and Nordic countries (Kantola and Seeck, 2010; Streeck, 1998, pp. 438–440), and in the EU (Heidersohn and Hibbert, 1997, pp. 25–26). In the developing countries, talk of competitiveness developed into discussions of national development (Lall, 2001), the core question boiling down to making a national plan to choose the right kind of "technological avenue" to prosperity (Knudsen and Kotlen, 2006).

Many claims introduced in the name of competitiveness seem to belong politically to right-wing market liberalism. Governmental social insurance, income distribution and welfare benefits have been questioned in the face of a need for lower taxes and higher productivity (Rodrick, 1997, pp. 6–7). At the same time competitiveness has ranked particularly high in the political vocabularies of the Left. In the US competitiveness was embraced by the Clintonites (Krugman, 1994) and more recently by Barack Obama.

In the UK the Thatcher governments were not very interested in competitiveness policies, which were considered an unnecessary, state-led form of intervention. New Labour, however, embraced such policies, as the government attempted to gain credibility in financial markets and create competitiveness in a productive economy (Hay, 2004, p. 41). The Labour government set out a new industrial policy, and later, competitiveness policies addressed virtually every aspect of government policy (Oughton, 1997, p. 1487). Michael Porter was also brought in to map the UK's competitiveness (Beath, 2002; Porter and Ketels, 2003).

In Germany competitiveness entered the political arena in 1998 with a new red–green government. The government established a tripartite body made up of representatives of government, trade unions and employers' associations. The "Alliance for Jobs, Training and Competitiveness" would issue numerous directives on education, tax policies, pension schemes, working-time policies, health insurance, and economic development in East Germany. The Alliance was not, however, very successful. Internal disagreements undermined it as trade unions insisted on collective bargaining, and employers disagreed (Eiro, 2002).

The regimes of competitiveness have thus been set up by leftist parties, which have been winding down the class-based political concepts and have instead searched for concepts that would not divide the populace but rather create a sense of the common good. Laura d'Andrea Tyson, a Clintonite who later joined Barack Obama's council on competitiveness, explained the concept of competitiveness in 1995:

Like most buzzwords, competitiveness has symbolic significance. It draws national attention to the unassailable fact that the position of the United States in the world economy is weakening.

(D'Andrea Tyson, 1995, p. 96)

The leftist governments, most recently that of President François Hollande of France, have all used competitiveness to build up working relations with the business and industry sectors and to make their policies respectable in the new globalized economic conditions. Competitiveness has been introduced as a new "peace formula," which tries to define a social consensus between employers and workers and jointly search for "win–win" strategies in the markets (Streeck, 1998, pp. 438–440). At the same time the adoption of competitiveness has served the power interests of governments seeking to gain credibility, legitimacy, and power in an era when competitiveness has become a way of reaching out for the floating and shifting middle-class voters (Kantola, 2003).

In Foucauldian terms, policies aiming at improving national competitiveness have become a project of betterment typical of the idea of Progress: a range of techniques that map the state of the nation, its weaknesses and strengths, and endeavor to provide guidelines on how nations and their populations can increase their wealth and welfare. At the same time competitiveness functions as a rhetorical tool that naturalizes policies made in its name as part of a universal, necessary and irreversible trajectory of modernization (Alasuutari, 2011), particularly in its emphasis on rational planning. Competitiveness is an idealized simplification, a modern state plan that seems to offer a scientific and rational way of solving social problems, which an expert can discover and execute. As such, it is also a map allied with state power: it guides and legitimates political action and thus offers a sound basis for actual political power (Scott, 1998, pp. 112–113).

On the global level national competitiveness has been constructed as a transnational project that overcomes national barriers with its strategies and tactics (Foucault, 2004b, p. 121). The techniques of governance are carried on by the hypermobile international elites: professionals, researchers, scientists as well as managers, legislators, and policy-makers, who believe in high-modernist rational planning and science (Meyer et al., 1997, pp. 162, 174; Scott, 1998, pp. 4–5). International organizations such as the OECD and other administrative bodies act as mediators as they collect statistics and give policy recommendations. Moreover, competitiveness indicators and ratings make the concept politically effective by giving a clear target and a race track on which the contest can easily be followed up. Numbers make the difference in modern political life, as they appear to disclose the truth about our society (Rose, 1999, pp. 198–199).

When numbers are not enough, the gurus appear. Transnational consultants such as Michael Porter move swiftly from country to country, suggesting that their planning and expertise can solve societal problems (Kantola and Seeck, 2010). Management gurus and consultants have gained a rather visible role in societies and in politics as mediators, enablers, catalysts, and brokers of ideas

(Ernst and Kieser, 2002; Huczynski, 1998; Saint-Martin, 2000). Policy fashions are carefully planned and orchestrated, attracting attention and making a communicative difference (Osborne, 2004, pp. 440–441).

Many Foucauldian studies have examined the transmission of ideas from one sector to another, especially the influx of economic, enterprise, and business management models in the public sector (Barnett, 2002; Burchell, 1993; Foucault, 2004a, pp. 246–251; Longstreth, 1990; Miller and Rose, 1990, 1995; Rose, 1999, 2000). Competitiveness is one of those traveling concepts that have permeated politics, and the international models are used in local power politics (Sum, 2010).

A growing body of research has also analyzed the current interplay of ideas, knowledge and political power and pointed out how political ideas are depoliticized and irrelevant to left–right policy divisions, and how they circulate globally and cross national borders and sectoral barriers (Green-Pedersen and Wilkeson, 2006; Lyngard, 2007; Timmermans and Scholten, 2006) as policy-makers hook on to an idea to legitimize their actions (Holm Pedersen, 2007). Competitiveness has clearly become a world model, built on the rationalistic idea of development and peaceful co-existence (Meyer et al., 1997).

The case of competitiveness is also a good example of the productivity and creativity of power. Power does not reside in institutions, but rather works as strategies and techniques that go across institutional boundaries and turn into regimes with a variety of practices (Foucault, 2004b, pp. 121–122). New ideas are taken up and molded into new formulas and practices to gain power in the political system as local power relations come into play when ideas are domesticated on the national level. Looking at the way in which competitiveness is domesticated in different national contexts shows that nation-states are not mere conformists that unthinkingly copy models from other countries. Rather, buzzwords such as national competitiveness circulate between local regimes if and when policy-makers find them useful as a means to govern other actors, stakeholders, and the citizens by acting upon their beliefs, hopes, or desires (Dean, 1999, pp. 22–29; see also Rose, 1999, pp. 20–60).

In the case of national competitiveness, this is evident in the way it has been used in politics to create "unholy alliances"—that is, political agreements that cross traditional party lines and political divisions, and therefore, are useful in gaining political power. Competitiveness became a buzzword used by leftist and conservative governments, and by governments, industries and trade unions to create a common understanding. Some political actors, especially on the Left, adopted it in order to appear credible in the eyes of other political actors. Thus, competitiveness was useful in helping to create alliances that were needed to exercise power.

Competitiveness is a non-divisive concept of the common national good and, at the same time, a very flexible concept. The wide range of variables in transnational indicators as well as in the Porterian theory open up a wide array of possibilities in interpreting policy tasks, and the case of Finland demonstrates that political actors have seized on this possibility creatively. This also has to do with the obscure nature of national competitiveness. The validity of the notion has been contested in many ways, as it has been questioned whether a nation's competitiveness can be assessed or advanced in a meaningful way (see Kantola and Seeck, 2010). Finland, however, is just a case example. Most political systems have interwoven balancing qualities, which means that rulers need to take into account other actors and persuade them. This need is most pressing in political systems based on coalition governments that include a mix of parties. On the other hand, in some countries the president and the parliament balance each other, and thus the need to find compromises is crucial. There is always a search for uniting concepts that help to create alliances of power. The need to find a common unifying rationale has increased with the downfall of class-based party ideologies and the increasing importance of centrist and middle-class politics (Kantola, 2003).

The case of national competitiveness thus shows that the formula of power cannot dictate in advance, but rather the exercise of power evolves over time with unexpected outcomes and developments as well as through the dynamic relationships within organizations (Clegg, Courpasson, and Phillips, 2006, pp. 400–401). As Rose (1999, p. 11) has pointed out, one needs to pay attention to the humble, the mundane, and the small shifts in ways of thinking and understanding, the petty and contingent struggles, and the tensions and negotiations that give rise to something new and unexpected. In studies of domestication one should thus focus on the real uses of power: how transnational regimes of knowledge and expertise are translated into techniques of power in local settings.

References

Alasuutari, P. (2011). Modernization as a tacit concept used in governance. *Journal of Political Power, 4*(2), 217–235.

Alasuutari, P. (2013). Spreading global models and enhancing banal localism: The case of local government cultural policy development. *International Journal of Cultural Policy, 19*(1), 103–119.

Barnett, N. (2002). Including ourselves: New Labour and engagement with public services. *Management Decision, 40*(4), 310–317.

Beath, J. (2002). UK industrial policy: Old tunes on new instruments? *Oxford Review of Economic Policy, 18*(2), 221–238.

Burchell, G. (1993). Liberal government and techniques of the self. *Economy and Society, 22*(3), 267–283.

Clegg, S., Courpasson, D., and Phillips, N. (2006). *Power and Organizations.* London: Sage.

D'Andrea Tyson, L. (1995). Competitiveness: An analysis of the problem and a perspective on future policy. In M.K. Starr (ed.), *Global Competitiveness: Getting the US Back on Track.* New York: W.W. Norton.

De la Mothe, J., and Dufour, P. (1995). Techno-gobalism and the challenges to science and technology policy. *Daedalus, 124*(3), 219–234.

Dean, M. (1999). *Governmentality: Power and Rule in Modern Society.* London: Sage.

Eiro (2002). Future of National Alliance for Jobs under debate. Retrieved 9 August 2013 from www.eurofound.europa.eu/eiro/2002/12/feature/de0212205f.htm.

Ernst, B. and Kieser, A. (2002). In search of explanations for the consulting explosion. In K. Sahlin-Andersson and L. Engwall (eds), *The Expansion of Management Knowledge* (pp. 47–73). Stanford, CA: Stanford University Press.

Fagerberg, J. (1988). International competitiveness. *Economic Journal, 98*(391), 355–375.

Flyvbjerg, B. (1998). *Rationality and Power: Democracy in Practice*. Chicago, IL: University of Chicago Press.

Foucault, M. (2000). *Essential works of Foucault 1954–1984* (edited by D. Faubion). New York: New Press.

Foucault, M. (2004a). *Naissance de la Biopolitique: Cours au Collège de France, 1978–1979*. Paris: Seuil/Gallimard.

Foucault, M. (2004b). *Sécurité, Territoire, Population: Cours au Collège de France, 1977–1978*. Paris: Seuil/Gallimard.

Francis, A. (1992). The process of national industrial regeneration and competitiveness. *Strategic Management Journal, 13*(Special issue: Fundamental themes in strategy process research), 61–78.

Freeman, C. (1984). Prometheus unbound. *Futures, 16*(5), 494–500.

Freeman, C. (1990). *The Economics of Innovation*. Brookfield, VT: Edward Elgar.

Freeman, C. and Soete, L. (1987). *Technical Change and Full Employment*. Oxford: Basil Blackwell.

Godin, B. (2004). The obsession for competitiveness and its impact on statistics: The construction of high-technology indicators. *Research Policy, 33*, 1217–1229.

Green-Pedersen, C. and Wilkeson, J. (2006). How agenda-setting attributes shape politics: Basic dilemmas, problem attention and health politics developments in Denmark and the US. *Journal of European Public Policy, 13*, 1039–1052.

Hay, C. (2004). Credibility, competitiveness and the business cycle in "Third Way" political economy: A critical evaluation of economic policy in Britain since 1997. *New Political Economy, 9*(1), 39–56.

Heidersohn, K. and Hibbert, E. (1997). A sectoral analysis of Europe's international competitiveness. *Competitiveness Review, 7*(2), 25–37.

Helsingin Sanomat (1990, 23 September). Suomen ovea kolkutetaan (Editorial).

Helsingin Sanomat (1998, 25 February). Mikä onkaan Suomen kilpailukyky? (Johannes Koroma).

Helsingin Sanomat (1999, 21 April). Kilpailukykykilpailussakin Suomen sijoitus riippuu kilpailun säännöistä.

Helsingin Sanomat (2001, 19 April). Luonto ei odota eikä neuvottele (Satu Hassi).

Helsingin Sanomat (2001, 19 October). Suomen kilpailukyky taas maailman paras. Etlan tutkija: Oikea sijoitus on kymmenen parhaan joukossa.

Helsingin Sanomat (2004, 16 October). Korkean tason huvia (Editorial).

Helsingin Sanomat (2005, 10 September). Heinäluoma: Taloudessa ei aihetta synkistelyyn (Laura Pekonen).

Helsingin Sanomat (2012, 30 September). Työn hinta on saatavissa kilpailukykyiseksi.

Helsingin Sanomat (2012, 14 October). Ollila vaatii työmarkkinauudistusta.

Helsingin Sanomat (2012, 3 November). SAK:n kysely: Työn mielekkyyden koetaan vähentyneen.

Hernesniemi, H., Lammi, M., and Ylä-Anttila, P. (1995). *Kansallinen kilpailukyky ja teollinen tulevaisuus*. Helsinki: Taloustieto.

Hindess, B. (1996). *Discourses of Power, From Hobbes to Foucault*. Oxford: Blackwell Publishers.

Hindess, B. (1998). Neo-liberalism and the national economy. In M. Dean and B. Hindess (eds), *Governing Australia, Studies in Contemporary Rationalities of Government* (pp. 210–226). Cambridge: Cambridge University Press.

Holm Pedersen, K. (2007). Ideas are transformed as they transfer: a comparative study of eco-taxation in Scandinavia. *Journal of European Public Policy, 14*, 59–77.

Huczynski, A.A. (1998). Management gurus: What makes them and how to become one. In S. Segal-Horn (ed.), *The Strategy Reader* (pp. 430–437). Oxford: Blackwell Publishing.

Hämäläinen, T. (2003). *National Competitiveness and Economic Growth*. Cheltenham: Edward Elgar.

Kananen, J. (2011). *Modern Societal Impulses and their Nordic Manifestations*. Doctorate, Helsinki University, Helsinki.

Kantola, A. (2002). *Markkinakuri ja Managerivalta: Poliittinen hallinta Suomen 1990-luven talouskriisissä*. Helsinki: Loki.

Kantola, A. (2003). Loyalties in flux: The changing politics of citizenship. *European Journal of Cultural Studies, 6*(2), 205–217.

Kantola, A. (2010). The disciplined imaginary: The nation reconfigured for the global condition. In A. Roosvall and I. Moring (eds), *Communicating the Nation* (pp. 237–254). Gothenburg: Nordicom.

Kantola, A. and Kananen, J. (2013). Seize the moment: Financial crisis and the making of the Finnish competition state. *New Political Economy*, DOI:10.1080/13563467.2012.753044.

Kantola, A. and Seeck, H. (2010). Dissemination of management into politics: Michael Porter and the political uses of management consulting. *Management Learning, 42*(1), 25–47.

Keep, E. and Mayhew, K. (1999). The assessment: Knowledge, skills, and competitiveness. *Oxford Review of Economic Policy, 15*(2), 1–18.

Kirzner, I. (1997). Entrepreneurial discovery and the competitive market process: An Austrian approach. *Journal of Economic Literature, 35*, 60–85.

Knudsen and Kotlen. (2006). Systems of production and international competitiveness: Prospects for the developing countries. In D. Conway and N. Heynen (eds), *Globalization's Contradictions* (pp. 65–76). London: Routledge.

Kravis, I. and Lipsey, R. (1967). A report on the study of international price competitiveness. *American Economic Review, 57*(2), 482–491.

Kravis, I. and Lipsey, R. (1971). *Price Competitiveness in World Trade: Studies in International Economic Relations, 6*. New York: National Bureau of Economic Research.

Krugman, P. (1994). Competitiveness: A dangerous obsession. *Foreign Affairs, 73*(2), 28–44.

Krugman, P. (1995). Technological change in international trade. In P. Stoneman (ed.), *Handbook of the Economics of Innovation and Technological Change* (pp. 342–365). Oxford: Blackwell.

Lall, S. (2001). Competitiveness indices and developing countries: An economic evaluation of the Global Competitiveness Report. *World Development, 29*(9), 1501–1525.

Lemola, T. (2001). Tiedettä, teknologiaa ja innovaatioita kansakunnan parhaaksi. Katsaus Suomen tiede ja teknologiapolitiikan lähihistoriaan (Vol. 57/01): VTT *Työpapereita*.

Lodge, M. (2007). The importance of being modern: International benchmarking and national regulatory innovation. *Journal of European Public Policy, 12*(4), 649–667.

Longstreth, F.H. (1990). Historical political economy and liberal democratic capitalism. *Economy and Society, 19*(1), 95–120.

Lyngard, K. (2007). The institutional construction of a policy field: A discursive institutional perspective on change within the common agricultural policy. *Journal of European Public Policy, 14*, 293–312.

Meyer, J.W. (2004). The nation as Babbitt: How countries conform. *Contexts, 3*(3), 42–47.

Meyer, J.W., Boli, J., Thomas, G.M., and Ramirez, F.O. (1997). World society and the nation-state. *American Journal of Sociology, 103*(1), 144–181.

Miller, P. and Rose, N. (1990). Governing economic life. *Economy and Society, 19*(1), 5–31.

Miller, P. and Rose, N. (1995). Production, identity and democracy. *Theory and Society, 24*(5), 427–467.

Määttä, S. (2005). Strategian ja strategisen informaation tulkintahorisontteja. Case Valtiovarainministeriö. *Turun Kauppakorkeakoulun julkaisuja, A*(2).

OECD (1997). *Industrial Competitiveness in the Knowledge-based Economy: The New Role for Governments*. Paris: OECD.

Osborne, T. (2004). On mediators: intellectuals and the ideas trade in the knowledge society. *Economy and Society, 33*(4), 430–447.

Oughton, C. (1997). Competitiveness policy in the 1990s. *Economic Journal, 107*, 1486–1503.

Perez, C. (1983). Structural change and the assimilation of new technologies in the economic and social system. *Futures, 15*(4), 357–375.

Porter, M.E. (1990). *The Competitive Advantage of Nations*. London: Macmillan Press.

Porter, M.E. and Ketels, C. (2003). UK competitiveness: Moving to the next stage. DTI Economics Paper 3: Economic and Science Research Council.

Reubi, D. (2010). The will to modernize: A genealogy of biomedical research ethics in Singapore. *International Political Sociology, 4*, 142–158.

Richardson, J.D. (1972). [Review]. [Kravis, I. and Lipsey, R. (1971) Price competitiveness in world trade. *Studies in International Economic Relations, No. 6*]. *Journal of the American Statistical Association*, 490–491.

Rodrick, D. (1997). *Has Globalization Gone Too Far?* Washington, D.C.: Institute for International Economics.

Rose, N. (1999). *Powers of Freedom*. Cambridge, UK: Cambridge University Press.

Rose, N. (2000). Governing liberty. In R. Ericsson (ed.), *Governing Modern Societies* (pp. 141–176). Toronto, ON: Toronto University Press.

Saint-Martin, D. (2000). *Building the Managerialist State*. Oxford: Oxford University Press.

Schmidt, V. (1995). The new world order, incorporated: The rise of business and the decline of the nation state. *Daedalus, 124*(2), 75–106.

Schumpeter, J. (1992/1943). *Capitalism, Socialism and Democracy*. London: Routledge.

Scott, J. (1998). *Seeing Like a State*. New Haven, CT: Yale University Press.

Seeck, H. and Kantola, A. (2009). Organizational control: Restrictive or productive? *Journal of Management and Organization, 15*(2), 241–257.

Sharp, M. (1997). Technology, globalization and industrial policy. In M. Talalay, C. Farrands and R. Tooze (eds), *Technology, Culture and Competitiveness* (pp. 90–106). London: Routledge.

Sklair, L. (2002). The transnational capitalist class and global politics: Deconstructing the corporate–state connection. *International Political Science Review, 23*(2), 159–174.

Starr, M.K. and Ullmann, J.E. (1988). The myth of US industrial supremacy. In M.K. Starr (ed.), *Global Competitiveness: Getting the US Back on Track* (pp. 43–71). New York: W.W. Norton.

Stoneman, P. (1995). *Handbook of the Economics of Innovation and Technological Change*. Oxford: Blackwell.

Strange, S. (1996). *The Retreat of the State: The Diffusion of Power in the World Economy*. Cambridge: Cambridge University Press.

Streeck, W. (1998). The internationalization of industrial relations in Europe: Prospects and problems. *Politics and Society, 26*(4), 429–459.

Sum, N.-L. (2010). A cultural political economy of transnational knowledge brands. *Journal of Language and Politics, 9*(4), 546–573.

Timmermans, A. and Scholten, P. (2006). The political flow of wisdom: Science institutions as policy venues in the Netherlands. *Journal of European Public Policy, 13*, 1104–1118.

VNK (2005a). Julkinen hyvinvointivastuu sosiaali- ja terveydenhuollossa [Public welfare responsibility in social and health care] *Valtioneuvoston kanslian julkaisusarja 5/2005*. Helsinki: Valtioneuvoston kanslia [Prime Minister's Office].

VNK (2005b). Tuottavuus ja työllisyys. Mitä opittavaa muista Pohjoismaista? [Productive and employment: What can we learn from other Nordic countries?] *Valtioneuvoston kanslian raportteja 3/2005*. Helsinki: Valtioneuvoston kanslia [Prime Minister's Office].

VNK (2007). Pääministeri Matti Vanhasen hallituksen ohjelman seuranta [The follow-up of Prime Minister Matti Vanhanen's governmental program] *Valtioneuvoston kanslian julkaisusarja 6/2007*. Helsinki: Valtioneuvoston kanslia [Prime Minister's Office].

Warf, B. (1999). The hypermobility of capital and the collapse of the Keynesian state. In R. Martin (ed.), *Money and the Space Economy* (pp. 227–239). Chichester: John Wiley and Sons.

4 The sociogenesis of the nation-state in European social policy

Stefan Bernhard

Introduction

In this chapter, a world culture perspective is applied to alternative forms of governance within the EU. In contrast to the widely held view in governance research that the Open Method of Coordination (OMC) constitutes a more or less successful arrangement for policy learning, I propose the hypothesis that mechanisms of "soft" governance (Trubek and Trubek, 2003) are both means and results of the diffusion (by transposition) of a global culture. The OMC surrounds EU member states with a complex array of expectations that constitute a framework for legitimate action. Ultimately, the member states' adoption of the OMC leads to a reconstitution of the idea of who an actor is and what an actor does. The European Commission, researchers, and International Non-Governmental Organizations (INGOs) play a decisive part in this process of actor formation by taking on the role of "cultural others" (Bernhard and Münch, 2011; Meyer, 1996). Their work can be understood in reference to the work of George H. Mead as a contribution to the sociogenesis of the nation-state in a European community. These cultural others contribute to the dissemination of scripts, which can be defined by three key elements: first, the EU member states are expected to behave as actors that learn strategically and formulate policy prospectively in a learning-based manner. Second, the coordination of national social policies offers transnational actors diverse and lasting opportunities to act as cultural others and thereby contribute to the new self-understanding of the member states. Third, through the process of OMC, central terms and concepts are established as legitimizing European frames of reference that allow for coordination in the form of a "standardization of differences." (Schwinn, 2006) The actual impact of these scripts in national contexts depends on complex processes of domestication that can be analyzed with Bourdieu's concept of fields (Bourdieu, 1977; Bourdieu and Wacquant, 1992). All in all, the world culture perspective and governance research thus share the view that OMC is a process of diffusion, but according to the world culture perspective advocated here diffusion is not primarily of instrumental policy-making knowledge but rather of "existential knowledge" (Büttner, 2012).

The contribution has three sections. The following section introduces the neoinstitutional idea of actorhood with an emphasis on the role of cultural others in the process of becoming a legitimate actor. The next section turns to the empirical object of investigation, the OMC in EU social and employment policies. It elaborates the world cultural script of good European nationhood and shows how the OMC as a learning procedure serves as a structural base for the diffusion of this script. The section also argues that the domestication of this script depends on the dynamic of power struggles in national fields. Finally, in the last section the core assertions of the world culture perspective are summarized with a view to explaining processes of domestication.

The sociogenesis of the EU nation-states

World culture theory incorporates a number of theoretical premises that have far-reaching implications. Three issues are of particular importance to the argument here. First, neoinstitutionalists see actors (i.e. individuals, organizations, and nation-states) as units that are constructed by and subject to social expectations. Rather than being primordial entities, they gain prominence and relevance only in very concrete social settings (Meyer and Jepperson, 2000). As these settings change over time so do the actors embedded in them (Boli, 1987; Boli and Thomas, 1997; Dobbin, Simmons, and Garrett, 2007; Drori, Meyer, Ramirez, and Schofer, 2003). Secondly, scripts (in the neoinstitutionalist sense) can only be diffused when cultural others enter the picture as their circulators. Cultural others continually develop actor identities and spheres of action with reference to world culture principles. These identities and spheres then become resources for actors in national field struggles. Thirdly, world-cultural actors assimilate the social expectations that cultural others produce, and assign to them in a way analogous to the constitution of the self in ontogenesis as described by George H. Mead (1967): They become who they are by "internalizing" (globally disseminated) social scripts in constant (inner) dialogue with others. Since this third point is essential to the argument here, I will elaborate on it in greater detail.

Meyer's idea of nation-states is inspired by Mead's path-breaking perspective on the co-constitution of individuals and society. Global society precedes the existence of the nation-states in both logical and historical terms, and it is only by participating in that society that nation-states can become legitimate actors. Participating here means that nation-states adopt the expectations of their social environment. To do this, they develop a formal structure (which Mead would call a "me") that corresponds to the social expectations directed towards them by third parties. This dissolves the actor–society duality: just as in Mead's theory, society is not external to the self; the nation-state does not act in global society as a primordial unit. By internalizing third-party expectations as a formal structure, the nation-state can make itself an object; as Mead was eager to stress, having a self means that one can judge oneself on the basis of social expectations. "That is to say, self-criticism is essentially social criticism, and behavior controlled by self-criticism is essentially behavior controlled socially" (Mead, 1967: 255). The formal structure of the nation-state is thus primarily a kind of checklist for the nation-state to work towards, and by doing so the state is undergoing social control in the sense of world culture theory. With this formal structure, the nation-state declares the noble ideals of global society to be its own ideals. In so doing, it opens both to self-criticism and criticism with reference to these ideals. Creating a formal structure transposes the dynamic tension between the authority to act and the resulting legitimate authority (the two components of Meyer's actor model) inside the nation-state itself. Thus, the nation-state can be conceived of as an ongoing process of optimization in the pursuit of general, i.e. world cultural, goals. The actor is embedded in its environment by turning itself into its own object.

Cultural others play an important part in this process. They embody (some-times literally) the ambitious goals of the global society that constitute nation-states (Boli and Thomas, 1999). It is their reactions that tell nation-states what progress and justice, the overriding principles for actors in rationalized moder-nity, actually mean (Meyer, Boli, Thomas, and Ramirez, 1997). Nation-states can communicate and interact with cultural others, and thus test their scope for legitimate action. Through the social acts (in Mead's sense) that they undertake with generalized cultural others, they can develop the social expectations that make them fully adequate individuals, capable of action, within the globally embedded European community of states. Cultural others form the raw material for social control.

Cultural others thus have a dual function. Firstly, they convert world cultural values into specific expectations, which, once internalized, guide behavior. Sec-ondly, they keep these expectations relevant, because their ongoing presence constantly triggers renewed criticism and self-criticism (Bernhard, 2009). Taking the analogy between Mead's generalized other and Meyer's cultural other one step further, one could perhaps even read a passage in Mead on the relationship between the individual and society as a description of the relationship between the nation-state and the global or European society, respectively:

> The self-conscious human individual [or, the nation-state], then, takes or assumes the organized social attitudes of the given social group or com-munity (or of some one section thereof) [or, of the world society] to which he belongs, toward the social problems of various kinds which confront that group or community at any given time, and which arise in connection with the correspondingly different social projects or organized co-operative enter-prises in which that group or community as such is engaged [i.e. the pursuit of equity and progress]; and as an individual participant in these social pro-jects or co-operative enterprises, he governs his own conduct accordingly.
>
> Mead, 1967: p. 156

The diffusion of world culture occurs because scripts are rendered specific and relevant by cultural others, and because nation-states internally orientate them-selves towards these scripts.

We can now formulate the main thesis of this chapter with greater precision. As noted in the introductory section, the OMC is both a means and a result of the diffusion of world culture. It attains this status by creating space for cultural others who communicate specific world culture expectations with the member states of the EU. To the extent that nation-states domesticate these scripts in national fields, world culture values spread, and the OMC acts as a means. To the extent that the OMC is regarded as a legitimate way of shaping policy, it is itself also an indicator of global society. Successful diffusion ultimately leads to the result that nation-states claim to work towards the expectations contained in the world culture scripts. This does not necessarily mean that their (here: political) practices necessarily correspond to these formal structures. Following on from these preliminary considerations, we can now analyze the OMC as an empirical object in terms of world culture.

Soft forms of governance and nation-state selves in the EU

In this section, I will first lay out what the OMC is—or what it is proclaimed to be by those cultural others that helped to develop and implement it at the European level. I will show how the world culture perspective breaks with and transcends the commonly held view on the method. Subsequently, I present three main elements of the OMC script and then advance the idea that their domestication hinges upon the dynamics of national field struggles.

The OMC: procedures and types of knowledge

What is the OMC and how does it work? Commonly, the OMC is described as a new (or alternative) form of governance that could replace power-based policy-making by learning-based policy-making (e.g. Mosher, 2003). Four elements are considered essential (European Council, 2000): First, goals (Common Objectives) are set at European level to lay out a general framework for the entire process of exchanging experiences. Examples of such Common Objectives are the goal of achieving an employment rate of 70 percent (CEU, 2008: 4) or the goal of effectively combating exclusion (CEC, 2006: 18; CEU, 2002). Second, member states draw up National Action Plans or National Reform Strategies that should outline how they try to achieve the Common Objectives. Ideally, these action plans include a description of fundamental problems, political goals possibly with target indicators, an evaluation of previous policy evaluations and, finally, a list of good policy practices. On the basis of these reports, third, the European Commission draws up Joint Reports in cooperation with member states. These Reports gather the experiences of member states and distribute them so that every other member state can profit from them. Then, fourth and finally, topics suitable for direct bilateral and multilateral learning processes in a Peer Review are selected. These four institutionalized steps take different forms in different policy areas. For example, the Joint Report on pension policies is scarcely more than a paper outlining the differences between the states (CEU, 2009b), while for employment policy, specific recommendations can be given to individual member states (CEU, 2009a). What is more important than these nuances is the fact that in all cases the OMC is designed to be a recursive process, i.e. that after one cycle of the process, from defining objectives to Peer Review, there are new Common Objectives for the next cycle. Thus, every goal and every political instrument to achieve these goals is embedded in a trial-and-error process, while the goals and instruments of previous cycles are revisited at a later point in time. Moreover, this means that the process is permanent.

The OMC is treated as a learning process both by officials and scholars. Consequently, reflections on the process deal with the conditions for recipro-cal policy learning and the limitations to that principle in a political environ-ment. Kerber and Eckhardt, for example, put it as follows: "For the OMC the most interesting aspects concern (1) the incentives for actors to actively parti-cipate in learning about better policies; and (2) the incentives to actually implement such better policies" (Kerber and Eckardt, 2007). The research interest is thus formulated in such a way that it sparks off academic debates on the potential of the method. Authors who do not consider learning to be an appropriate form of policy-making then become critics: "It is not reasonable to expect far-reaching results of a mechanism which is not legally binding, which remains rather vague about its goal(s), which does not foresee a mandate for independent evaluation as well as for the dissemination of information, etc." (Kröger, 2006: 13).

These quotes illustrate that scholarly debate about the OMC aims at a specific form of knowledge, which I, following Büttner (2012), dub instrumental know-ledge. Contrary to existential (identity) knowledge, instrumental knowledge is not about what things are and where they come from, but rather on how to achieve something in a given social setting. With this conceptual distinction we can see that researchers as well as participating bureaucrats and politicians deal with optimizing the OMC not with reflecting upon its social conditions of exist-ence. Hence, for the great majority of policy researchers we can say that they are epistemically so close to their object of scrutiny that they share its perspective on the OMC (Bernhard, 2010, 2011).

The world culture perspective takes a different stance. Here, instrumental knowledge is secondary material. Of greater importance are issues of existential knowledge. More generally, neoinstitutionalism is not concerned with the effec-tiveness of the method but with its formative effects upon reality (Djelic and Sahlin-Andersson, 2006b). Leading questions are: What principles of good policy underlie the OMC (Jacobsson and Sahlin-Andersson, 2006: 253–262)? How is the nation-state envisaged (Jacobsson, 2006: 209–218)? What actors in what capacity are defined as relevant actors (Djelic and Sahlin-Andersson, 2006a: 8–12)? The world culture perspective *breaks* with the perspective of the participants and of the researchers surrounding the OMC. The price for this change of perspective is a different kind of knowledge that might be of little interest to participants but is all the more important to evaluating the overall sociological effect of the method. This implies that the world culture perspective treats mainstream research as part of the object of investigation. In this sense, governance research is part of the empirical processes observed.

The OMC as a means and a result of the diffusion of world culture

At the level of existential knowledge, we can identify three effects of the OMC: (1) the OMC produces a large number of expectations, which center on the expectation that nation-states reconfigure as strategically learning actors; (2) it creates social spaces where EU officials, researchers and INGOs can act as cultural others; and (3) it establishes new legitimating references for national social policy.

The strategically learning nation-state

The OMC helps to ensure that EU member states move from being isolated entities in a diffuse global environment to members of a European family of nations. The guiding principle behind this transformation is that nation-states participate voluntarily in learning processes, and that they prepare to make policy reforms in a pragmatic, non-ideological manner that is evidence-based. As strategically learning states EU member states are expected to be the driving force behind the learning procedures of the OMC. Thus, there should be no need for carrot-and-stick types of sanctions. The OMC script postulates three issues for the strategically learning nation-state. By defining Common Objectives, the European nation-states are joined together as equals to form a common European family of nations that faces common problems. Such equality is operationalized by creating comparability and equivalence among states as a basis for learning processes. Finally, codified styles of behavior suggest how each state should behave.

The point of Common Objectives, the first step in the continuing process of the OMC, is not their actual content but rather the fact that they are formulated and communicated as European objectives. In world cultural terms, they circumscribe nation-states' legitimate scope of action by marking areas where action is most legitimate. Seen this way, for instance, the goal of "making pensions policies sustainable" signals a legitimate sphere for agency that has to be filled with concrete policies on the national level. The same holds true for the objective to "promote social inclusion." If member states announce an intention to reduce social exclusion, they demonstrate their willingness to stick to this part of the OMC script. In practical terms, the need for action in such policy fields results in considerable efforts to document attempts at action that are being made. These include National Action Plans, which should, whenever possible, be based on regional action plans and drawn up after extensive consultation with actors from civil society. They also include the Joint Reports.

Neoinstitutionalism summons such processes under the umbrella term of excessive structuring (for example Meyer et al., 1997). One effect of all this activity is that in the course of undertaking voluntary political actions towards framework objectives, European nation-states implicitly consent to be part of a European whole. Hence, the world of the European nation-state is one in which the supranational context of national social policy can now be determined more precisely than ever before, namely as a group of European member states that are willing to learn. In this "community of the willing" and under the approving gaze of cultural others, European nation-states develop new or additional selves.

Another fundamental assumption behind the OMC's learning dynamics is that EU member states are equal and that they have to see themselves as equal. If this were not the case, learning from the experiences of others would become much more difficult. Strang and Meyer (1993) have emphasized the importance of this assumption for the diffusion of concepts and ideas: "States subscribe to remarkably similar purposes ... And while these cultural definitions can be and are in fact violated, they provide fertile ground for the rapid diffusion of public policies and institutional structures. Consider how much diffusion would be slowed if nation-states were wholly primordial, or if they occupied formally differentiated positions within a hierarchical global political structure" (Strang and Meyer, 1993: 491). In this respect, the OMC is a mechanism for creating equivalences. It ensures that nation-states represent their historical developments, current situation and policy approaches in a uniform manner and that they offer them to other member states as a resource for experience-based learning.

Outlines for National Action Plans give detailed instructions about what these should contain (CEC, 2006). A complex apparatus of knowledge production about a wide variety of social policy issues further supports this standardization. First and foremost is, of course, the Joint Report, the explicit objective of which is to create a shared pool of knowledge that is accessible to all those interested in learning at any time. The Joint Reports are accompanied by expert reports created by a network of independent national experts (EC, n.d.(a)). The European Commission regularly contributes reports on the social situation in Europe (for example CEC, 2007). It also finances transnational projects at local levels, focusing on implementation and knowledge, as part of its action program PROGRESS (EC, n.d.(b)). A large number of research reports deal with individual issues. And the Peer Review process is an occasion to bring researchers, practitioners and politicians together (EC, n.d.(c)). The European Observatory on the Social Situation and Demography and the knowledge-oriented work of the INGOs (for example FEANTSA, 2007) ensure that there is a constant flow of comparable information about each nation-state in the EU. Finally, the continual expansion of the European statistical infrastructure will, in the medium and long term, help to spread acceptance of the idea of Europe as a common social space (Bernhard, 2012). With all this, national peculiarities appear as differences against shared scales of measurement and comparison.

Finally, the OMC script includes very specific expectations about the types of behavior expected of member states. They should develop a pragmatic attitude towards policy reforms, proceed in a strategic manner and yet be willing to learn, and involve regions and NGOs. Moreover, where possible, they should ground their policies on the results of scholarly research.

The institutional structures of the OMC encourage EU member states to question not only their methods of policy implementation but also their policy objectives. This is in line with the pragmatic view that policy goals and their implementation should be seen in relation to one another. In other words, policy objectives change with the means deployed in their cause (Dorf and Sabel, 1998). This presupposes, of course, that member states embrace criticism. It is evident that nation-states have to get used to this way of thinking about and making policy, and the European Commission does its best to assist them in this process (as it does for Eastern Enlargement: CEC, 2004). *Pars pro toto*, the case of the new member states shows how cultural others assist nation-states in becoming members of the European club.

The primary condition for the OMC is that member states act strategically in a manner that is focused on learning. In general, the entire system of knowledge production accompanying the OMC is advertised as an opportunity for member states: Learning from experience is voluntary, but acquiring knowledge stipulates and facilitates further learning. So improving a nation's policies is a promising occasion with obvious merits. The most explicit requirement for experience-based learning can be found in the guidelines for the National Action Plans on pensions, social inclusion and health policies. Here, member states are requested to set clear and, where possible, quantifiable output and input targets and to evaluate these afterwards (CEC, 2006: 6).

Another feature of legitimate governance in the OMC is the cooperative and inclusive nature of the process. This orientation has long been characteristic of the European Union. Think, for example, of the complex system of committees, the social and civil dialogues, or the attempts to enrich EU governance activities with increasingly far-reaching and increasingly systematic attempts to work in cooperation with civil society, the regions of the member states, and local instances (for example CEC, 2001a: 4). With the OMC, the European Commission has found a way to disseminate this attitude. The "involvement of all actors" is in fact one of the four common European framework objectives (CEU, 2002).

Finally, an essential element of nation-states that are willing to learn and that behave in a strategic manner is that they ground their actions in research. This means, first of all, that expert advice is needed and compatible at all stages of policy formulation (from planning to evaluation). The increasingly scientific nature of governance is reflected in the fact that knowledge produced by scientific means and presented by researchers has become the primary source of legitimate justifications for decisions. Science has become the language for legitimizing policies. And there is a second, deeper sense in which governance is becoming "scientific:" literature on the knowledge society has indicated that it is not just that science as a part of society is becoming more influential, but that individuals are increasingly behaving like scientists (Büttner, 2012). The OMC asks politicians at all levels to use an evidence-based approach to policy, which means that they (just like actual researchers) are supposed to collect, compare and interpret data in order to draw conclusions. The increasing influence of science is thus a style of action, not just an external product of advice external to politics. It is part of the self of OMC-participants at all levels.

Spaces for cultural others

Not only does the OMC reconstitute member states as strategically learning actors, it also defines who else is a relevant actor in the transnational learning process, and what is expected of him/her. The political style of alternative governance sees governance as a cooperative process between state actors and non-state actors at all levels. The OMC brings in researchers and policy advisors, NGOs, social movements and international bureaucracies, based on the idea that policy learning is best done in a dense and diversified network of peers. Of particular importance at European level are INGOs, researchers and the European Commission. These actors take a comprehensive advisory function within the governance architecture that is intended to help member states "to progressively develop their own policies" (CEC, 2003b: 9). INGOs like the European Anti-Poverty Network (EAPN) and the homeless organization FEANTSA (the European Federation of National Organisations working with the Homeless) collect information from their national member organizations, use reports to criticize and praise policies, and contribute to monitoring the process. In addition, INGOs get involved in transnational networks, and in practice and research projects at European level, and make suggestions about how the procedures for the European coordination process should be improved (for example EAPN, 2000, 2004; FEANTSA, 2006). With all these activities they make reference to scholarly expertise or compile their own research (Bernhard, 2009: 40–50). In addition researchers are consulted repeatedly in the processes of policy-learning, most prominently when projects are being evaluated for peer review, and when statistics for comparative descriptions of the social situation in Europe are being prepared.

In cooperation with the EU, INGOs and researchers are thus constantly involved in the coordination process. They continually remind the nation-states of the expectations of the script of the strategically learning nation-state: the iterative process of the OMC offers them a range of opportunities to do so. Thus, these actors can become cultural others for the nation-states. Their activities drive the internalization of what is expected of a modern, future-oriented nation-state. The advisors (cultural others) help determine which world cultural expectations, in what form, are adopted by the nation-states for self-criticism or third-party criticism. Through constructive criticism and guidance for self-criticism, a "me" is created, which the nation-states can then use as a monitoring point for their own actions. The task of the cultural others is not primarily to monitor; rather, they offer the opportunity for self-monitoring. With each National Action Plan, in which member states attempt to show that they have set themselves quantitative goals, with each identification of examples of good practice, with each participation in a Peer Review, and with each proof that policy learning has taken place, it becomes evident that the EU member states have accepted the script as an integral part of themselves. Their behavior shows how world cultural expectations become relevant in practical terms: that is, as self-evident, and self-applied, scales for measuring their own behavior.

New references for legitimating national social policy

Despite the vagueness of the OMC process with regard to policy content, it does manage to create some directions for policy in the form of references (for EU gender policy see Wobbe, 2007). It does not determine what policies member states should pursue, but it does relate their efforts within a common European framework. Their influence does not take the form of stipulating particular goals or methods; it is limited to defining the background of member states' attempts to make policy. Due to the fact these references are made again and again (and not just occasionally), and in a systematic form (not as vague references), European definitions of social and political situations become common points of reference. Standardization takes place through the "standardization of differences" (Schwinn, 2006: 225–227). This means that national policies are not legitimized in and by themselves, but by their proximity or distance to a common European vanishing point. The shared framework creates a uniform system of coordinates within which each state takes a clearly identifiable place: national idiosyncrasies thus turn into local European particularities.

Core ideas in European discourse include the development of a knowledge society and the need to invest (and invest in) human capital (CEC, 1997, 2001b, 2003a; European Council, 2000). Key concepts include flexicurity, social inclusion, knowledge, life-long learning, and equal opportunities (Daly, 2006; Dräger, 2007; Jensen, 2008; Szyszczak, 2001). Any entity that translates its policies into this language is acting legitimately in the sense of the European scripts. The fact that the terms and concepts used are ambiguous is not a disadvantage; indeed it is a necessary condition for the standardization of difference. Almost any kind of policy can be described as being in accordance with the vague goal of "flexicurity." One just needs to lay out which part of a policy is designed to improve security and which is targeted at flexibility. Of course, critics may argue that the concept is meaningless, and this cannot be denied. But this is not why the concept of "flexicurity" is productive for script diffusion. If all EU member states define their policies with reference to the same conceptual dimension (flexibility–security), a new overall picture is created, which is qualitatively different from those before. The construction takes place not at the level of "what," but at the level of "what for," "to what end." National social policies are literally *thought through* and thus become part of *one* European flexicurity policy. Seen from this perspective, the vague character of the main concepts of European social policy is not a regrettable problem, but a prerequisite to standardization in European social policy.

The most important exercise in the standardization of differences is the creation of the National Action Plans and Reform Strategies. As has been shown, member states have been required to demonstrate, within a precisely defined framework, the attempts they make to meet the Common Objectives. This means that they describe their experiences within a common system of reference. Whether this actually changes policy-making is an open empirical question.

Either EU member states use the European objectives to rethink their policies; or the creation of the national Reform Strategies remains merely a formal exercise, in which old policies are redressed and are subsumed under European goals. Empirically, both tendencies have been found, depending on the member state and on the area of policy involved (Heidenreich and Zeitlin, 2009). How, when, and to what degree national differences are standardized depends on actor strategies in national fields (see below).

Domestication in national fields

So far we have considered how an EU script develops around the OMC. Thereby, the argument focused exclusively at the European level and did not address the question when, how, and to what extent nation-states actually adopt the EU script. To investigate these processes of domestication one needs to complement the world polity approach with other theoretical perspectives. As argued elsewhere (Bernhard, 2009; Jepperson, 2002), Bourdieu's theory of field is well equipped to fill the gaps of Meyer's approach: analytically speaking, the domestication of EU scripts is the result of complex interdependencies between a European field that shapes the OMC script and national fields that need to process the respective expectations. In all fields less privileged actors (challengers in Fligstein's terms: Fligstein and McAdam, 2012) struggle with dominant actors (incumbents) over the distribution of resources as well as over the rules of the game, i.e. the whole social setting that has made one set of actors *dominant* and another one *dominated* actors. Each field defines and rates resources in a specific way; each is built on tacit assumptions and consent but also on histories of manifest conflict, and each is characterized by the interplay of dynamic forces (namely the strategic actors) and conservative forces (namely the power imbalances in the field).

Now, how does the constellation of national and European fields influence the adoption of the OMC script? A simple reference to different levels of governance might in fact oversimplify things. Scripts are not simply up- or downloaded; rather *national fields function as prisms* for EU scripts so that they do not arrive as such in national fields but as representational reconstructions. Since actors embedded in field contexts draw upon them, EU scripts are always interpreted or translated according to positions and the interests these actors have. Analytically, EU scripts multiply through such processes of domestication. They occur in the European field but also in modified versions in national fields, and thus become multifocal social phenomena. How a script arrives in a field varies. There might be explicit references to the EU script, silent borrowing, banal nationalism, or externalization (see Takayama, this volume). The question is whether, and how, embedded actors succeed in using the European script as a resource for their cause, in their context, at a particular point in time. For example, if a challenger pursues a revolutionary strategy aiming at overcoming dominant national traditions championed by an incumbent group, he/she might find it helpful to draw explicitly on the OMC script, postulating for example that the national legacy lags behind in international comparison. In this situation the incumbents on their part might have recourse to "banal nationalism" and stress national idiosyncrasies as a comparative advantage. The example demonstrates that latent and manifest negotiations in national fields shape the representation of an EU script in a national field.

Conclusion

This chapter presented the OMC as a means and result of world culture. It deliberately took a perspective that allows for a sociologically distanced view on mutual learning processes in EU social policy. To mark the difference from other research perspectives it is useful to distinguish instrumental from existential knowledge. For participants and many scientific observers the OMC is about the diffusion of instrumental knowledge. These actors are interested in finding and advocating examples of good policy practices, standards of comparative policy measurement and the like. This kind of knowledge is *instrumental* because it addresses practical needs of policy-makers. The diffusion processes that can be observed from a perspective of global culture by contrast refer to *existential* knowledge. Here, the main issue is not techniques of evidence-based learning but rather the question as to *who* acts, *how*, and what processes legitimize these actions. Nation-states are invited to rethink their ways of policy-making and reorient themselves according to the model of strategically learning actors. Also, the OMC establishes new standardizing frameworks for observing and developing social policies. Furthermore, cultural others, such as EU officials, researchers, and INGOs, use the OMC as a platform for counseling member states throughout the process of policy coordination.

The OMC script discussed here is an invention at the European level, or—to be more precise—an invention in a European field. To be effective in national contexts the script has to be transposed and linked to national discourses and institutional heritages. To follow the OMC script "through Europe" I suggested reconstructing these multiple processes of transposition from a field-analytical perspective: interested actors, embedded in unequal national power configurations and struggles for hegemony, take up, ignore, mold, reinterpret, orient towards, or fight what they, from their field position, consider to be the European script. In so doing, they domesticate—and this means here also—duplicate it. The essence of the script—the identification as a learning nation-state, the positions for cultural others, the standardization of differences—is but a *potential* resource for national actors. Just like any other resource it has to be used in field struggles to yield profit. Thereby, one has to bear in mind that the OMC script has characteristics that suggest its transposition in national fields. It recasts the recipient of the diffusion process (as learning nation-state), it establishes the carriers of diffusion (i.e. cultural others) and it does not exclude policy positions (via the deliberate ambiguity of key terms such as flexicurity). Clearly, the likelihood of diffusion is conditioned by the object of diffusion.

References

Bernhard, S. (2009). Die symbolische Inszenierung als kultureller Anderer—Zur Definition weltkultureller Skripte im Feld der europäischen Inklusionspolitik. *Berliner Journal für Soziologie, 19*(1), 1–26.

Bernhard, S. (2010). *Die Konstruktion von Inklusion. Europäische Sozialpolitik aus soziologischer Perspektive*. Frankfurt a.M.: Campus.

Bernhard, S. (2011). Beyond Constructivism—The Political Sociology of an EU Policy Field. *International Political Sociology, 5*(4), 426–445.

Bernhard, S. (2012). Informationelles Kapital als transnationale Ressource. In S. Bernhard and C. Schmidt-Wellenburg (eds), *Feldanalyse als Forschungsprogramm 2: Gegenstandsbezogene Theoriebildung* (pp. 195–216). Wiesbaden: VS.

Bernhard, S. and Münch, R. (2011). Die Hegemonie des Neoliberalismus. Ein gesellschaftstheoretischer Erklärungsansatz. *Sociologia Internationalis, 49*(2), 165–197.

Boli, J. (1987). Human Rights or State Expansion? Cross-National Definitions of Constitutional Rights, 1870–1970. In G.M. Thomas, J.W. Meyer, F.O. Ramirez, and J. Boli (eds), *Institutional Structure. Constituting State, Society, and the Individual* (pp. 133–149). London: Sage.

Boli, J. and Thomas, G.M. (1997). World Culture in the World Polity: A Century of International Non-governmental Organization. *American Sociological Review, 62*(2), 171–190.

Boli, J. and Thomas, G.M. (1999). INGOs and the Organization of World Culture. In J. Boli and G.M. Thomas (eds), *Constructing World Culture. International Nongovernmental Organizations since 1985* (pp. 13–49). Stanford: Stanford University Press.

Bourdieu, P. (1977). *Outline of a Theory of Practice*. Cambridge: Cambridge University Press.

Bourdieu, P. and Wacquant, L. (1992). *An Invitation to Reflexive Sociology*. Chicago, IL: Chicago University Press.

Büttner, S. (2012). *Mobilising Europe: A world-culture perspective on regional development in Poland*. London/New York: Routledge.

CEC (Commission of the European Communities) (1997). The Social and Labour Market Dimension of the Information Society. *COM(1997) 390 final*.

CEC (Commission of the European Communities) (2001a). European Governance. A White Paper. *COM (2001) 428*.

CEC (Commission of the European Communities) (2001b). Realising the European Union's Potential: Consolidating and Extending the Lisbon Strategy. *COM (2001) 79 final*.

CEC (Commission of the European Communities) (2003a). Choosing to grow: Knowledge, innovation and jobs in a cohesive society. Commission Staff Working Paper in support of the report from the Commission to the Spring European Council, 21 March 2003, on the Lisbon Strategy of economic, social and environmental renewal. *SEC(2003) 25*.

CEC (Commission of the European Communities) (2003b). Strengthening the social dimension of the Lisbon Strategy: Streamlining Open Coordination in the field of social inclusion. *COM(2003) 261/2 final*.

CEC (Commission of the European Communities) (2004). Social Inclusion in the New Member States. A synthesis of the joint memoranda on social inclusion. *SEC(2004) 848 final*.

CEC (Commission of the European Communities) (2006). Guidelines for Preparing National Reports on Strategies for Social Protection and Social Inclusion. Retrieved 21 May 2007 from http://ec.europa.eu/employment_social/social_inclusion/docs/2006/guidelines_en.pdf.

CEC (Commission of the European Communities) (2007). *The social situation in the European Union 2005–2006. The balance between Generations in an Ageing Europe.* Luxembourg: Office for Official Publications of the European Communities.

CEU (2002). Objectives in the fight against poverty and social exclusion. Council of the European Union: *14110/00, SOC 470.*

CEU (2008). Council Decision on guidelines for the employment policies of the Member States. Council of the European Union: *10614/2/08 REV 2.*

CEU (2009a). Country-Specific Integrated Recommendations—Report from the Council to the European Council. Council of the European Union: *7444/09,* 10 March 2009, Brussels.

CEU (2009b). Joint Report on Social Protection and Social Inclusion 2009. Council of the European Union: *7503/09,* 13 March 2009, Brussels.

Daly, M. (2006). EU Social Policy after Lisbon. *Journal of Common Market Studies, 44*(3), 461–481.

Djelic, M.-L. and Sahlin-Andersson, K. (2006a). Introduction: A world of governance: The rise of transnational governance. In M.-L. Djelic and K. Sahlin-Andersson (eds), *Transnational Governance. Institutional Dynamics of Regulation* (pp. 1–28). Cambridge: Cambridge University Press.

Djelic, M.-L. and Sahlin-Andersson, K. (2006b). *Transnational Governance. Institutional Dynamics of Regulation.* Cambridge: Cambridge University Press.

Dobbin, F., Simmons, B., and Garrett, G. (2007). The Global Diffusion of Public Policies: Social Construction, Coercion, Competition, or Learning? *Annual Review of Sociology, 33,* 449–472.

Dorf, M.C. and Sabel, C.F. (1998). Constitution of Democratic Experimentalism. *Columbia Law Review, 98*(2), 267–473.

Drori, G.S., Meyer, J.W., Ramirez, F.O., and Schofer, E. (eds) (2003). *Science in the Modern World Polity. Institutionalization and Globalization.* Stanford, CA: Stanford University Press.

Dräger, K. (2007). Europäisches Sozialmodell, Wettbewerbsfähigkeit und die neoliberale "Modernisierung." *Kurswechsel, 1,* 16–26.

EAPN (2000). A Europe for all: For a European strategy to combat social exclusion. EAPN contribution to the Round Table Conference of 6–7 May 1999. In EAPN (ed.), *Combating poverty and social exclusin. A new momentum in the European Union* (pp. 165–174). Brussels: European Anti-Poverty Network.

EAPN (2004). Streamlining. Strengthening a Social Europe while maintaining a visible Social Inclusion Strategy. *Position Paper, October.* Brussels: European Anti-Poverty Network.

EC n.d.(a). Social Protection and Social Inclusion. European Commission. Retrieved 19 December 2012, from http://ec.europa.eu/social/main.jsp?langId=en&catId=750.

EC n.d.(b). PROGRESS Programme. European Commission. Retrieved 19 December 2012, from http://ec.europa.eu/social/main.jsp?catId=327&langId=en.

EC n.d.(c). Employment, Social Affairs and Inclusion. European Commission. Retrieved 19 December 2012, from http://ec.europa.eu/social/main.jsp?catId=1023&langId=en.

European Council (2000). Lisbon European Council 23 and 24 March. Presidency Conclusions. Lisbon.

FEANTSA (2006). The Right to Health is a Human Right: Ensuring Access to Health for Homeless People. FEANTSA Conference, 13 October.

FEANTSA (2007). ETHOS 2007. European Typology of Homelessness and Housing Exclusion. Retrieved 19 December 2012 from www.feantsa.org/files/indicators_wg/ETHOS2007/general/EN_2007EthosLeaflet.pdf.

Fligstein, N. and McAdam, D. (2012). *A Theory of Fields*. Oxford: Oxford University Press.

Heidenreich, M. and Zeitlin, J. (2009). *Changing European Employment and Welfare Regimes. The influence of the open method of coordination on national reforms.* London and New York: Routledge.

Jacobsson, B. (2006). Regulated Regulators: Global Trends of State Transformation. In M.-L. Djelic and Sahlin-Andersson (eds), *Transnational Governance. Institutional Dynamics of Regulation* (pp. 205–224). Cambridge: Cambridge University Press.

Jacobsson, B. and Sahlin-Andersson, K. (2006). Dynamics of Soft Regulations. In M.-L. Djelic and Sahlin-Andersson (eds), *Transnational Governance. Institutional Dynamics of Regulation* (pp. 247–265). Cambridge: Cambridge University Press.

Jensen, J. (2008). The European Union and the social investment perspective. A historical–institutionalist approach is sociology too. Paper presented at the Workshop: Does European integration theory need sociology? Towards a research agenda, ECPR, 11–16 April 2008, Rennes.

Jepperson, R.L. (2002). The Development and Application of Sociological Neoinstitutionalism. In J. Berger and M. Zelditch (eds), *New Directions in Contemporary Sociological Theory* (pp. 229–266). Lanham, MD: Rowman and Littlefield.

Kerber, W. and Eckardt, M. (2007). Policy Learning in Europe: the Open Method of Co-Ordination and Laboratory Federalism. *Journal of European Public Policy, 14*(2), 227–247.

Kröger, S. (2006). When Learning Hits Politics or: Social policy Coordination Left to the Administration and the NGOs? *European Integration Online Papers, 10*, No. 3.

Mead, G.H. (1967). *Mind, Self, and Society from the Standpoint of a Social Behaviorist.* Chicago, IL and London: University of Chicago Press.

Meyer, J.W. (1996). Otherhood: The Promulgation and Transmission of Ideas in the Modern Organizational Environment. In B. Czarniawska-Joerges and G. Sevón (eds), *Translating Organizational Change* (pp. 241–258). Berlin/New York: Walter de Gruyter.

Meyer, J.W. and Jepperson, R.L. (2000). The "Actor" of Modern Society: The Cultural Construction of Social Agency. *Sociological Theory, 18*(1), 100–120.

Meyer, J.W., Boli, J., Thomas, G.M., and Ramirez, F.O. (1997). World Society and the Nation State. *American Journal of Sociology, 103*(1), 144–181.

Mosher, J.T., David M. (2003). Alternative Approaches to Governance in the EU: EU Social Policy and the European Employment Strategy. *Journal of Common Market Studies, 41*(1), 63–88.

Schwinn, T. (2006). Konvergenz, Divergenz oder Hybridisierung? Voraussetzungen und Erscheinungsformen von Weltkultur. *Kölner Zeitschrift für Soziologie und Sozialpsychologie, 58*(2), 201–232.

Strang, D. and Meyer, J.W. (1993). Institutional Conditions for Diffusion. *Theory and Society, 22*, 487–511.

Szyszczak, E. (2001). The New Paradigm for Social Policy: a Virtuous Circle? *Common Market Law Review, 38*, 1125–1170.

Trubek, D.M. and Trubek, L.G. (2003). Hard and Soft Law in the Construction of Social Europe: the role of the Open Method of Co-ordination. *European Law Journal, 11*(3), 343–364.

Wobbe, T. (2007). Die Metamorphosen der Gleichheit in der Europäischen Union. Genese und Institutionalisierung supranationaler Gleichberechtigungsnormen. *Kölner Zeitschrift für Soziologie und Sozialpsychologie, 59*(4), 565–588.

5 Global trends in European regional development

EU Cohesion Policy and the case of region-building in Poland[1]

Sebastian M. Büttner

Introduction

Subnational communities and regions are often regarded as sites of primary cultural and social integration. Accordingly, processes of regionalization are often conceived as the outcome of bottom-up political mobilization, or rather as deliberately particularistic strategies putting forward "local" collective identities against allegedly "alien" forces of central state politics and "globalization." In marked contrast to these conventional views it is argued here that subnational regions do not develop independently from their wider social surroundings. In fact, in times of worldwide connectivity and multi-faceted transnational integration the assumption of independent and self-sufficient regional cultures no longer holds true. Regionalization has become a global trend, and some practices of regional mobilization have become global models that decisively influence the character of regionalization and how regional mobilization is performed these days. Thus, the question is how can we make sense of the huge standardization and global spread of certain models of regionalization without losing our sense of the distinctiveness of regional contexts? And how can we explain why regional development strategies are so similar, especially in Europe today, although subnational regions are usually regarded as sites of cultural difference and particularity?

Based on a macro-phenomenological research perspective in the tradition of the so-called "world polity" approach, first proposed by John W. Meyer and colleagues, this contribution focuses on the emergence of global models of regional development and how they are domesticated in existing regional development practices in Europe today. It is argued that during the past three decades a strong common sense of major principles and standards of "good" regional development practice has emerged in the academic world and circles of experts in regional development. On the European continent, these principles and models have found their way into official regional development programs on all administrative levels, especially since the establishment of a common European framework of regional mobilization at the European Union (EU) level under the heading of EU Cohesion Policy, which constitutes in itself a highly standardized project of regional mobilization. This is finally illustrated in the example of region-building and regional mobilization in Poland in the course of EU integration. This case study exemplifies how global models of regional development are domesticated and put in place in a particular national context under the condition of far-reaching Europeanization and demonstrates the importance of scientific experts and standardized institutional procedures, such as strategy building, in this process of domestication.

Regional mobilization in a global context

In contrast to popular interpretations of a tremendous shrinking or even disappearance of "fixed space" (Castells, 2002) in times of intensifying global integration it can be observed that the importance of geographical demarcations and concrete local and regional sites of interaction has not decreased so far. Rather, from regional integration at the supra-state level down to political and economic mobilization at the subnational level we have witnessed a new wave of regionalization in many areas of the world since the mid-1980s. Economists, geographers, political scientists, and many other social scientists alike have detected a far-reaching rescaling of societal government both beyond and underneath established administrative structures of nation states and a peculiar resurgence of a "new regionalism" during the past three decades, world-wide but with more intensity on the European continent (c.f. Hooghe and Marks, 2001; Keating, 1998, 2004; Ohmae, 1995; Paasi, 2009).

Thus, we observe that apart from intensifying supranational integration subnational regions have also become more significant and more active in past decades, even in countries without strong regional or federal traditions (Börzel, 2002; Keating, 2001; LeGalés and Lequesne, 1998). Old territorial and cultural identities have been revived, and in some countries new regional identities have actually been created. Moreover, municipalities and regions all over Europe have set up similar technology parks, business incubators, and other types of knowledge transfer centers in order to attract new investors and to promote new business activities. Today, regions are widely considered as important political actors in multilevel systems of modern government and as an "appropriate" spatial unit of both effective and democratic governance on the European continent.

This transformation of established spatial logics of governance in Europe is widely interpreted as the result of a major shift of economic production by most advanced industrial societies since the beginning of the 1970s: the end of integrated Fordist mass-production and the rise of new post-industrial modes of production. Hence, most analysis and interpretation of the rise of a "new regionalism" is based, in one way or another, on materialist politico-economic accounts of social change (c.f. Brenner, Jessop, Jones, and MacLeod, 2003; Cox, 1997; Keating, 1998; Lagendijk, 2007; Paasi, 2009; Scott and Storper, 2003; Storper and Salais, 1997).

Certainly, the rules of the economic game have changed significantly in the past few decades. Economic activities have become more transnational in recent times. Moreover, there has been a massive relocation of mass production from highly industrialized Western countries to newly industrialized countries in Asia and other parts of the world. This has surely had a great impact on the development of localities, regions, and states all over the world, for instance in fueling the competition of business locations for human resources, investments and other elements of favorable economic value creation (Castells, 2002; Krugman, 1991; Storper, 1997). But it does not explain why in particular subnational territories have become more significant politically in recent years, and neither does it explain why most subnational regions implement more or less the same measures of development policy, even though competition is expected to increase diversity and inequality.

Hence, we need an analytical perspective that accounts for both the transnational rise of regions and the extension of development aspirations in the past decades without presupposing the supremacy of economic rationales. Before we predetermine social developments as primarily economically driven, it is important to explore which concepts are applied and adopted in political programs and how they find their way to political practice. Thus, it is suggested here that this can be achieved on the basis of a macro-phenomenological research perspective that puts the role of highly rationalized and active development agents as well as the translocal diffusion of concepts and models of organizational practice at the front and center of the analysis.

Institutional diffusion and domestication of global models: a macrophenomenological research perspective

The macrophenomenological research perspective is part of a broader strand of research that has developed during the past 30 years under the label of "world polity," or rather "world culture" studies (c.f. Krücken and Drori, 2010; Meyer, 2010; Thomas, Meyer, Ramirez, and Boli, 1987). In the center of this approach is the assumption of a worldwide expansion and diffusion of "world culture," the cultural account of modernity that endows social actors with highly rationalized scripts of actorhood (c.f. Meyer and Jepperson, 2000; Meyer and Rowan, 1977).[2] The expansion of "world culture," however, is not conceived as a teleological project that heads automatically towards certain predetermined goals. In explicit reference to contemporary culturalist sociological accounts, "world culture" is rather conceptualized as a particular cultural project that is legitimized by scientific authority and carried out by scientifically trained experts and other sorts of scientifically trained professionals.

Thus, on the basis of this analytical perspective the current phase of regional mobilization in Europe can be interpreted as a particular cultural project of social mobilization that is largely shaped by epistemes of contemporary development practice and carried out by various scientifically trained professionals, such as bureaucrats, scientists, development consultants, and the like (c.f. Büttner, 2012).

The diffusion of organizational practices and policy programs is usually studied and explained on the basis of relational agent- and network-based accounts (c.f. Finnemore and Sikkink, 1998; Rogers, 1995; Valente, 1995). From a macrophenomenological perspective, however, purely agent-based relational models of diffusion are not sufficient to explain the high speed and extensiveness of diffusion of many world-cultural principles and models in contemporary society, since diffusion often proceeds more immediately and on a more unstructured basis than predicted in agent-based relational accounts. Accordingly, David Strang and John W. Meyer (1993) have pointed out that relational models would be appropriate for explaining the diffusion of non-social elements such as viruses or infectious diseases. Where diffusion essentially involves the constitution of "social actors" and respective identities, however, it is the increasing approximation of cultural definitions and frames of actorhood amongst different and largely disconnected social entities that creates a tie between them in the first place: "[D]iffusion is importantly shaped and accelerated by culturally analyzed similarities among actors, and by theorized accounts of actors and practices. These institutional conditions are argued to be especially rife in 'modern' social systems" (Strang and Meyer, 1993, p. 487). This is the constitutive phenomenological condition and the absolute condition, the *sine qua non*, of endemic translocal diffusion of models of social organization. If there were no cultural-cognitive "apriorities," the objects of diffusion would simply not have any substance or significance for potential recipients of diffusion. And the availability of cultural–cognitive conceptions, such as certain abstract theoretical models and concrete scripts of social organization, facilitates the rapid diffusion of social practices without spatial restriction and independently of direct social bonding.

Yet the explication of the cultural–cognitive dimension is not sufficient for an empirical exploration of the diffusion and social significance of organizational models, especially when we are dealing with highly disputed and politicized issues, such as conceptions and models of development. "In some way, models must make the transition from theoretical formulation to social movement to institutional imperative," as Strang and Meyer (1993, p. 495) have also pointed out. Hence, since theoretical models gain social significance only if they have the support of powerful social forces and they are also established in authoritative institutions, Strang and Meyer suggest that macrophenomenological analysis must also be sensitive to processes of "authoritative institutionalization." This is also widely reflected in contemporary diffusion studies, where researchers have determined a whole range of structural conditions, social mechanisms and carriers of diffusion beyond discursive or cultural construction (Czarniawska-Joerges and Sevón, 1996; DiMaggio and Powell, 1983; Djelic, 2008; Dobbin, Simmons, and Garrett, 2007; Finnemore and Sikkink, 1998; Sahlin-Andersson and Engwall, 2002). And it is commonplace in contemporary institutionalist accounts to stress the importance of the *regulative* and *normative* dimensions of institutional diffusion apart from the above-mentioned *cultural–cognitive* dimension (c.f. Scott, 2001).

Beyond that, it must be noted that the diffusion of world-cultural models into concrete local (or regional and national) contexts neither constitutes a one-way track nor a one-to-one adaptation. Global models are never just "adopted" blindly, but turned into actual practices and attached to local conditions. Thus, in order to capture this transformative momentum of the adoption of global models in particular local contexts, the concept of "domestication" is used here in addition to institutional models of "diffusion" (Alasuutari, 2009, 2013; and see introduction to this volume). According to the domestication framework, the local adoption of globally standardized techniques and practices always entails a huge portion of naturalization, familiarization, and routinization of globally standardized models, which means that new technologies and practices usually become so natural and familiar to local actors that they are not considered as external, strange or alien after all (Alasuutari, 2009, p. 66f). This, however, requires the active engagement of local actors as agents of change, translating abstract, mostly scientifically grounded practical models into everyday language, practice, and routine, and actively advertising the benefits of new practices. And as Alasuutari and Qadir also point out in the introduction to this volume, "domestication" should not be understood as a concept that reproduces the old global–local dichotomy and the image of diffusion as transfer of external models to local contexts, as has often been suggested by proponents of the world-polity perspective (c.f. Meyer, 2010). In fact, with the notion of domestication we aim to overcome these old dichotomies and distinctions and rather point to the strong intermingling of global models and local actors. The proponents, translators, and institutional carriers of global models are already local; and the more institutional support and cultural legitimacy global models enjoy in a particular local context, the more social significance they gain in this particular social environment.

Based on these conceptual preconditions we analyze the emergence and diffusion of global standards of regional mobilization in the remainder of this chapter in more detail. In accordance with the phenomenological assumption of a preeminence of cultural–cognitive dimensions of diffusion, the subsequent section shows the epistemic foundations of contemporary regionalism, followed by a short portrayal of the institutionalization of regionalism in political programs, particularly in the rules, laws, and bureaucratic practices of EU regional policy.

Global trends in regional development and European contributions

If one looks for the major cultural–cognitive preconditions for the new regionalism, one of them is the innumerable and multifaceted research on subnational regions, which emerged since the end of the 1970s and beginning of the 1980s. It had a great impact on changing the common understanding of subnational spaces and local features of development. Alongside the academic discussion on post-Fordism and globalization, academics have (re-)discovered the region as a major object of research (for an overiew, see Dawkins, 2003; Keating, 2004; Pike, Rodríguez-Posé, and Tomaney, 2006; Storper, 1995). This scientific discourse constitutes the general epistemic field, so to speak, within which contemporary regional development practice has been shaped. In this sense it can be noted that the transformation of the former economic order was indeed a major catalyst of the upsurge of new research and a new way of thinking on regional development. However, this does not mean that these new research endeavors were just a derivate of economic interests. In fact, even though there are complex interrelations between business and sciences as well as economic interests and knowledge production, these two areas are by no means congruent with one another, and world-cultural models do not simply mirror hegemonic economic interests.

The scientific underpinnings of contemporary regional development practice

Indeed, the first generation of new regional research was mainly concerned with exploring the new challenges posed by the transition from integrated mass production to more mobile and flexible forms of economic production in existing business locations (c.f. Bagnasco, 1977; Hall and Markusen, 1985; Piore and Sabel, 1989; Saxenian, 1994; Zeitlin, 1990). The economic revival of some traditional industrial agglomerations as well as the rise of "new industrial districts" has inspired a whole range of researchers to explore and outline the particular features of these multi-faceted "regional worlds" of production (Storper and Salais, 1997). Consequently, regions were no longer considered as a mere background variable or a passive context for economic production and business activities. On the contrary, they were increasingly considered as the generic loci of economic value creation, as "key sources" (Storper, 1995) of development in post-industrial times, and as the "motors" (Scott, 1996) of contemporary global capitalism.

Some scientific vocabularies and scientifically sanctified "best practice" models of regional development have been taken up and further developed in practical contexts. One notion that has become a quasi-universalistic dictum of "modern" regional development practice is the notion of *flexible specialization* (Piore and Sabel, 1989). It suggests that in times of intensified global competition, all municipalities and regions must define their unique "core competences" and find their niche in the global economy.[3] Another key notion that has become particularly popular in the past three decades is the model of *innovative cluster economies*. Initially deriving from economic geography but vigorously proposed and promoted in a stylized and easily applicable way by figureheads of business studies at Harvard Business School (c.f. Porter, 1998, 2003), it definitely constitutes one of the most prominent world-cultural models of regional economic mobilization of contemporary times. Without doubt, the assumption that businesses should be concentrated in "clusters" and that innovativeness evolves out of intensified, multifaceted, and fruitful interlinkages between science and businesses is widely accepted these days. And the few successful and exceptionally vibrant business clusters, such as above all the famous Silicon Valley in Northern California, have become iconic reference models and prototypes of successful regional mobilization.

However, the new academic interest in regions, regional social practices and regional institutions has also widely transcended the narrow focus on business studies. Furthermore, enterprise development and the interdisciplinary scientific preoccupation with regions and regional questions of development have increased massively (c.f. Lawson and Lorenz, 1999; Morgan, 2004; Salais and Villeneuve, 2005). Consequently, it is a widely shared view these days that (regional) innovation and overall socio-economic wellbeing are decisively determined by certain *endogenous* relational, institutional, or cultural factors. Therefore, the notions of *trust* and *social capital* have also gained huge prominence in regional development practice (Putnam, 1993; Triglia, 2001).

Beyond that, researchers have also observed *and* evoked the emergence of new political actors, new corporatist arrangements and new forms of policy experimentation at local and regional levels. Consequently, scientific assumptions and interpretations of "good" regional governance have become widely shared world-cultural models and institutional imperatives over the past decade (c.f. Benz and Fürst, 2002; Crouch, LeGalés, Triglia, and Voelzkow, 2004). Hence, the rise of "new regionalism" in scientific debates has been accompanied by an increase of political practice at regional levels in advanced industrial societies. In this context also a huge variety of alternative concepts and models of regional development, such as models of *sustainable development* or *cohesion*, were put forward and made subject to multifaceted "regional experimentation." Thus, in the past decades, more and more "holistic," "progressive," and "sustainable" approaches have flourished in regional policy debates (Pike et al., 2006). These new approaches to regional development often explicitly aim to transcend the narrow focus on economic development by encouraging broader multidimensional conceptions of wellbeing and quality of life as well as long-term thinking in development strategies. Some approaches are actually highly critical of the destructive effects of one-dimensional economic development strategies (Barton and Dlouhá, 2011; Hadjimichalis and Hudson, 2007; Morgan, 2004; Salais and Villeneuve, 2005).

Last but not least, it can be pointed out that international agents of development, such as the OECD or the European Commission, also play an important role in promoting regional mobilization and certain notions and models of regional development. In fact, the OECD and the European Commission disseminate a whole range of information on regional development and regional reform. They also contribute vigorously to the establishment of transnational "fields" of organizational activity (c.f. DiMaggio and Powell, 1983), within which knowledge, experts, practices, and even financial resources fostering "regional mobilization" diffuse more directly and rapidly on a transnational scale than ever before. Through outlining common standards for regional reform, institutionalizing transnational channels of exchange and publishing reports, rankings, and huge amounts of statistical material on regional development, they create transnational linkages and new discursive fields in which states, and—ever more frequently—regions and other sub-state units can locate themselves and compare their own situation in relation to other similar political units (c.f. Alasuutari and

Rasimus, 2009).[4] And with the establishment of a common "cohesion policy" at the European level in the late 1980s a whole range of standards, principles, procedures, and practices of regional mobilization were institutionalized as standard practices and conditions (*sine qua non*) in European regional development.

EU Cohesion Policy as a catalyst of pan-European mobilization of subnational regions

Indeed, the introduction of the EU Cohesion Policy in 1989 has established a new pan-European multilevel system of regional mobilization based on a number of unitary organizing principles and standard procedures, such as subsidiarity, multi-annual planning, participation, partnership, and good governance (c.f. Büttner, 2012; EC, 2008a; Hooghe, 1996; Leonardi, 2005; Molle, 2007; Rumford, 2000). Initially introduced as a complementary side project of the European Single Market in order to counterbalance potential market failures and expected tensions resulting from the huge divergence between the most and the least developed areas of the EU territory, the Cohesion Policy has become one of the largest EU policy areas in terms of annual spending. In fact, since its introduction in 1989 until today more than 700 billion euros were spent on projects of spatial and regional development all over Europe. This accounts for more than one-third of the annual EU budget (EC, 2008a).

The territorial and regional scope of policy-making was always highlighted as an important element of the common European project since the beginning of the process of European integration.[5] However, for decades there was no distinct European approach to regional mobilization and regional development policy. This changed significantly with the creation of the common European market at the beginning of the 1990s. Efforts to establish a common European Single Market led to a strong reinforcement of the territorial or geographical levels of European government (c.f. Barry, 1993; Hooghe, 1996). The goal of reducing imbalances between the most advanced regions and areas that are "lagging behind the most" (measured by GDP per capita) was put forward as a fundamental condition for the functioning of the European Common Market. And the regional level has become the focal point for the perception and management of territorial disparities in contemporary EU policy-making (c.f. Molle, 2007; Rumford, 2000). Moreover, in the past decade the Cohesion Policy has gained even more importance in political terms. It was considered, first, as a means of supporting the integration of new member states into the existing institutional structure of the EU, and second, as a central means of spreading the strategic goals of the renewed Lisbon agenda to cities and regions all over the EU territory (EC, 2005, 2008d). Furthermore, it is central to the expansion of transport infrastructures and to the realization of common European transport policies (EC, 2011).

The strategic guidelines and funding priorities of Cohesion Policy mirror in an ideal-typical way the major global trends and standards of contemporary development thought. Thus, the Cohesion Policy aims to strengthen the "innovativeness" and "competitiveness" of European regions by co-financing countless initiatives of "regional specialization," "cluster building," and "human resource development," and by stimulating "regional learning" and "experimentation" (EC, 2006). It supports the increase of entrepreneurship and knowledge-based industries in areas all around Europe, but also the refurbishment of roads and basic local infrastructure, and the expansion of broadband internet connections. At the same time, it co-finances numerous projects for environmental protection, social and cultural activation, and inter- and trans-regional social exchange and cooperation (EC, 2008b, 2008c). Beyond that, it promotes the improvement of the "administrative capacity" of the national, regional, and local authorities involved in planning and implementation in order to ensure effectiveness and efficiency of funding. In short, the EU Cohesion Policy strongly contributes to the evocation and dissemination of many scripts and aspirations of contemporary regional development practices that are most prevalent in the development discourse, and it contributes to this discourse by promoting its own research and respective notions and concepts.[6] Furthermore, in line with the most important credo of the regional governance literature, "agency" is stimulated in order to foster "capacities of self-support," and to mobilize key regional actors to "work together" and "get active" for their common regional futures.

The most remarkable element of the Cohesion Policy, however, is the *conditionality* that is built into the system of funding and implementing regional development policies based on a multi-annual strategic vision. This constitutes an elaborate regulative institutional framework of the pan-European diffusion of global models and a whole range of standardized procedures and rationalized practices. The strategic goals of Cohesion policy are officially determined and adopted by the European Council, but they stem mainly from policy proposals of the Directorate-General for Regional Policy (DG Regio) and expert debates on the strategic objectives of Cohesion Policy in the forefront and in the aftermath of decision-making. Once the strategic objectives are determined in legal terms, they have to be adopted and transposed into national, regional, and local development practices by the political authorities in order to be eligible for receiving the financial support of one of the EU's structural and cohesion funds (EC, 2008d). In this way, the institutional framework of EU Cohesion Policy has become central to the rapid diffusion of world-cultural models to regional development agendas all around Europe. This will be shown in the next section, which depicts the process of region-building in Poland in the course of EU integration and some elements of the current system of regional development policy of the country.

The domestication of global models in national contexts: regionalization in Poland

The present Republic of Poland certainly constitutes an interesting research object for the exploration of the world-cultural foundations of region-building and the domestication of current global models of regional mobilization. On the one hand, the country was part of the Soviet bloc until the end of 1980s and, thus, belonged to a political project that was antagonistic to Western models of capitalism and democracy. On the other hand, it can be noted that 1989 constitutes a radical break in the history of the country, since it broke with the communist heritage and witnessed a rapid and fundamental transformation of society, leading to its accession to the EU in 2004.

From the very beginning of state transformation, external consultants and advisors were involved in the reform processes, consulting the new elites about how to implement most contemporary Western models of economic policy and accompanying the first steps of state reform (c.f. Sachs, 1992). In fact, during the 1990s a whole industry of both governmental and non-governmental development organizations entered the arena, promoting economic, democratic, administrative, and cultural change at all levels of society. Accordingly, the process of transformation was widely considered as a condensed reification of the processes of state-building and societal modernization in Western European countries. It was also celebrated enthusiastically as a "return to Europe" (c.f. Sztompka, 1993).

The reform of administrative structures has become a vital element of state reform from the very beginning, and all the more in the course of EU integration. Right after the fall of communism in 1990 the newly elected government rapidly passed legal acts in order to foster local democracy and to strengthen the local level of self-government in municipalities (Regulski, 2003; Swianiewicz, 2002). However, region-building as the establishment of self-governing administrations at the intermediate level and as a distinct regional policy approach on the part of the central state were not high on the agenda during the first years of state transformation. This changed markedly in the mid-1990s when the negotiations about EU accession had officially started. Apart from many other aspects, the creation of a "functional" administrative structure on the meso level was compelled by the standard requirements of EU structural policies. In this sense it can be noted that external institutional pressure was a crucial factor in region-building in Poland, and it was mainly initiated and driven forward by a small number of domestic and foreign experts (c.f. Batchler, Downes, and Gorzelak, 2000; Ferry, 2003). Thus, the process of regionalization was neither a purely "external" effect, nor an outcome of bottom-up mobilization. It was a process of domestication of global models of regionalism, largely dependent on both the "conditionality" of EU Cohesion Policy and the normative expectations connected with region-building.

The current regional structure of Poland was created on 1 January 1999. It was introduced in the course of a larger administrative reform (adopted by the Polish Parliament in July 1998). This reform replaced the former two-tier administrative system of 49 smaller voivodships [*województwa*] and approximately 2,400 municipalities [*gminy*], which had been in place since 1974, by a three-tier system of 16 new voivodships, 373 counties [(so-called) *poviaty*] and 2,489 local municipalities [*gminy*]. This administrative reform in 1999 marks an important milestone in the contemporary history of the country. It put to an end to the endless and heated political debates on the role of the state in post-communist Poland and to the need to create a new territorial division.

External funds as a major driving force of region-building

With a size of 312,679 square kilometers and a population of approximately 38 million inhabitants, Poland is by far the biggest of all post-communist countries that entered the EU in 2004. Due to its greater area and size of population Poland is by far the biggest receiver of external financial resources that are targeted at regional development in European policy-making in the EU. In fact, between 1990 and 2003 Poland received about 5.9 billion euros of EU pre-accession funding, which already brought about significant financial support for local and regional development initiatives. Between 2004 and 2006 11.3 billion euros in EU funds (7.6 billion euros in Structural Funds and 3.7 billion euros of the Cohesion Fund) were allocated to Poland. This money was distributed both nationally and regionally in accordance with the guidelines of the official EU Community Support Framework and the specifications of the so-called "National Development Plan," 2001–2006. It was distributed to municipalities, counties, voivodships, and individual beneficiaries who applied for funds. It has been invested in numerous projects of national, regional, and local development ranging from small infrastructure projects at the community level to large-scale investment in the construction of motorways, railway tracks, airports and business clusters (c.f. Büttner, 2012: 179–188). In some cases the latter even bear reference to their famous role model, the Silicon Valley, in their official name, such as "Aviation Valley," created in 2003 in south-eastern Poland.[7]

In the programming period from 2007 to 2013 Poland receives approximately 67 billion euros from the Structural Funds and the Cohesion Fund, which is about one-quarter of all funds assigned by the European Union to regional policy. It is the largest amount of EU structural funds ever paid to a single EU member state. So far, this huge amount of EU funding for local and regional initiatives has definitely had a huge impact on the overall infrastructural development of the country, and the mobilization of municipalities and regions in particular. The amount of projects and activities has further increased, due to the much higher level of funding provided between 2007 and 2013. Thus, we can assume that hundreds of thousands of projects, some small and some large, have been initiated or implemented since 2007.[8]

Yet region-building, infrastructural development, and the revitalization of prospective industries are far from being the only effects of regional mobilization in contemporary Poland. There has also been a complete restructuring of the governance of spatial development and the establishment of new approaches to regional development planning since the beginning of 2000. Regional mobilization has become a matter of all-encompassing and comprehensive planning under the heading of "strategic development planning." All Polish administrative constituencies from local municipalities up to the ministry of regional development at the central state level have drafted comprehensive strategies of development planning in 2000 and 2006/2007 in order to show that EU structural funds and other financial resources are spent in the most efficient and rational way, and to determine key aims and major objectives of future development. In this context, the subnational administrative entities have become important agents of development planning. The preparation of distinct subnational development strategies was enforced by law in the administrative reform in 1999. Thus, the individual regional governments were obliged to draft and implement their own development strategies from the very beginning of their existence. This process of strategizing is interpreted here as a major institutional funnel of world-cultural diffusion and a major component of the "domestication" of global models.

Strategy building as a major funnel of world-cultural diffusion

The regional development strategies (RDSs) are the major documents of development planning of the 16 Polish voivodships, and thus they are central to regional policy-making in Poland of today. They specify the major goals, objectives, and priorities of development policy of the regions, and they are supposed to serve as focal points of future development as well as guidelines for all operational development activities. Experts and policy-makers in Poland considered the preparation of distinct RDS as a milestone in the history of spatial development and planning of the country. The need to prepare the RDS was proclaimed in scientific debates that had ambitious aspirations for far-reaching social change and development. Moreover, they were promoted with a strong modernist impetus. This is evident in the following statement by the geographer Andrzej Klasik, a leading figure in the academic debate on the preparation of the RDS in 1999/2000:

> The restructuring and globalization of regions requires a holistic development approach. This entails, in fact, the development of regions in terms of international competitiveness and in all their general structural aspects. *The restructuring of Polish regions is finally leading to their cultural transformation . . .* The result will be the change in the identities of the regions which will entirely focus on new specializations of production and services, new qualifications and competences, and new life-styles of local societies. *The process of restructuring leads to a change in the regional leadership and governing elite.*
>
> (Klasik 2000: 7, translated from Polish by Sebastian Büttner, emphasis in original)

Though the whole process was politically steered and coordinated, the documents were mainly drafted and created by scientists and other scientifically trained "professionals:" thus, the process of strategic development started with a comprehensive, scientific diagnosis of the situation of the regions: an exploration of the particular development problems and challenges, as well as the strategic assets and options for future development. This culminated in the compilation of detailed "SWOT analyzes" outlining the future strategic options taking account of the given assets and resources available for development.[9] Subsequently, major strategic aims and special strategic objectives were formulated. This process was accompanied by consultations with experts and key actors in the given region in order to involve as many groups and people as possible in the process and to give them the opportunity to exchange opinions. Furthermore, the general strategic goals and priorities were specified in more concrete "operational priorities" and "action plans" in accordance with the funding guidelines of the National Strategy for Regional Development. Finally, the documents underwent a process of official political approval by the regional authorities. They were discussed and evaluated by the relevant committees of the respective regional parliaments and, after official approval by all parliamentary committees, each strategy was officially adopted by all of the individual regional parliaments as the official development strategies of the respective regions.

The first development strategies of the regions had been officially adopted and put in place in all 16 voivodships by the end of 2000; hence, just one year after the official introduction of the new administrative system. The individual regional governments did not have much room for maneuver to decide freely on the structure, content, and procedural regulations of their development strategies. In light of the huge levels of expected EU funding after Poland's EU accession, the regional governments were by and large forced to draw on the official standards, goals, regulations, and requirements of EU funding (c.f. Žuber, 2000). This becomes apparent also when we look at the content of the 16 individual strategies and the huge similarity and congruency that the individual strategies feature—even though the socio-economic conditions and challenges vary significantly amongst the 16 voivodships, especially between regions in eastern and western Poland (Gorzelak, 2006; Grosse, 2006). Hence, all regions place an emphasis on "raising the level of living conditions and the wealth of citizens," "improving the competitiveness of the regional economy," and "achieving sustainable and multifaceted growth." They all want to "improve the internal territorial cohesion" and the transport system as well as all other technical infrastructures. Moreover, all the regions want to "improve [the] social cohesion," "social activity," and "social participation" of their citizens, and so forth. In short, the individual regional development strategies mostly contain the usual key terms and notions of contemporary regional development, and especially the key terms of European regional development policy.

This shows strikingly the extent to which the subnational areas in contemporary Poland are shaped by EU policies and policy priorities, and how regional authorities define their own situation primarily on these grounds. This has not changed thus far, although all regional development strategies were revised in the meantime and replaced in 2006 by long-term strategies that envisage development processes until at least 2020. Thus, the existing regional development strategies are similarly equal in scope, structure, and in their specifications of major fields of activities. All regional development strategies are still built upon the same standards and principles of regional development. Furthermore, they all still proclaim relatively similar goals and ambitions for future development. This demonstrates a remarkably high level of standardization of regional development policies in contemporary Poland and the strong role of world-cultural principles in the whole process of regional mobilization.

Final remarks

This chapter has discussed the emergence, diffusion, and domestication of global models of subnational regional development. I showed that along with the transformation of economic logics of production during the 1970s and 1980s, subnational regions have gained more attention both in scientific research and in concrete social practice. Thus, it is widely accepted these days that subnational regions play a vital role in the governance of future developments. Regional governments are expected to plan regional development actively, strategically and in the most possible sustainable ways. Moreover, they are expected to define key areas of "regional specialization" and to mobilize regional resources of economic and social innovation. They are expected to protect their "natural landscapes" and foster their particular "cultural heritage." Last but not least, they are also expected to foster the "inclusiveness" of local and regional populations, and the "cohesion" of their particular social space. In short, regions are expected to comply, as much as possible, with all requirements and aspirations of "modern" development practices, regardless of any ambiguity or contradiction that might be inherent in the aforementioned list of expectations. This has been discussed throughout this chapter as the "world-cultural character" of regional mobilization; and it was argued, furthermore, that this particular world-cultural character of regional mobilization has been domesticated in the Europe of today through the institutional structures of EU Cohesion Policy.

In the case study on region-building in Poland we have identified the strong influence of "European" standards and requirements of regional mobilization. Without doubt, financial incentives have played a major role in the massive and rapid stipulation of diffusion of world-cultural principles of regional mobilization. Nonetheless, it must be noted that the institutional framework of EU Cohesion Policy also provides national governments and subnational regions with a whole range of notions, interpretations, and models of "modern" regional development practices as well as with standard routines and techniques of regional planning. In this sense, we can conceive of EU Cohesion Policy as a particular institutional framework that *reinforces*, *specifies* and *accelerates* the diffusion of world-cultural principles and standards to subnational areas all around the EU territory, and fosters the domestication of global models in "European" terms. We have traced in the example of Poland some elements of diffusion and domestication and how they affect planning efforts in particular local settings. This case study has just exemplified what has happened and is still happening in similar ways in many countries and in many regions all around Europe. The impacts of these efforts and concrete transformative long-term effects, however, will show up only in the future.

Notes

1 This chapter draws on research that was published in 2012 in my research monograph entitled *Mobilizing Regions, Mobilizing Europe: Expert Knowledge and Scientific Planning in European Regional Development* (Büttner, 2012). It is the first empirical analysis in the tradition of the world-polity perspective that addresses the global constitution of subnational regions and global models of regional mobilization. Until now, world-polity research has primarily focused on the construction of nation-states, organizations, and individuals as modern "rationalized" actors (c.f. Meyer, 2010; Meyer and Jepperson, 2000).

2 The approach is "macrophenomenological" in the sense that it rests upon the classical phenomenological assumption of an all-encompassing *cultural construction* of social reality on the one hand (Berger and Luckmann, 1966), and on the other hand on Max Weber's classical thesis of an increasing *cultural significance* of formal–rational models of social organization with the breakthrough of modernity (c.f. Meyer and Rowan, 1977; Thomas et al., 1987).

3 Most remarkably, most of the analytical models of "good" regional practice derive from research on best practice models of economic governance at the national level (c.f. Lundvall, 1992; Porter, 1990). The major assumptions and rationales of these models were transposed directly to subnational settings without any major changes or adaptations.

4 See European Commission, "Regional policy in your country," retrieved 15 January 2013 from http://ec.europa.eu/regional_policy/index_en.cfm, for a look at the activities of the European Commission in the field of regional policy; and OECD, "Regional, rural, and urban development," retrieved 15 January 2013 from www.OECD.org/regional/, for an overview of OECD activities.

5 In fact, even in the Preamble of the Treaty of Rome, the founding script of European economic integration signed in May 1957, the aim of reducing existing differences between regions and the "backwardness" of less favored regions is highlighted as one of the major policy objectives of the European Community.

6 One of newest "innovations" in the field of EU regional policy-making seems to be the notion of "smart specialization," which is supposed to link the notion of "smart growth" with references to "sustainable growth" (EC, 2012).

7 More information at the webpage of the DG Regio of the EU Commission: retrieved 15 January 2013 from http://ec.europa.eu/regional_policy/atlas2007/poland/index_en.htm.

8 For more information on the utilization of EU structural funds in Poland see: "How is the European funds implementation system organised in Poland?" retrieved 15 January 2013 from www.funduszeeuropejskie.gov.pl/English/Introduction/Strony/Programmes.aspx.

9 A SWOT analysis is an analysis of "strengths," "weaknesses," "opportunities," and "threats." It is a standard technique of planning in business studies, and it has also become a standard technique and an obligatory requirement of strategic planning in the governance system of EU structural and regional development policies. For more information, see Büttner (2012, p. 98f).

References

Alasuutari, P. (2009). The domestication of worldwide policy models. *Ethnologia Europea, 39*(1), 66–71.

Alasuutari, P. (2013). Spreading global models and enhancing banal localism: The case of local government cultural policy development. *International Journal of Cultural Policy, 19*(1), 103–119.

Alasuutari, P. and Rasimus, A. (2009). Use of the OECD in justifying policy reforms: The Case of Finland. *Journal of Power, 2*(1), 89–109.

Bagnasco, A. (1977). *Tre Italie*. Bologna: Il Mulino.

Barry, A. (1993). The European Community and European government: Harmonization, mobility and space. *Economy and Society, 22*(3), 314–326.

Barton, A. and Dlouhá, J. (eds) (2011). *Multi-actor Learning for Sustainable Regional Development in Europe: A Handbook of Best Practice*. Guildford: Grosvenor House.

Batchler, J., Downes, R., and Gorzelak, G. (eds) (2000). *Transition, Cohesion and Regional Policy in Central and Eastern Europe*. Aldershot: Ashgate Publishing.

Benz, A. and Fürst, D. (2002). Policy learning in regional networks. *European Urban and Regional Studies, 9*(1), 21–35.

Berger, P.L. and Luckmann, T. (1966). *The Social Construction of Reality: A Treatise in the Sociology of Knowledge*. Garden City, NY: Anchor Books.

Brenner, N., Jessop, B., Jones, M. and MacLeod, G. (eds) (2003). *State/Space: A Reader*. Malden, MA: Blackwell Publishing.

Börzel, T.A. (2002). *States and Regions in the European Union: Institutional Adaptation in Germany and Spain*. Cambridge: Cambridge University Press.

Büttner, S. (2012). *Mobilizing Regions, Mobilizing Europe: Expert Knowledge and Scientific Planning in European Regional Development*. London: Routledge.

Castells, M. (2002). Local and global: Cities in the network society. *Tijdschrift voor Economische en Sociale Geografie, 93*(5), 548–558.

Cox, K.R. (1997). *Spaces of Globalization: Reasserting the Power of the Local*. New York: Guilford Press.

Crouch, C., LeGalés, P., Triglia, C., and Voelzkow, H. (eds) (2004). *Changing Governance of Local Economies: Responses of European Local Production Systems*. Oxford: Oxford University Press.

Czarniawska-Joerges, B. and Sevón, G. (1996). *Translating Organizational Change*. Berlin: Walter de Gruyter.

Dawkins, C.J. (2003). Regional development theory: Conceptual foundations, classic works, and recent developments. *Journal of Planning Literature, 18*, 131–172.

DiMaggio, P.J. and Powell, W.W. (1983). The iron cage revisited: Institutional isomorphism and collective rationality in organizational fields. *American Sociological Review, 48*(2), 147–160.

Djelic, M.-L. (2008). Sociological studies of diffusion: Is history relevant? *Socio-Economic Review, 6*, 538–557.

Dobbin, M., Simmons, B.A., and Garrett, G. (2007). The global diffusion of public policies: Social construction, coercion, competition, or learning? *Annual Review of Sociology, 33*, 449–472.

EC (2005). Relaunching the Lisbon Strategy: A Partnership for Growth and Employment. *COM(2005) 330*. Brussels: Commission of the European Communities.

EC (2006). Innovative Strategies and Actions: Results from 15 Years of Regional Experimentation. *EC Working Document*. Brussels: DG Regio, Commission of the European Communities.

EC (2008a). EU Cohesion Policy 1988–2008: Investing in Europe's Future. *Inforegio Panorama 26*. Luxembourg: Office for Official Publications of the European Communities.

EC (2008b). Regional Policy, Sustainable Development and Climate Change. *Inforegio Panorama 25*. Luxembourg: Office for Official Publications of the European Communities.

EC (2008c). Turning Territorial Diversity into Strength: Green Paper on Territorial Cohesion. *COM(2008) 616*. Luxembourg: Office for Official Publications of the European Communities.

EC (2008d). Working for the Regions: EU Regional Policy 2007–2013. Brussels: Commission of the European Communities.

EC (2011). Connecting Europe: Transport and Regional Policy. *Inforegio Panorama 38.* Luxembourg: Office for Official Publications of the European Communities.

EC (2012). Smart Specialization: The Driver of Future Economic Growth in Europe's Regions. *Inforegio Panorama 44.* Luxembourg: Office for Official Publications of the European Communities.

Ferry, M. (2003). The EU and recent regional reform in Poland. *Europe–Asia Studies, 55*(7), 1097–1116.

Finnemore, M.J. and Sikkink, K. (1998). International norm dynamics and political change. *International Organization, 52*(4), 887–917.

Gorzelak, G. (2006). Poland's regional policy and disparities in the Polish space. *Studia Regionalne i Lokalne* (Special Issue), 39–74.

Grosse, T.G. (2006). An evaluation of the regional policy system in Poland: Challenges and threats emerging from participation in the EU's Cohesion Policy. *European Urban and Regional Studies, 13*(2), 151–165.

Hadjimichalis, C. and Hudson, R. (2007). Rethinking local and regional development: Implications for radical political practice in Europe. *European Urban and Regional Studies, 14*(2), 99–113.

Hall, P.G. and Markusen, A.R. (eds) (1985). *Silicon Landscapes.* Boston, MA: Allen & Unwin.

Hooghe, L. (ed.) (1996). *Cohesion Policy and European Integration: Building Multi-level Governance.* Oxford: Clarendon Press.

Hooghe, L. and Marks, G. (2001). *Multi-level Governance and European Integration.* Lanham, MD: Rowman & Littlefield.

Keating, M. (1998). *The New Regionalism in Western Europe: Territorial Restructuring and Political Change.* Aldershot: Edward Elgar.

Keating, M. (2001). Rethinking the region: Culture, institutions and economic development in Catalonia and Galicia. *European Urban and Regional Studies, 8*(3), 217–234.

Keating, M. (ed.). (2004). *Regions and Regionalism in Europe.* Cheltenham: Edward Elgar.

Klasik, A. (2000). Strategia rozwoju regionu [Regional development strategy]. *Studia Regionalne i Lokalne, 3*(3), 7–22.

Krugman, P. (1991). *Geography and Trade.* Cambridge, MA: MIT Press.

Krücken, G. and Drori, G.S. (eds) (2010). *World Society: The Writings of John W. Meyer.* Oxford: Oxford University Press.

Lagendijk, A. (2007). The accident of the region: A strategic relational perspective on the construction of the region's significance. *Regional Studies, 41*(9), 1193–1208.

Lawson, C. and Lorenz, E. (1999). Collective learning, tacit knowledge and regional innovative capacity. *Regional Studies, 33*(4), 305–317.

LeGalés, P. and Lequesne, C. (eds) (1998). *Regions in Europe.* London: Routledge.

Leonardi, R. (2005). *Cohesion Policy in the European Union: The Building of Europe.* New York: Palgrave Macmillan.

Lundvall, B.-A. (1992). *National Systems of Innovation: Towards a Theory of Innovation and Interactive Learning.* London: Pinter.

Meyer, J.W. (2010). World Society, institutional theories, and the actor. *Annual Review of Sociology, 36*, 1–20.

Meyer, J.W. and Jepperson, R.L. (2000). The "actors" of modern society: The cultural construction of social agency. *Sociological Theory, 18*(1), 100–120.

Meyer, J.W. and Rowan, B. (1977). Institutionalized organizations: Formal structures as myth and ceremony. *American Journal of Sociology, 82*(2), 340–363.

Molle, W. (2007). *European Cohesion Policy*. London: Routledge.

Morgan, K. (2004). Sustainable regions: governance, innovation and scale. *European Planning Studies, 12*(6), 871–889.

Ohmae, K. (1995). *The End of the Nation State: The Rise of Regional Economies*. New York: Free Press.

Paasi, A. (2009). The resurgence of the "region" and "regional identity": Theoretical perspectives and empirical observations on the regional dynamics in Europe. *Review of International Studies, 35*(Supplement 1), 121–146.

Pike, A., Rodríguez-Posé, A., and Tomaney, J. (2006). *Local and Regional Development*. London: Routledge.

Piore, M.J. and Sabel, C.F. (1989). *The Second Industrial Divide*. New York: Basic Books.

Porter, M.E. (1990). *The Competitive Advantage of Nations*. London: Macmillan Press.

Porter, M.E. (1998). Clusters and the new economies of competition. *Harvard Business Review* (November/December), 77–90.

Porter, M.E. (2003). The economic performance of regions. *Regional Studies, 37*(6/7), 549–578.

Putnam, R.D. (1993). *Making Democracy Work: Civic Traditions in Modern Italy*. Princeton, NJ: Princeton University Press.

Regulski, J. (2003). Local government reform in Poland. *Local Government and Public Service Reform Initiative*. Budapest: Open Society Institute.

Rogers, E.M. (1995). *Diffusion of Innovations* (4th ed.). Detroit, MI: Free Press.

Rumford, C. (2000). *European Cohesion?* London: Macmillan Press.

Sachs, J.D. (1992). The economic transformation of eastern Europe: The case of Poland. *Economics of Planning, 25*, 5–19.

Sahlin-Andersson, K. and Engwall, L. (eds) (2002). *The Expansion of Management Knowledge: Carriers, Flows, and Sources*. Stanford, CA: Stanford University Press.

Salais, R. and Villeneuve, R. (eds) (2005). *Europe and the Politics of Capabilities*. Cambridge: Cambridge University Press.

Saxenian, A. (1994). *Regional Advantage: Culture and Competition in Silicon Valley and Route 128*. Cambridge, MA: Harvard University Press.

Scott, A.J. (1996). Regional motors of the global economy. *Futures, 28*(5), 391–411.

Scott, A.J. and Storper, M. (2003). Regions, globalization, development. *Regional Studies, 37*(6/7), 579–593.

Scott, W.R. (2001). *Institutions and Organizations* (2nd edn). London: Sage Publications.

Storper, M. (1995). The resurgence of regional economies, ten years later: The region as a nexus of untraded interdependencies. *European Urban and Regional Studies, 2*(3), 191–221.

Storper, M. (1997). Territories, flows, and hierarchies in the global economy. In K.R. Cox (ed.), *Spaces of Globalization: Reasserting the Power of the Local* (pp. 19–44). New York: Guilford Press.

Storper, M. and Salais, R. (1997). *Worlds of Production: The Action Frameworks of the Economy*. Cambridge, MA: Harvard University Press.

Strang, D. and Meyer, J.W. (1993). Institutional Conditions for Diffusion. *Theory and Society, 22*(4), 25.

Swianiewicz, P. (2002). Consolidation or Fragmentation? The Size of Local Governments in Central and Eastern Europe. *Local Government and Public Service Reform Initiative*. Budapest: Open Society Institute.

Sztompka, P. (1993). Civilisational incompetence: The trap of post-Communist societies. *Zeitschrift für Soziologie, 22*(2), 85–95.

Thomas, G.M., Meyer, J.W., Ramirez, F.O., and Boli, J. (eds) (1987). *Institutional Structure: Constituting State, Society, and the Individual*. London: Sage Publications.

Triglia, C. (2001). Social capital and local development. *European Journal of Social Theory, 4*, 427–442.

Valente, T.W. (1995). *Network Models of the Diffusion of Innovations*. New York: Hampton Press.

Zeitlin, J. (1990). *Industrial Districts and Local Economic Regeneration: Models, Institutions and Policies*. Geneva: International Institute for Labour Studies.

Žuber, P. (2000). Teoria i praktyka opracowania strategii rozwoju województwa—prace nad strategiami rozwoju województw w oewietle ankiety Ministerstwa Gospodarki. [Theory and practice for the preparation of the voivodships' regional development strategies: Work on the voivodships' development strategies in the light of a survey by the Ministry of the Economy]. *Studia Regionalne i Lokalne, 3*(3), 87–97.

6 The role of PISA publicity in forming national education policy

The case of Finnish curriculum reform

Marjaana Rautalin

Introduction

Since the beginning of the 2000s, Finland has done outstandingly well in PISA assessment (Programme for International Student Assessment). In the study led by the Organisation for Economic Co-operation and Development (OECD) that assesses how far students near the end of compulsory education have acquired some of the knowledge and skills essential for full participation in society, Finland has been consistently at or near the top of all nations tested and in all areas assessed so far (OECD, 2001, 2004, 2007, 2010).[1] In the Finnish Ministry of Education and Culture, Finland's success in PISA has been explained mainly by the successful national education policy, for instance the autonomy enjoyed at the local level. In a Ministry bulletin from 2006, the background to Finland's PISA success is discussed in the following way:

> The education system is flexible and the administration is strongly based on delegation and support. Centralised steering is conducted through the aims set by laws and degrees as well as by the national core curriculum. Municipalities are responsible for the organisation of education and the implementation of the aims. Schools and teachers have a lot of independent autonomy in the provision and contents of education.
>
> (Ministry of Education and Culture, Finland, 2006)

Yet, soon after the release of the first PISA result, a curriculum reform was introduced by the central administration that excessively curtailed the autonomy of Finnish schools and teachers. Where the earlier national framework curriculum of 1994 (NBE, 1994) was perhaps the lightest in the world, enabling Finnish municipalities and, ultimately, individual schools to set their own curricula on the basis of the national core curriculum, the framework curriculum introduced in 2004 (NBE, 2004) was much more detailed and binding. The new curriculum set educational objectives not just for the whole nine years of basic education, as in the earlier framework curriculum, but also, for instance, for the second, sixth, and ninth grades. The cut-off points chosen for assessing achievement in different subjects also varied.

In the Finnish central administration, the introduction of the new framework curriculum was justified particularly by the fact-finding work that the Finnish National Board of Education (NBE) conducted in the late 1990s, the results of which indicated that the previous reform, i.e. the framework curriculum of 1994, was moving in the right direction but did not meet the requirements of the new millennium. That is to say, in the NBE it was believed that although Finland had achieved good results in PISA just at the time when basic education was nationally governed by very liberal curricular guidelines (Laukkanen, 2008), the new detailed framework curricula would meet the challenges emerging in Finnish future education even better (Lindström, 2005, p. 33).

In this chapter I examine how it was possible in Finland to carry through a curriculum reform that strongly conflicted with how national educational experts have interpreted the reasons for Finland's PISA success. I will gloss the paradox by examining the national PISA publicity, particularly the ways in which PISA has been discussed and thus constructed in the Finnish media. I will also examine how this publicity about PISA affected the publicity surrounding the national curriculum reform and, hence, the decisions made concerning that reform. I argue that the role of the national media is crucial in the process of forming national policies. In their reporting of global news events, the national media put forward interpretations of these events, thereby constructing out of them a meaningful and comprehensible public story. Some of these stories or discourses can achieve dominance that further determines how other (related) issues can be discussed with the national public. This way, the national media serve as a forum by which foreign news events are introduced into domestic settings (Clausen, 2004; Gans, 1979; Liebes, 1992; Nossek, 2004) and through which they become incorporated in the national public discourse, thus affecting people's perceptions of society as well as of desirable policy solutions (for example, Alasuutari, Qadir, and Creutz, 2013; Qadir and Alasuutari, 2013).

This case links to recent discussions about how national public PISA debates allegedly affect domestic education policies. For instance, Takayama (2008, and Chapter 8 in this volume) has studied how the Japanese media has covered PISA and argues that biased media writing on PISA enabled the Japanese Ministry of Education to halt an unpopular curriculum reform known as *yutori*. According to Takayama (2008, p. 401), the misleading media coverage "not only enabled its (the Ministry's) reorientation of the unpopular *yutori* reform but facilitated its institutional shift to the market-based output-management mode of educational administration." Similarly, German researchers have examined national public debates on PISA and the ways in which these have affected German education policy. For instance, Martens and Niemann (2010) show that PISA results led to an intense public outcry in Germany. According to them, the PISA finding that the socioeconomic background of teenagers in Germany seems to have more effect on national learning performances than on average in OECD countries was picked up by the national public to demand reforms. As a result, the political elite in Germany has been forced to take measures to improve the country's standing in future comparisons (see also Ertl, 2006; Gruber, 2006; Niemann, 2010).

However, existing studies approach the influence of public PISA debates mainly from the perspective of how *poor* PISA results affect national policies. For instance, Martens and Niemann (2010, p. 5) argue that performing well in PISA does not seem to entail the need for further analysis or discussion in the domestic sphere. Instead, the claim is that poor results seem to prophesy reforms, but only if the country's poor performance is framed as crucial in the domestic public and if there is a gap between the country's self-perception and the empirical results evinced by PISA (Dobbins and Martens, 2010; Martens and Niemann, 2010, p. 2). Furthermore, the existing studies do not address the question of how the ways in which PISA is framed in the national media also affects the ways in which other issues regarding national education can be discussed in the domestic public and hence, the decisions to be made concerning these issues.

Finally, these and many other studies on the local uses of PISA (e.g. Dobbins and Martens, 2012; Grek, 2009; Takayama, 2010), assume that the comparison, after being accepted locally, harmonizes national education policies. This idea of PISA affecting national policies is based on the notion that the OECD is a very (or even the most) influential actor in shaping national policies. By contrast, I argue here that the active and creative role of local actors is central to national policy formation. Local actors do not simply implement ready-made global policy ideas but instead draw on them in the local political field in line with their interests. The final policy outcome depends on these local developments, in which all kinds of counter discourses are mobilized to negotiate the shape of policy reforms. Consequently, as emphasized by Alasuutari (2011) and discussed in the introduction to this volume, the end result may be a far cry from the original ideals (as promoted by the OECD) and there may be considerable differences between countries in which the same policy idea or model has been introduced.

In this study, I focus on how *good* results in an international comparison can affect national policies. I explore how the ways in which the Finnish media frame Finland's PISA results also affects the framing of other (related) issues in the domestic public and, consequently, informs new policies and practices. In this, I also wish to contribute to the theoretical discussion of how positive publicity about events such as cross-national comparisons can have an effect on the processes in which national policies are formed. In this context, I draw on Ari Adut's theory of the public sphere (Adut, 2012), and discuss how PISA publicity has made it possible for Finnish politicians and decision-makers to continue reforming despite the publicly evinced explanations for the national PISA success.

The remainder of the paper proceeds as follows. First, I briefly introduce the data and methods used in the empirical analysis. Next, I present the main results of the analysis, i.e. how PISA was discussed and constructed in the Finnish media and then how the national curriculum reform was discussed in the same media. I am particularly interested in the different ways in which the reform was attacked by Finnish actors during the time period analyzed. I then discuss how the interpretations of PISA in the Finnish media may have influenced interpretations of the national curriculum reform in the same forum, and how Finnish education policy can be seen as an outcome of that process. By way of conclusion, I consider the overall role of international comparisons such as PISA in forming domestic policies.

Data and methods

The empirical data here consist of stories with reference to PISA and stories with reference to the curriculum for Finnish basic education appearing in *Helsingin Sanomat, Suomen Tietotoimisto*, and *Suomen Kuvalehti*. Both news stories and letters to the editor are included.[2] The texts cover the time period January 2001– April 2009.[3]

Helsingin Sanomat, Suomen Tietotoimisto, and *Suomen Kuvalehti* are all prestigious national media with large circulations. *Helsingin Sanomat* is the biggest quality daily newspaper in Finland with more than 380,000 readers daily. *Suomen Tietotoimisto* is the leading national press agency in Finland, providing news services to nearly all media houses in the country, besides having international clients. The total circulation of media that published news provided by *Suomen Tietotoimisto* in 2011 was more than 2.5 million. Finally, *Suomen Kuvalehti* is one of the most respected and followed weekly periodicals in Finland, with around 320,000 readers a week. All three publications cite freedom of speech and independent communication as operating principles. They all require that the news they publish be based on verified information and be impartial (*Suomen Kuvalehti*, 2011; *Suomen Tietotoimisto*, 2011; Sanoma, 2011) and, taken together, they offer a comprehensive picture of PISA and curriculum reform publicity.

In the analysis I make no distinction between arguments in "traditional" news stories and those in letters to the editor. Rather, I see all arguments put forward when discussing PISA and the curriculum reform as reflections of how these events are discussed by the national audience. That is to say, if a viewpoint is not highlighted by journalists in the news stories, it is typically raised by readers in letters to the editor.

I analyze media texts discussing the curriculum reform over about eight years, instead of only from the time when the reform was introduced, since I want to examine how the national public reform discussion evolved. There are cases in which political decisions do not become public issues immediately but only with a delay and in the context of some other (related) issue (Gans, 1979). Thus, I want to ensure that I also include any stories in which the reform becomes a subject of critical scrutiny even later, for instance possibly when discovering some misfit between the main objectives of the reform and national success factors for PISA.

The data were collected using the media's own electronic archives. In collecting the data I ensured that all stories discussing both the PISA study and the curriculum for Finnish basic education were included (not just the "reform," since otherwise I might have missed numerous stories where the reform was discussed but not referred to as such).[4] By collecting all stories with references to PISA and the curriculum, I eventually had two separate text corpora; one consisting of stories with references to the PISA study, and the other with references to the curriculum for Finnish basic education.[5] In my final analysis, however, I focus on examining how PISA and the actual reform were discussed in the Finnish media.

I analyzed the data by identifying inductively the different types of contexts or *frames* in which PISA or the curriculum occurred. The frames present in the media texts are ideal objects of the study as these organize the world both for news workers who report on the events (Scheufele, 2006) and more importantly, for readers who aim to make sense of the events reported (Entman, 1989; Gamson, Croteau, Hoynes, and Sasson, 1992; Gamson and Modigliani, 1989; Iyengar, 1991; Tuchman, 1978). Having inductively identified different frames within which PISA and the curriculum appeared in the collected stories, I had an all-embracing typology to which all stories referring to PISA and the curriculum could be assigned. After that, I coded the stories of each corpus according to this typology using systematic random sampling.[6] The different types of typologies were not mutually exclusive. Rather, by coding each story I marked all the contexts in which PISA or the curriculum was referred to. This way, one story could be coded to several parallel typologies.

This method relates to approaches broadly known as rhetorical analysis (Perelman, 1982; Perelman and Olbrechts-Tyteca, 1969) and discourse analysis (Foucault, 1972; Potter, 1996; Wood and Kroger, 2000). In my empirical analysis, I pay special attention to the types of justifications or *premises* used in the various arguments evinced by various audience members that are perceived to be so convincing that they are taken up and reported by the media. This becomes important as I seek to find how the dominant interpretations made of PISA and the national curriculum reform turn into organizational forms, thus shaping Finnish education policy (Rautalin and Alasuutari, 2007, 2009).

The superiority of Finnish basic education

Considering how PISA was discussed both in the news stories and letters to the editor, my analysis shows that PISA appears in nine distinct frames in the Finnish media. Mostly, however, PISA emerges in the frames "Finnish education the best in the world" and "all is not well in Finland." The overwhelming majority of stories discuss PISA in one or both of these frames. The former occurs in more than 94 percent of all the sample stories with references to the PISA study. One prominent way of coming to terms with PISA in this context is to highlight how Finland and its education system, due to PISA, attract countries worldwide, and how international experts visit to learn about the Finnish education system:

> The PISA comparisons conducted by the OECD on what fifteen-year-olds can do have caused thousands of experts to come to Finland to witness, for example, special teaching, teacher training and in general how schools are run … Even before 2001, when the results of the first PISA survey on

literacy were publicized, Finland was a fairly popular destination for educationists, but thereafter the number has increased many times over ... Since 2004 some 1,200 visitors from some 60 countries have come annually to Finland through the Ministry of Education and Culture. Last year there were some 1,800.

(*Helsingin Sanomat*, domestic news, 24 February 2008)

Discussions about the potential reasons contributing to Finland's PISA success are often highlighted in the media. Some of these are reported to be the successful Finnish education policy, and the successful work done at the local level (the role of Finnish teachers is especially emphasized), as well as the many factors outside the education sector, such as a strong national culture of reading newspapers. One factor that is particularly underlined in the media as being part of the successful Finnish education policy is the autonomy given to Finnish teachers. An argument put forth in this context is that we had achieved good learning outcomes due to the trust Finnish teachers enjoy:

The confidence in teachers is great. In Finland teachers deservedly enjoy a great deal of power, responsibility and freedom. There is no need for a cumbersome inspectorate. In many countries inspections and constant testing stifle teachers' creativity and misdirect energy.

In Finland teachers plan their teaching from the curriculum level right up to the individual lessons. Here they are capable of it. In Finland subject teachers take the same studies in those subjects as other degree students. Thus the teachers' networks include people active in the world of science and scientific achievements seep through unofficial channels to school.

(*Helsingin Sanomat*, opinion, December 2007)

In this text, the writer links the autonomy given to Finnish teachers with the trust Finnish teachers enjoy. However, instead of attributing the trust and autonomy Finnish teachers enjoy to the work done by the teachers, the writer attributes them to the high quality national teachers' training organized by the state. Hence the text constructs Finnish decision-makers, particularly the Finnish education policy, as the hero rather than Finnish teachers who, at least according to their own interpretations (Rautalin and Alasuutari, 2007), have done self-sacrificing work despite scarce resources for basic education.

Besides discussing the superiority of Finnish basic education, the media also reports potential deficiencies in basic education. The frame "all is not well in Finland" occurs in about 67 percent of the sample stories mentioning PISA. In these stories, the media reports different actors' interpretations of potential deficiencies in Finnish education despite the PISA success. However, the deficiencies claimed vary greatly, and do not constitute any uniform "grand design" for how Finnish basic education should be developed. One concern highlighted in this context is that by neglecting issues potentially endangering basic education, Finland will lose its leading position in international learning assessments:

"School closures, bigger groups in teaching and mergers of upper secondary schools planned in many municipalities are causing many teachers to ask themselves if they have strength enough," says Professor Eira Korpinen of the Teacher Education Department of the University of Jyväskylä.

"Teachers, school heads and pupils need humane and encouraging conditions when they recommence their work this autumn," she says.

Professor Korpinen points out that although the international PISA study on school achievement showed that our country's comprehensive school pupils' skills are top class in reading and mathematics, things look quite different for future surveys. If special teaching and extra coaching are neglected, as is now the case, international studies will not be so complimentary to us Finns.

(*Suomen Tietotoimisto*, domestic news, August 2002)

Here, a professor in a Finnish teacher training college makes a distinction between good national learning performance and existing political practices. By highlighting Finnish teenagers' high learning outcomes in reading and mathematics on one hand, and the retrenchments to be made in schools and teaching on the other, the professor implies that Finnish decision-makers are hindering rather than assisting schools and teachers from producing good learning performances in the future. This way, the professor raises Finland's future ranking in PISA as a political asset that can be used to call for more resources for national education.

Other frames appear notably more seldom in the stories discussing PISA. On the whole, the analysis reveals that PISA is covered in a very positive manner. PISA results are used particularly to argue how the Finnish education system is superior to others, although the media also highlights potential deficiencies. However, again, the critical views are highly fragmentary in nature. If anything, Finland's PISA ranking is used to argue how education is in good shape in Finland, how the Finnish education system is internationally acknowledged, and that any shortcomings should be remedied in order to do well in future assessments.

The moderate national curriculum discussion

In covering PISA there is hardly any mention of the curriculum reform in the media, let alone its seemingly inconsistent nature. In none of the stories discussing PISA is the argument evinced that Finnish teachers and schools have too much autonomy. Against this background, it is interesting that a curriculum reform was implemented that goes against how national educational experts, and the national media, explain Finland's PISA success. In order to understand how such a contradictory reform could be introduced, I argue that one needs to study the publicity emerging on that reform, i.e. how the reform was constructed in the Finnish public and how this publicity, together with other publicity, enabled its introduction.

The issue of the Finnish basic education curriculum is very much present in the national public and is covered in diverse contexts. Interestingly, the actual curriculum reform is discussed relatively little. The reform appears in only about one-third of the sample stories where curricula are mentioned. Although the reform itself is discussed in diverse contexts, it appears mostly within the frame of being seen as advantageous—potentially enhancing equality in Finnish basic education—or in negative terms—as a threat or burden for Finnish teachers and pupils. Each frame occurs in about 40 percent of the sample stories with references to the curriculum. I am particularly interested in whether the national curriculum reform, especially its seemingly inconsistent nature, was publicly contested in Finland either at the time of preparing the reform, or afterwards. Therefore, I concentrate here particularly on the latter frame, i.e. how the menace of the reform is validated in the Finnish public during this period, and how PISA is used as a weapon when attacking the reform.

Amazingly, the argument that the reform runs contrary to the way Finnish educational experts parade Finland's high PISA ranking is not made in any story. That is, neither the news stories nor letters to the editor ever raise the argument that Finnish education policy decisions contradict how Finland's PISA success is explained by national educational authorities. Instead of being seen as politically incorrect or disharmonious, the reform is interpreted as having other faults. One very prominent point presented in this context is that the proposed reform increases compulsory subjects in schools at the expense of electives:

> The editorial addressed the new proposal for the allocation of hours in comprehensive school ... Attention was paid to the main feature of the proposal, reduction of elective subjects in favour of subjects compulsory for all. Arts subjects, pictorial art and music are an important group of elective subjects. These subjects are being removed from the upper classes of comprehensive school as consequences of the reduction in elective subjects ... Doing away with artistic subjects in the upper classes of comprehensive school is to do away not only with the joy of creation and expression, but also to dumb down the level of national cultivation. Are Finnish society and cultural life conceivable without a high level of musical and artistic life, without Finnish design, film and architecture? Not everyone becomes a professional in these subjects, but everyone does indeed need the ability to comprehend and enjoy culture and the products of the arts.
>
> (*Helsingin Sanomat*, opinion, 16 May 2001)

In this extract, a music teacher and an art teacher attack the new proposal for its distribution of hours in Finnish comprehensive schools by linking the elective subjects, particularly the arts subjects, to the level of national cultivation. By highlighting the areas in artistic life in which Finns have achieved merit nationally and internationally, the argument is that the very arts subjects that the new curriculum proposes to reduce are the ones that can ensure a high level of national cultivation in the future. The text aims to show the myopia of the planned reform and, hence, to stop it from being implemented.

Finland's PISA ranking is barely referred to in criticisms of the reform. In fact, PISA appears in only seven of the 25 sample stories in which the reform is seen as a threat to Finnish basic education. One dominant way of coming to terms with PISA in this context is to claim that the new core curriculum excessively curtails the autonomy of Finnish schools and teachers, thus endangering future PISA results. However, even in this discussion the point is never made that the national decision runs contrary to how national education experts explain the country's high PISA ranking. In fact, the fact that the PISA success is explained in contradictory terms to the logic of the reform is not even used as political capital in the domestic field to oppose the reform. Rather, the counter-arguments are made only in terms of the negative effects of pupils' future performance:

> Addressing an international seminar in Helsinki entitled *Education in Finland—the best in Europe?* Professor Reijo Wilenius warned against the consequences of the excessive unification of curricula ... In Wilenius' opinion one reason for the good findings on competence is that the Finnish comprehensive school system has been relatively open. Schools and teachers have also enjoyed independence ... According to Wilenius, standardized or uniform curricula might restrict schools' autonomy too much, and competence findings might deteriorate. "Freedom is the best method" Wilenius assured his audience, as befits a discussion session of the European Forum on Freedom in Education.
>
> (*Helsingin Sanomat*, domestic news, 9 June 2006)

Considering the Finnish media discourse as a whole, PISA and the curriculum seem to appear in two separate discussions. Both issues are present in the media but clearly separate from each other. Interestingly, the reform itself does not receive as much media attention as one would anticipate. Its appropriateness is questioned in places, but the reform and its aims are also defended.

Discussion

In this study, I set out to examine how it was possible to carry through a curriculum reform in Finland that ran contrary to how national educational experts have interpreted the reasons behind the country's resounding PISA success. The paradox was glossed by analyzing the national PISA publicity, particularly the ways in which PISA was framed and, thus, constructed in the national media, and how this national PISA publicity may have affected the national curriculum reform publicity and the decisions made concerning that reform.

The analysis shows that in the national media, PISA was used mainly to argue how Finnish basic education serves as the best in the world and how Finnish education policy has been successful. The media also reported on the potential problems existing in Finnish education despite Finland's PISA success. Nevertheless, the problems claimed to exist in Finnish education did not form any uniform "grand design" for how Finnish education should be improved. Rather, the focal story told in the media delivered an image of Finnish education being in good shape, how the Finnish education system was internationally acclaimed, and that any shortcomings in the Finnish system should be remedied in order to do well in future assessments.

The reform discussion, for its part, was very moderate in nature, comprising both arguments for and against the reform. Interestingly, PISA was hardly invoked as a weapon when attacking the reform. PISA was used to argue that the new standardized curricula curbed the autonomy of Finnish schools and teachers too much, thus endangering Finland's future prospects in PISA. However, even in this connection the argument was not made that the reform introduced invalidated the virtues highlighted by national educational experts as leading to Finland's good PISA performance. Rather, the reform was debated like any education policy issue in the domestic media, where different national actors expressed their views concerning the reform while simultaneously aiming to safeguard their interests and future prospects.

It is difficult to understand why the national PISA success was not articulated as a political weapon rolled out sensationally in the Finnish press, where it might have impeded the national curriculum reform; I argue that there are two distinct reasons for this. First, due to Finland's high ranking in PISA, the interpretation that Finnish education is superior to others and that this is largely due to successful Finnish education policy was firmly rooted with the Finnish public. In this connection, it would have been outrageous to put out a story that was completely at odds with the public view, denying that Finnish education policy was unified. This kind of coverage was peculiar to countries in which the preliminary estimates concerning the domestic education system were relatively high as shown, for instance by German and Japan researchers (Dobbins and Martens, 2010; Martens and Niemann, 2010; Takayama, 2008). In these countries, after PISA revealed that the national education system may not be as good as expected, it was easy for the national media to debate this unexpectedly poor performance and seek reasons for the bad results.

In Finland, on the contrary, the general assumption was that the national education system was working well, and thus the country would rank quite high in the PISA comparison. However, probably only a few anticipated that Finland would rank at the very top in all rounds conducted and in each area assessed. Since this was the case, it was perfectly natural for the Finnish media to highlight how well Finnish pupils were doing against their foreign peers and seek to explain the factors behind Finland's PISA success.

Second, the reason why the curriculum reform caused no uproar in the Finnish press may be that after the first PISA results were publicized in December 2001, no overall explanation was forthcoming for Finland's success, and the public discussion did not focus on the controversy between the publicly evinced explanations for Finland's PISA success and the new curriculum in the making. Rather, the media discussion focused on marveling at the superiority of the Finnish education system and its specific characteristics.

As a result particularly of this positive public image of Finnish education and education policy as successful and reliable, and the absence of any public consensus on which particular factor best explained Finland's high scores in PISA, the work of Finnish decision-makers and reformers was not questioned by the public. Hence, they could continue uninterrupted with their reform work.

The interpretations made in this chapter are, of course, only based on readings of how the *media* work and how this affects national policy-making. Needless to say, there are plenty of other equally plausible reasons that have contributed to the reform, but which are not examined in this case study. For instance, as emphasized in the introduction, the curriculum reform may be due to the fact that the needs analysis conducted by the NBE had revealed that the former framework curriculum was moving in the right direction but was still inadequate to meet future challenges. Hence, the NBE launched a reform to address these challenges and to continuously improve the learning outcomes of Finnish basic education. On the other hand, the preparation of the reform was also started long before the first PISA results came out. For this reason, when the first PISA results were released in 2001, the spirit of the 2004 curriculum reform was already decided and work was underway. On those grounds, one may argue that the reform was not called off since, according to the findings of the central administration, there were strong national reasons for it, and because there were no reliable explanations—let alone a national consensus—that the autonomy given to the local level, rather than other factors, would best explain Finland's PISA success.

To prove the correctness of these reasons would, however, require examination of different research material. However, these explanations in any case do not sufficiently account for why the media did not seize on the topic and report how Finnish education policy decisions are not consistent with how Finnish educational experts explain Finland's PISA success. As I have emphasized earlier, the national media serve as a forum where different nationally important issues come up and where they are discussed actively. The national media particularly highlight issues in which, according to the general interpretation, there lies something mysterious or even scandalous (e.g. Adut, 2008; Lull and Hinerman, 1997; Thompson, 2000; Tumber and Waisbord, 2004). In light of Finland's success in PISA, however, it would appear that an interpretation totally at odds with what has been stated about our national education and especially its success in connection with PISA could not be publicly accommodated or condoned in Finland. As a consequence of this, the reform of the national curriculum was not accorded criticism, and could be pushed through without interruption.

This case study also enhances our understanding of how good PISA performance can have an influence on national policies. As I discussed earlier, existing studies propose that only poor success in PISA appears to have an effect on domestic policies, and this if and only if national PISA performance is framed as crucial in the domestic media, and if a substantial gap between the national self-perception and the empirical results can be observed. Based on the findings made in this case study, however, I argue that good national PISA performance can also have an effect on domestic political decision-making. It can make possible national reforms totally devoid of any direct connection to the international assessment. Drawing particularly on Adut's theory of the public sphere, I argue that the positive publicity of national policy-making, in this case of Finnish education policy, always entails power. When the domestic media construct national policy-making as successful and reliable, national policy-makers have the freedom to practice their policy uninterrupted (Adut, 2012, p. 247). As PISA revealed that the Finnish education system is of higher quality than expected, public discussion in Finland did not focus on the workings of the central government. Instead, the media highlighted the unexpected success of Finnish education and the potential reasons behind it.

However, as underlined by Adut, the consequences of positive publicity can be double-edged. While positive publicity for domestic policy-making can guarantee industrial peace for policy makers under some circumstances, it also increases expectations of them. "The publicity that a political actor enjoys, while potentially glorifying and immunizing him in the short run, will also ultimately saddle him with unrealistically high expectations from the audience. This will often eventuate in dissatisfaction and distrust" (Adut, 2012, p. 248). By this Adut means that when policy makers fail to meet public expectations, everything they do falls under the public's inspection. This seems to be so for Japan and Germany. In these countries, public expectations of the national education system were rather high before PISA. After PISA revealed that German and Japanese teenagers did not perform as well as expected, the entire education system went under public scrutiny as politicians and decision-makers were called to account. If and when politicians and decision-makers succeed in meeting the expectations of the audience, or even exceeding them, which seems to be again the case in Finland, the national reform work can be continued interrupted. Without specific opposition from the public, politicians and other actors responsible for the national curriculum reform could pursue their objectives and continue uninterrupted with the work they claimed to be nationally justified.

This case study also enriches our understanding of how international comparisons such as PISA work in national contexts. Instead of claiming that international organizations and the comparisons they produce harmonize national policies, based on the findings made in this case study, I argue, they contribute to synchronizing national policies. International assessments such as PISA trigger policy debates in the local contexts in which comparisons are invoked when defending or criticizing existing policies. However, not all comparisons, ideas, models, or trends circulating in the world catch attention, let alone trigger a debate in the nation-state. The "success" of a comparison or idea depends on whether local players see it as potentially advantageous both for their own national policies and, more importantly, for their political interests and positions. If the points highlighted by the comparisons are favorable for domestic actors and their interests, these are easily taken up. In the cases of Germany and Japan, the poor results in international comparisons are easily utilized by reformers, actors who aim to justify the necessity of the reforms by the poor ranking of their own country. This case, for its part, shows that good results are also easily taken up by national actors. By the good results achieved in international assessments, different national actors justify the functionality of existing systems, although these good results are also used to substantiate the need for changes to the existing systems in order to do even better in future comparisons. Through these local applications, globally shared images of desirable national education systems and practices become assumed in national contexts, thus leading to synchronization of national policies. In other words, by reacting to PISA, nation-states make similar political moves. However, due to the varied natures of local field battles, nation-states may end up introducing quite different policy reforms. In Japan and Germany, different reforms have been introduced in the wake of PISA, whereas in Finland, PISA does not seem to have set off reforms. By this, I do not mean that in Finland PISA has not had an effect. If anything, it seems that in Finland the national PISA success has made it easy for politicians and decision-makers to continue with their policy as before. As PISA did not provide any worthy assets for criticism, the workings of the Finnish central administration were not interfered with by the public and the Finnish curriculum reform could be followed through uninterrupted.

Notes

1 For what PISA assesses, see: "OECD: Programme for International Student Assessment (PISA): background and basics," retrieved 4 August 2013 from www.OECD.org/pisa/pisafaq/#background_and_basics.
2 From the selected media only *Helsingin Sanomat* and *Suomen Kuvalehti* publish letters to the editor.
3 The data from *Suomen Kuvalehti* cover only the time period April 2002–April 2009; the stories published prior to this were not electronically filed and thus not available.
4 In the media, the curriculum reform was referred to, for instance, by using expressions such as "the new curriculum" or "the new proposal for the allocation of hours."
5 The total number of stories discussing PISA is 602. The curriculum for Finnish basic education is discussed in 761 stories. All text extracts included in the final analysis have been translated by a native speaker.
6 I coded a significant sample of the stories to identify the frames in my analysis, which I confirmed are evident throughout the stories in each corpus.

References

Adut, A. (2008). *On Scandal: Moral Disturbances in Society, Politics, and Art*. New York: Cambridge University Press.
Adut, A. (2012). A theory of the public sphere. *Sociological Theory, 30*(4), 238–262.
Alasuutari, P. (2011). Modernization as a tacit concept used in governance. *Journal of Political Power, 4*(2), 217–235.
Alasuutari, P., Qadir, A., and Creutz, K. (2013) The Domestication of Foreign News: News Stories Related to the 2011 Egyptian Revolution in British, Finnish and Pakistani Newspapers. *Media, Culture & Society, 35*(6), 692–707.
Clausen, L. (2004). Localizing the Global: "Domestication" Processes in International News Production. *Media, Culture & Society, 26*(1), 25–44.

Dobbins, M. and Martens, K. (2010). A contrasting case—the USA and its weak response to internationalization process in education policy. In K. Martens, A. Nagel, M. Windzio, and A. Weymann (eds), *Transformation of Education Policy* (pp. 179–195). Basingstoke: Palgrave Macmillan.

Dobbins, M. and Martens, K. (2012). Towards an education approach à la finlandaise? French education policy after PISA. *Journal of Education Policy, 27*(1), 23–43.

Entman, R.M. (1989). How the media affect what people think: An information processing approach. *Journal of Politics, 51*, 347–370.

Ertl, H. (2006). Educational standards and the changing discourse on education: The reception and consequences of the PISA study in Germany. *Oxford Review of Education, 32*(5), 619–634.

Foucault, M. (1972). *The Archaeology of Knowledge*. London: Tavistock.

Gamson, W. and Modigliani, A. (1989). Media discourse and public opinion on nuclear power: A constructionist approach. *American Journal of Sociology, 95*(1), 1–37.

Gamson, W., Croteau, D., Hoynes, W., and Sasson, T. (1992). Media images and the social construction of reality. *Annual Review of Sociology, 18*, 373–393.

Gans, H. (1979). *Deciding What's News: A Study of CBS Evening News, NBC Nightly News, Newsweek, and Time.* New York: Pantheon Books.

Grek, S. (2009). Governing by numbers: the PISA 'effect' in Europe. *Journal of Education Policy, 24*(1), 23-37.

Gruber, K.-H. (2006). The German "PISA-Shock": some aspects of the extraordinary impact of the OECD's PISA Study on the German education system. In H. Ertl (ed.), *Oxford Studies in Comparative Education* (Vol. 16, pp. 195–208). Oxford: Symposium Books.

Helsingin Sanomat (2001, 16 May). Kerho ei korvaa taideopetusta [Opinion: The club is no substitute for art instruction].

Helsingin Sanomat (2006, 9 June). Wilenius: Opetussuunnitelmia ei saa liikaa yhtenäistää [Report: Wilenius: Curricula cannot be standardized in excess].

Helsingin Sanomat (2007, 2 December). Suomen peruskoulu on ylivertainen [Opinion: The Finnish comprehensive school is beyond compare].

Helsingin Sanomat (2008, 24 February). PISA-vertailu on tuonut tuhansia turisteja Suomeen [Report: The PISA comparison has brought thousands of tourists to Finland].

Iyengar, S. (1991). *Is Anyone Responsible? How Television Frames Political Issues.* Chicago, IL and London: University of Chicago Press.

Laukkanen, R. (2008). Finnish Strategy for High-Level Education for All. In N.C. Soguel and P. Jaccard (eds), *Governance and Performance of Education Systems* (pp. 305–324): Springer.

Liebes, T. (1992). Our war/their war: Comparing the Intifadeh and the Gulf War on US and Israeli television. *Critical Studies in Mass Communication, 9*, 44–55.

Lindström, A. (2005). Kansalliset opetussuunnitelmat yhteiskunnallisina uudistajina [National curricula as social reformers]. In K. Hämäläinen, A. Lindström, and J. Puhakka (eds), *Yhtenäisen peruskoulun menestystarina [The national comprehensive education, the Finnish success story]* (pp. 18–35). Helsinki: Yliopistopaino Kustannus.

Lull, J. and Hinerman, S. (1997). The search for scandal. In J. Lull and S. Hinerman (eds), *Media Scandals* (pp. 1–33). Cambridge: Polity Press.

Martens, K. and Niemann, D. (2010). Governance by comparison: How ratings and rankings impact national policy-making in education. *TransState working papers*, (139), 1–22. Retrieved 12 March 2012 from http://hdl.handle.net/10419/41595.

Ministry of Education and Culture (2006). *OECD PISA Survey, Bulletin.* Helsinki:

Ministry of Education. Retrieved 15 November 2006 from www.minedu.fi/OPM/Kou-lutus/artikkelit/pisa-tutkimus/?lang=en.

NBE (1994). *Framework Curiculum for the Comprehensive School*. Helsinki: National Board of Education.

NBE (2004). *Framework Curriculum for the Comprehensive School*. Helsinki: National Board of Education.

Niemann, D. (2010). Turn of the tide: New horizons in German education policy through IO influence. In K. Martens, A. Nagel, M. Windzio, and A. Weymann (eds), *Transformation of Education Policy* (pp. 77–104). Basingstoke: Palgrave Macmillan.

Nossek, H. (2004). Our news and their news: The role of national identity in the coverage of foreign news. *Journalism, 5*(3), 343–368.

OECD (2001). Knowledge and skills for life: First results from PISA 2000. Paris: OECD.

OECD (2004). Learning for Tomorrow's World: First Results from Pisa 2003. Paris: OECD.

OECD (2007). PISA 2006. Science Competences for Tomorrow's World (Vol. 1). Paris: OECD.

OECD (2010). PISA 2009 Results. What Students Know and Can Do: Student Performance in Reading, Mathematics and Science (Vol. 1). Paris: OECD.

Perelman, C. (1982). *The Realm of Rhetoric*. Notre Dame, IN: University of Notre Dame Press.

Perelman, C. and Olbrechts-Tyteca, L. (1969). *The New Rhetoric: A Treatise on Argumentation*. Notre Dame, IN: University of Notre Dame Press.

Potter, J. (1996). *Representing Reality: Discourse, Rhetoric and Social Construction*. London: Sage.

Qadir, A. and Alasuutari, P. (2013). Taming terror: domestication of the war on terror in the Pakistan media. *Asian Journal of Communication*. doi:10.1080/01292986.2013.764905.

Rautalin, M. and Alasuutari, P. (2007). The curse of success: The impact of the OECD's Programme for International Student Assessment on the discourses of the teaching profession in Finland. *European Educational Research Journal, 6*(4), 348–363.

Rautalin, M. and Alasuutari, P. (2009). The uses of the national PISA results by Finnish officials in central government. *Journal of Education Policy, 24*(5, September), 539–556.

Sanoma (2011). Helsingin Sanomain Periaatelinja [Operating principles of *Helsingin Sanomat*]. Helsinki: Sanoma Oyj.

Scheufele, B. (2006). Frames, schemata and news reporting. *Communications: European Journal of Communication Research, 31*, 65–83.

Suomen Kuvalehti (2011). *Ajattelevien Ihmisten Lehti* [*Journal of Thinkers*]. Retrieved 16 November 2011 from www.otavamedia.fi/web/guest/suomenkuvalehti.

Suomen Tietotoimisto (2002, 13 August). Opettajat tarvitsevat inhimilliset ja kannustavat olot [Report: Teachers need humane and encouraging conditions].

Suomen Tietotoimisto (2011). Kansallinen Uutistoimisto [The National News Agency]. Retrieved 16 November 2011 from www.stt.fi/fi/mika-on-stt/kansallinen-uutistoimisto.

Takayama, K. (2008). The politics of international league tables: PISA in Japan's achievement crisis debate. *Comparative Education, 44*(4), 387–407.

Takayama, K. (2010). Politics of externalization in reflexive times: reinventing Japanese education reform discourses through "Finnish PISA success." *Comparative Education Review, 54*(1), 51–75.

Thompson, J. (2000). *Political Scandal: Power and Visibility in the Media Age*. Cambridge: Polity Press.

Tuchman, G. (1978). *Making News: A Study in the Construction of Reality*. New York: Free Press.

Tumber, H. and Waisbord, S.R. (2004). Introduction: Political scandals and media across democracies, Volume II. *American Behavioral Scientist, 47*(9), 1143–1152.

Wood, L.A. and Kroger, R.O. (2000). *Doing Discourse Analysis: Methods for Studying Action in Talk and Text*. Thousand Oaks, CA: Sage Publications.

Part II

Domestic field battles and naturalization

7 The local politics of domesticating global models

The struggle over central bank independence in Israel[1]

Daniel Maman and Zeev Rosenhek

Central bank independence is considered a critical component of the worldwide spread of the neoliberal policy paradigm that has taken place since the 1990s. This is manifested in the growing number of countries that enacted legislative amendments aimed at making their central banks legally independent, providing evidence for what can be called a global wave of central banking reform (Carruthers, Babb, and Halliday, 2001; Marcussen, 2005; Polillo and Guillen, 2005). This process can be seen as a particularly salient instance of the worldwide diffusion of ideational frameworks and institutional models that come to be defined by powerful actors as necessary for the rational and efficient governing of the political economy. In terms of effects, the adoption of central bank independence has been enormously consequential for the most important dimensions of the local political economies, constituting a key element in the transformation of the state institutional configuration and of state–economy relationships since the 1990s (e.g. Hall, 2008; Maman and Rosenhek, 2011).

It is recognized today that processes of diffusion of institutional blueprints are neither automatic nor deterministic, but rather the result of complex and multi-faceted political dynamics in which diverse actors, both local and international, are involved. Hence, the politics of domesticating worldwide dominant models constitutes a fundamental facet of processes of institutional diffusion. Examining these political processes, where influential actors promote or contest particular ways of implementing global models, is essential to comprehensively capturing the complexities of institutional change at the state level and its connections to global processes.

In this chapter we examine the politics of domestication of the dominant global standard of central bank independence in Israel. Based on a detailed process-tracing analysis of the intensive and long-lasting struggle over the legal status of the Israeli central bank that took place between mid-1990s and 2010, we show that intra-state politics function as a key factor structuring and affecting processes of domestication of global models in the local political–economic field. Furthermore, while addressing the strategies deployed by state agencies, particularly the central bank and the Ministry of Finance, we show how global processes and logics serve them as resources to be mobilized in the struggle over the adoption of the model. This indicates the importance of globalization in the politics of institutional change—not as a causal factor determining changes at the state level, but rather as a political resource mobilized by local actors striving to promote institutional transformations.

Globalization, intra-state politics and central bank independence

Over the last two decades the model of central bank independence has emerged as a dominant global standard of rational statehood, that came to be regarded as a necessary institutional arrangement to guarantee the implementation of sound macroeconomic policy. The basic idea underpinning the model is that only a central bank that is independent of the government, and hence insulated from political pressure, is capable of formulating and implementing proper monetary policy aimed at maintaining price stability (e.g. Cukierman, 1992). This reflects the general notion that macroeconomic management should be depoliticized and put in hands of experts with recognized objective knowledge, which is one of the key tenets of the neoliberal dogma. Since the 1980s, and at least till the global financial crisis that erupted in 2007, the model of central bank independence was widely regarded as an undisputed standard of best practice by mainstream macro and monetary economists, international economic organizations, central banks all over the world, and other influential actors.

The worldwide diffusion of the model of central bank independence, as well as of other neoliberal practices, has been considered by numerous scholars as causally linked to several dimensions of globalization and the different power dynamics associated with them. The first dimension of globalization that is often regarded as having caused the adoption of central bank independence is the emergence and growth of global financial markets (Bell, 2004; Weiss, 2003). The basic claim is that the enormous expansion of global financial markets and the growing mobility of capital impose on states the adoption of a wide array of institutional arrangements and policies that conform to the interests of local and foreign investors. Therefore, the structural power enjoyed by mobile capital forces governments to grant independence to central banks, allowing them to implement monetary and other policies that benefit investors, as this is considered a necessary condition to attract and retain capital needed by the national economy (Maxfield, 1997).

The institutional–cultural explanation suggested by the world polity approach focuses on the emergence and diffusion of institutional models that are consensually perceived at the global level as rational, legitimate, and appropriate. Due to their normative power, the adoption of these models becomes nearly mandatory for states (Meyer, Boli, Thomas, and Ramirez, 1997). With the strengthening of neoliberal institutional practices within the global normative order, the model of central bank independence gained the status of self-evident standard of effective and rational macroeconomic management (King, 2005; Marcussen, 2006). As a result, this approach asserts, governments around the world are compelled to grant independence to their central bank as a necessary means to gain and maintain legitimacy in the international system. Furthermore, within the framework of processes of global isomorphism, states look at other states considered successful as models for learning appropriate institutional arrangements and policies (Dobbin, Simmons, and Garret, 2007). Hence, the independent US "Fed" (Federal Reserve Bank) and the even more independent European Central Bank (and previously the German Bundesbank) serve as sources of inspiration for states seeking efficient institutional arrangements for macroeconomic management.

A third explanation emphasizes the institutional–political dimension of globalization, claiming that the diffusion of neoliberal policies and institutional models is grounded on the coercive power upon states enjoyed by international agencies. According to this explanation, international financial organizations, such as the IMF (International Monetary Fund) and the World Bank, enforce central bank independence upon peripheral and semi-peripheral states through conditional lending practices, surveillance, and technical assistance, as part of their efforts to impose the neoliberal doctrine of free market, financial stability and fiscal and monetary discipline (Barnett and Finnemore, 2004; Kahler, 1992).

A major shortcoming common to these globalist approaches is that they see institutional change at the nation-state level as a simple and straightforward result of global forces, overlooking the key role of local actors, their conflicting institutional interests, and the concrete political interactions between them in the processes of institutional change. Furthermore, these explanations tend to see the relationship between the global and the local in a mechanistic or even deterministic way, while ignoring the complex and reciprocal relations between the global and local fields. As put by Pertti Alasuutari and Ali Qadir in the introductory chapter to this volume, these approaches do not address the concrete political dynamics in the local field that underlie the adoption and domestication of global standards, treating them as a black box. Therefore, they cannot account for the interactions between local political actors seeking to promote, or alternatively, resisting particular modes of domestication of global institutional models. To fill this gap, we seek in our analysis to open this black box, examining in-depth the politics of the legislation of a new central bank law in Israel as it evolved in the local field. This complex politics of domestication, in which the Israeli central bank and the Ministry of Finance played key roles, cannot be explained as resulting in a direct and straightforward manner from global forces. We argue that the domestication of the model of central bank independence was structured by political processes taking place mainly within the state, that is, by the struggles among state agencies that strove to strengthen their position in the political–economic field vis-à-vis competing agencies. As the strengthening of the central bank involves an important reconfiguration of the state institutional architecture, particularly concerning the power balance between its different economic agencies, the legal framework that defines the authority, the roles and the institutional resources of the central bank, is likely to turn into a prominent contested issue. Domesticating the model of central bank independence becomes, therefore, a key locus of conflict within the state apparatus.

While the focus of our analysis is on the dynamics of the local political field, we do not ignore forces and processes emerging and acting in the global field. We contend that global processes and logics function as resources that can be mobilized and deployed by local actors interested in promoting institutional change. As we show below, the notion that the adoption of central bank independence is imposed and made necessary by the structural power of global financial markets, the normative power of dominant global institutional models, and the coercive power of international financial organizations was deployed by the central bank as a main strategy to legitimize and promote its political project of institutional change. The analysis of these practices highlights the importance of political processes that take place in the local field—especially conflictive interactions between different state agencies—and their connections with the global field in the domestication of global models and the embedding of global logics into the state apparatus.

The struggle over the legal status of the Bank of Israel

As characteristic of developmental states, since its establishment in 1954 and up to the mid-1980s the Bank of Israel (hereafter, BoI) functioned under the effective control of the Ministry of Finance (hereafter, MoF), playing a key role in the monetization of fiscal deficits and the allocation of subsidized credit according to the development policy of the state. Since the mid-1980s, however, the Israeli central bank underwent a dramatic process of strengthening, and accumulated a great deal of institutional and political power (Maman and Rosenhek, 2011). Yet, in contrast to large numbers of central banks all over the world that gained legal independence, in the Israeli case, after 1985, there were no fundamental changes in the legal status of the central bank. Furthermore, since the mid-1990s, attempts to legislate a new Bank of Israel Law have been extremely salient on the political agenda, and became a prominent bone of contention between the central bank and the MoF. This intra-state conflict would be resolved only in 2010, with the passing of a new law that formally anchored the independent and powerful status attained by the BoI. It should be stressed from the outset that the intense conflicts over central bank independence were not the result of MoF opposition to the neoliberal policy paradigm per se. In fact, both agencies were equally enthusiastic supporters of the liberalization of the political economy and collaborated in advancing important liberalizing reforms, for example in the financial realm. However, with regard to the legal independence of the central bank, the MoF and BoI developed distinct, even clashing, political and organizational interests.

The struggle over the legal status of the central bank began in 1995, when several members of the Israeli parliament (Knesset) from both coalition and opposition parties, who opposed the BoI's strict anti-inflationary monetary policy proposed the establishment of a monetary council, with the aim of restricting the Governor's exclusive authority over monetary policy. In response, the central bank called for an overall legislative change that would legally enshrine the BoI's full independence. The central bank's main demand was to redefine its tasks in relation to macroeconomic management. The original Bank of Israel Law, which had been designed in the 1950s under the then dominant model of the developmental state, defined the bank's objectives as employing monetary policy in order to advance the stabilization of the value of the local currency, and promoting high levels of production, employment, national income, and capital investments (Bank of Israel Law 1954, Clause 3). Now, though, the BoI demanded that the attainment and long-term preservation of price stability be defined as its exclusive or primary objective.

These two issues—the establishment and composition of a monetary council, and the definition of the objectives of the central bank and its monetary policy— became the key bones of contention in the long-lasting dispute over the legislation of a new Bank of Israel Law. Both issues were directly related to the BoI's position within the state's institutional configuration and to the power balance with other state agencies, particularly the MoF. The first issue entailed the possibility that actors external to the central bank might be members in the monetary council in charge of defining monetary policy, thereby limiting the BoI's autonomy. The second issue touched on one of the most fundamental principles of the model of central bank independence as derived from neoliberal economic thought: namely, the rigid assertion that monetary policy is able only to influence inflation, and therefore the central bank's sole objective should be attaining and preserving price stability.

In our examination of the conflict over the proposed changes to the Bank of Israel Law, we shall focus on the patterns of action among the major players and the strategies they used in promoting their ends. Three particularly prominent political practices in play point to the mobilization and use of globalization by local actors as a key resource in their efforts to further their interests. The first one was to resort to institutional globalization, drawing on existing models in other countries as a source of legitimacy for institutional change at the local level. The phrase, "as every country in the world does," became a kind of mantra that was uttered almost every time any of the various actors sought to justify the particular change in the law that they were promoting as imposed by global standards. The second practice, employed mainly by the central bank, was to invoke financial globalization, portraying the global financial markets and their relevant actors—investors and credit ranking agencies—as an omnipotent disciplining force that imposes the adoption of neoliberal institutional arrangements and policies, such as central bank independence. The third practice at the disposal of the central bank was to mobilize the support of international organizations, particularly the IMF, as a source of legitimization for its agenda of institutional change.

Efforts to limit the central bank's independence

As suggested earlier, the struggles over the Bank of Israel Law emerged in mid-1995, when a group of legislators from various parties, supported by representatives of business interests, submitted a bill to the Knesset with the aim of limiting the BoI de facto independence and gaining influence over monetary policy-making through the establishment of a monetary council. Minister of Finance Avraham Shochat supported the private bill, though he rejected the idea that business interests should be represented on the monetary council. Shochat justified his backing of the proposal by referring to the necessity of adopting the same institutional arrangements implemented in developed countries like Japan, Germany, and the USA.

Just like the Minister of Finance, though with quite the opposite intent, the central bank also deployed a rhetoric of compulsory institutional convergence and declared that the proposed bill squarely contradicted global trends assuring central bank independence, emphatically stating on many occasions that Israel cannot remain an exception to this trend of convergence towards global standards of best practice in central banking. Furthermore, the central bank also drew on the rhetoric of financial globalization while highlighting the disciplinary force of international capital markets and countries' financial rankings. It intimated that, since the credit rating agencies attribute a great deal of importance to central bank independence, the establishment of a monetary council that would limit its autonomy was liable to harm Israel's status in the international financial markets. Its own proposal for a new Bank of Israel Law, in contrast, would strengthen Israel's economic reputation in the eyes of the international financial community.[2]

The central bank also mobilized the support of influential actors from the community of central banks and international financial organizations. The IMF offered its unequivocal support for the central bank's position, and asserted that the law had to be changed so as to include three key principles: central bank independence, the definition of price stability as the bank's primary objective, and the provision of all the tools required to implement autonomous and effective monetary policy to the central bank. For instance, an IMF statement concerning the Israeli economy stressed that:

> [It] is most important that policy-makers take the experience of other countries into account (especially countries like New Zealand and England, where significant amendments have been made to the law). This experience highlights the importance of the central bank's autonomy in striving to attain its objective, namely, price stability…[3]

The central bank's efforts to block the moves to limit its autonomy and initiate a comprehensive amendment to the law that would strengthen its legal status bore fruit in December 1997, when, as the Governor had demanded, the government decided to establish a public committee to examine options for a new Bank of Israel Law.

Defining the contours of the debate

The work and conclusions of the public committee—dubbed the Levin Committee after its chairperson, retired Supreme Court Justice Dov Levin—are a particularly instructive prism through which to observe the intra-state struggles over the domestication of the model of central bank independence, and the ways in which the BoI succeeded in establishing the range of feasible options in relation to its legal status. The central bank's overwhelming influence was most notable in the committee's frame of reference, its recommendations and its justifications for them, which perfectly reflected the ideational foundations of the institutional model of central bank independence and its specific practices.

In the government's resolution to establish the public committee it was emphasized that there was an urgent need to formulate an up-to-date Bank of Israel Law that accorded with legislative changes in other countries over the previous decade.[4] Furthermore, in the committee's letter of appointment, it was explicitly determined that it should consider the European Union's approach, which affords the central bank complete autonomy from all elected political bodies, as the main reference model. The list of experts who were invited from overseas to appear in front of the committee also testifies to its basic a priori approach. These experts included Professor Stanley Fischer, who had publically expressed his support for the Bank of Israel's position prior to the establishment of the committee, Professor Charles Goodhart, an expert in monetary economics and a member of the Bank of England's Monetary Policy Committee, and Donald Brash, the Governor of New Zealand's central bank, who promoted a strict anti-inflationary policy. It was not by chance that senior officials from these two specific central banks were invited: during the 1990s, significant changes in their legal status had given them a great degree of independence (in 1989 in New Zealand, and in 1998 in Britain).

At the end of 1998, the Levin Committee submitted its report to the government, which distinctly reflected the central bank's positions. The committee put forward a number of reasons for the need to initiate a comprehensive reform of the Bank of Israel Law according to the model of central bank independence, all of which were the same as those suggested by the BoI at every possible opportunity. First, the committee adopted the ideational underpinnings for the model; that is, the unequivocal belief that central bank independence is the only institutional arrangement that leads to price stability without harming growth, and that monetary policy is able to impact on inflation, and inflation alone, and hence it should be used only for this purpose. Second, the committee deployed the rhetoric of institutional globalization noting that, since the end of the 1980s, many countries had carried out far-reaching legislative reforms pertaining to their central banks so as to provide them with more independence, and emphasizing that Israel could not afford to ignore this global trend of institutional convergence. In this regard, and following the lead of the BoI, the committee defined the rules laid out in the Maastricht Treaty concerning the status of the European central banks as a binding standard that Israel must adopt. Finally, in order to stress the necessity to ensure price stability, the committee used the rhetoric of financial globalization, pointing out that countries with high levels of inflation find it impossible to participate in the international financial markets. Therefore, Israel's integration into the global economy required it to define price stability as the main objective of macroeconomic management. Based on these arguments, the report concluded that "the law must enable Israel to be integrated within the community of developed nations, and this task will be hard to carry out if the Bank of Israel Law significantly contradicts the central bank laws of those countries."[5]

Reflecting this ideational frame of reference, in the specific recommendations regarding the new law, the committee adopted the BoI demands that the attainment and preservation of price stability be defined as the central bank's main role, and that the central bank would have the authority to independently select and implement the policy instruments that it saw fit. The committee also recommended the establishment of a monetary council with a majority of external members, but giving the Governor of the central bank the right of veto in the nomination of those external members.[6]

Given the Levin Committee's recommendations, the reactions of the BoI and MoF were entirely predictable. While the former warmly embraced the recommendations, the latter reaction was much less enthusiastic, and noted the existence of significant professional disagreements.[7] The cool response was but the first manifestation of the uncompromising and lasting struggle that the MoF would wage from now on against the implementation of the recommendations. Indeed, a new central bank law would only be legislated more than a decade after the submission of the committee's report. Nonetheless, the Levin Committee's recommendations have defined the terms of debate for all of the actors involved in the struggle ever since. In this sense, through its influence over the committee, the BoI succeeded in determining the contours of the dispute and in shaping its content.

Enduring struggle and settlement

The struggle over the Bank of Israel Law intensified in the early 2000s, within a context of economic instability and slowdown, and especially increasing criticism of the restrictive monetary policy implemented by the central bank, with various political actors blaming it for the rise in unemployment.[8] In July 2001, the Prime Minister and Minister of Finance decided to push ahead with amendments to the Bank of Israel Law that did not accord with the recommendations of the Levin Committee and the central bank interests. The key sensitive issue in the proposal was that the central bank's objectives would include growth and employment, and not only price stability.

The government's decision was fiercely opposed by the BoI, which argued that the government was obliged to adopt the proposal formulated by the Levin Committee intact. Governor David Klein portrayed the attempts by the MoF to limit the governor's authority as the "politicization" of monetary policy, which would place Israel among the world's undeveloped countries. He further warned that any amendment that lacked the central bank's support might harm price stability as well as the stability of the financial markets. He even threatened that the stability of the financial institutions in which the public holds its savings might be in danger.[9] The IMF lent its backing to the BoI's efforts and called on the government to submit a bill based on the Levin Committee's recommendations as soon as possible so that the central bank's independence would be explicitly guaranteed.[10]

After a failed attempt in 2002 to reach an agreement between the government and the BoI that would result in a less restrictive monetary policy, the government renewed its efforts to amend the Bank of Israel Law in a manner that would deviate from the established model of central bank independence. The MoF once more proposed that the government be responsible for laying down conditions and qualifications to the objective of attaining price stability according to the goals of growth and employment promotion,[11] explaining that the "sole objective" doctrine that had guided the BoI's policies had seriously damaged the Israeli economy's ability to fulfill its potential for growth (Sharel, 2002). The MoF sought to legitimize its proposals by referring to prevalent institutional arrangements throughout the Western world, and stressed that many countries acknowledge the need for monetary policy to have other objectives than just price stability.[12] It further emphasized that monetary policy had a central role as an anti-cyclical policy tool during times of recession. This argument was backed up with the example of the USA, where, after the dot-com bubble burst in 2000, the Fed implemented an expansionary monetary policy that succeeded in pulling the US economy out of a recession in a very short period of time.[13]

The central bank responded with an assertive public campaign to delegitimize the MoF proposal. It made extensive use of the rhetoric of financial globalization, describing the international markets as an omnipotent force that punishes countries with "unsuitable" institutional arrangements while rewarding the adoption of "correct" neoliberal blueprints. To be sure, this was not a practice that the BoI had invented; indeed, it functioned as an important means in diffusing neoliberal policies and institutional blueprints throughout the global field. For instance, in the IMF's *World Economic Outlook* for 1997 it was argued:

[I]nternational financial markets can serve to "discipline" governments (either by raising default premiums or by forcing adjustments in exchange rate), encouraging the adoption of appropriate policies, and ultimately rewarding good policies.

(IMF, 1997, p. 66)

Drawing on the notion of the disciplinary power of the financial markets, the BoI presented dreadful apocalyptic scenarios concerning the consequences that the adoption of the MoF proposal would have. For instance, in a press release it stated that the bill subordinates the central bank to the directions of the MoF, and painted a chilling picture of the damage that the proposed law might cause, most importantly a reduction in Israel's credit rating in the international markets, which would lead to a deep financial crisis.[14] In this spirit of political fearmongering, the Governor added that the proposed legislative amendment would impact on each and every family in Israel through its negative repercussions for the stability of the financial institutions and the value of the public's financial assets (Atted, 2002b). The MoF's bill even brought the IMF into play (or perhaps the BoI got it involved), when, at a press conference, the IMF's External Relations Director, Thomas Dawson, referred to the difficult period that Israel was going through in terms of the threat to the central bank's independence.[15]

These blunt public statements were issued in the context of a deepening economic crisis and reports of an impending financial crisis. As a consequence of the second Intifada and a worldwide slowdown, 2002 was marked by a significant drop in output, a continuing decline in investments, a reduction in private consumption, a rise in unemployment to more than 10 percent, and a significant increase in inflation during the first half of the year (Bank of Israel, 2003). The BoI exploited the atmosphere of crisis and posited a direct link between the worsening economic situation, including the lowering of Israel's international credit rating, and the submission of the government bill. According to the central bank, the threat to its independence implied by the proposed new law was one of the main factors undermining confidence among the public and investors in the government's commitment to a sound macroeconomic policy aimed at preserving price stability; this, it was argued, was causing accelerated devaluation, a rise in expected inflation, and a contraction in flows of capital for long-term investment.[16]

Another particularly instructive step taken by the central bank sheds light on how local actors shape the relationship between the global field and local politics. In order to eliminate the threat to its status, the BoI appealed directly to the global sphere and officially asked the legal department of the European Central Bank (ECB) to assess whether the MoF's proposal accorded with the standards for central banks in EU countries. Although Israel was not a candidate for joining the EU, the central bank nonetheless argued that it was worthwhile drawing on the ECB's legal expertise and opinion regarding the government bill.[17] Obviously, the BoI approached the ECB because the model upon which it was built, which represents the archetype of the independent central bank, closely matched its own interests. The ECB's conclusions, which were translated into Hebrew and distributed to the press by the BoI, were thus unsurprising. Its report concluded that most of the clauses of the proposed law, and especially the one that defined the bank's objectives, did not meet the relevant criteria.[18] Mobilizing the support of international financial organizations, especially the IMF, as a resource in its struggles with the MoF was a strategy that the BoI frequently employed. However, the current episode represented a significant innovation in this regard. This was the first time that the central bank had openly and officially approached an external actor so that it might undermine a government-approved bill in the name of the global standard of central bank independence. The message conveyed by the BoI was impossible to misinterpret: globalization has knocked down the borders of the local field, giving external actors both the power and the right to ratify or disqualify institutional arrangements that the national government wishes to implement. It should be emphasized that this involvement, which would appear to deny the state its freedom of choice, was in fact instigated by an official invitation by a state agency, the central bank, which, acting as a key mediator between the local and global fields, inserted and endo-genized global logics into the state apparatus.

The BoI's efforts bore fruit, and the MoF withdrew from its intention to submit its bill to the Knesset. It would seem that the rhetoric regarding the omnipotent disciplinary power of the global financial markets that the BoI deployed so often and so forcefully was particularly effective. The MoF was concerned that the international rating agencies would indeed decrease Israel's credit rating because of the economic crisis and its much-reported conflict with the central bank, and that this might cause a chain reaction among both foreign and local investors, eventuating in a financial crisis.[19]

For eight years since 2002 there was a balance of deterrence between the MoF and the BoI that has led to a stalemate, with neither side able to further the legislation of a new law in accordance with its interests. Because of their key location in the political field and the resources available to each of them, both state agencies were able to neutralize each other's initiatives and proposals. It would take several more years of negotiations and public quarrels between the two until they finally settled their differences, allowing for the legislation of the new Bank of Israel Law—which marked the domestication of the model of central bank independence at the legal level—on 16 March 2010.

In the course of 2009, in the midst of the global financial crisis, the MoF and the BoI were finally able to formulate a joint proposal for a new law, and the government bill submitted to the Knesset was passed in a rapid legislative process and with no substantive changes. In accordance with the model of central bank independence, and in a manner that reflects the ideational frame of reference inserted and promoted in the local field by the BoI since the 1990s, the new law stipulates that the primary goal of the central bank is to maintain price stability. An additional objective defined for the central bank is to "support the stability and orderly activity of the financial system," an issue that had obviously become particularly relevant given the circumstances of the financial crisis during which the law was formulated. Furthermore, the new law states that the central bank shall be autonomous in choosing its actions and in exercising its powers to attain its goals (Bank of Israel Law 2010, Chapter 2). The law estab-lishes a monetary committee with the responsibility for determining the policies to be implemented for the attainment of the bank's objectives. Whereas the law establishes parity between the internal and external members of the committee, as demanded by the MoF, it grants the governor an additional vote in the event of a tied vote, thus assuring the central bank's effective control over the new monetary policy-making body.

The enactment of the law was the result of several factors. First, the struggles between the MoF and the BoI over the objectives of the central bank lost their acuteness once the anti-inflationary stance promoted by the central bank had been institutionalized and price stability had been attained and maintained since the late 1990s. Furthermore, the diminished relevance of that conflict became even more evident in light of the functioning of the BoI, along with most other central banks in the world, during the global financial crisis of 2007–2010. It followed the lead of the main central banks around the world, particularly the Fed, and implemented an extremely expansionary monetary policy of negative real interest rates, with the aim of saving the financial system and staving off a deep and long-lasting recession. This showed that when faced with a severe and menacing crisis the central bank would not refrain from deploying monetary tools to alleviate the situation, even if this contradicted its monetarist doctrine.

Moreover, in the context of the global financial crisis, the enactment of the new law was seen by all state agencies involved as a means to bring a degree of stability to the economy and to restore public confidence in economic policy by putting an end to the constant public quarrels and mutual accusations between the MoF and the BoI. This need to reassure public confidence was particularly pertinent given the fact that throughout 2009 Governor Stanley Fischer openly used his personal prestige as a political resource, repeatedly insinuating that he would not agree to serve a second term of office, beginning in May 2010, if the law formalizing the independence of the central bank had not been enacted, as promised to him by the Prime Minister upon his appointment in 2005 (Bassock, 2010). Under severe crisis conditions, the MoF and the government in general, were in no position to take the political risk that Fischer—a highly esteemed governor, both locally and internationally—might decline the offer to serve a second term, as this might cause a loss of public confidence and add dangerous jitteriness to an already unstable economy and financial system. And indeed, the day after the enactment of the new law by the Knesset, the Prime Minister, the Minister of Finance, and the Governor held a joint press conference in which they announced that Fischer would remain in office for a second term.

To sum up, because of the intensive intra-state struggles between the BoI and the MoF and the deadlock that these struggles reached, it took a long period of time until the central bank's legal status was fundamentally reformed in a way that formally enshrined its de facto independence. Throughout this period the BoI successfully instilled the institutional logic of global neoliberalism in the local field, thereby defining the contours of the debate over its independence and authority. One of the most important strategies used by the central bank in this endeavor was to construct the adoption of the model of central bank independence as absolutely necessary to assure the success of the national economy within a context of economic globalization and institutional convergence.

Conclusions

A new central bank law was legislated in Israel after 15 years of stormy relations between the Bank of Israel and the Ministry of Finance, with the severe conflicts between them taking center stage in the public arena. These conflicts evolved not only around specific macroeconomic policy measures, but mainly over the institutional arrangements that regulated the relations between these two powerful state agencies. Both agencies were competing over their positioning within the state's institutional configuration and the political economy. These intensive struggles show us that processes of domestication of global models are driven by deep conflicts between various institutional, political, and economic interests operating primarily at the local level. The politics of domestication thus indicates that local actors are pivotal players in these processes: they select the policy models to be promoted, and adapt and translate them to accommodate local conditions and according to their own interests. Moreover, while particular local actors can be motivated by global ideas and discourses, the adoption and implementation of global models is the result of interactions and conflicts in the local field, in which those institutional blueprints are also contested and resisted. When the institutional models at issue directly concern the architecture of the state and the power relations between its agencies, as in the case of the model of central bank independence, their domestication is structured mainly by intra-state politics.

A central feature of the struggle over the legal status of the Israeli central bank was the way the actors involved used rhetorical strategies that referred to various aspects of globalization in order to strengthen and legitimize their positions. These strategies related to three central dimensions of the globalization of the capitalist political economy: the normative power of global institutional models, the influence of international organizations, and the structural power of capital and financial markets. The strengthening of the processes and forces that constitute and act within the global field was represented by the central bank as an omnipotent factor that strongly delimited the possible institutional arrangements and policies that the state could adopt. The deep meaning of this politics of inevitability is the depoliticization of institutional arrangements and policies; that is, their displacement from the relatively open political space of interests and worldviews to the seemingly apolitical and closed sphere of the necessary and the inevitable.

The nature of the struggle over the legal status of the central bank and its protraction for more than a decade shed light on the complexity of processes of institutional change and the institutionalization of new policy paradigms. While these processes are often seen as the direct and inevitable outcome of institutional and/or economic globalization, our analysis has indicated that the relationship between globalization and institutional change and the transformation of the political economy in general is far more complex than that. The BoI's use of the strategies we have discussed throughout this article reveals the full extent of the active role that local actors play in bringing global logics and processes to bear on the local political field. Hence, global forces do not impose particular institutional arrangements on the state from the outside, but rather become factors that are endogenous to the local field and state apparatus through the purposive political practices of local actors, very often state agencies, who use globalization as a resource. As these actors engage in the politics of domestication of global institutional blueprints, they promote the insertion of global logics into the local field. It is through this political process taking place at the local level, therefore, that global dynamics play an instrumental role in institutional change.

Notes

1 This article partially draws on Chapter 6 of our book *The Israeli Central Bank: Political Economy, Global Logics and Local Actors* (Maman and Rosenhek, 2011).

2 Bank of Israel, Office of the Spokesperson and Economic Information, press release (untitled), 18 July 1995.

3 IMF: Concluding statement of the IMF mission, Israel 1997, p. 4 (Bank of Israel, Press release, 12 November 1997).

4 Government of Israel, Government resolution no. 2977, 14 December 1997.

5 Final Report, Committee for examining the Bank of Israel Law, December 1998, p. 13.

6 The three members from outside the central bank would be recognized experts in the monetary, financial, or macroeconomic fields, and would be appointed by the government in agreement with the Governor (Final Report, Committee for examining the Bank of Israel Law, December, 1998, p. 22).

7 Ministry of Finance: The Ministry of Finance's reaction to the report of the committee for examining the Bank of Israel Law, Press release, 28 December 1998.

8 See, for instance, the 15th Knesset, Third sitting, Protocol no. 274 of the Knesset Finance Committee, 26 June 2001.

9 Bank of Israel, Office of the Spokesperson and Economic Information, "The Governor's speech at a colloquium at Tel Aviv University," 10 February 2002.

10 IMF, "Concluding report of the IMF management's discussions in consultancy with Israel" (Bank of Israel, Press release, 6 August 2001).

11 Ministry of Finance, Spokesman department, "The proposal for amending the Bank of Israel Law compared to the Levin Committee's recommendations and the current law," 11 March 2002.

12 Ministry of Finance, Spokesman department, "The Deputy Prime Minister and Minister of Finance's speech at the government meeting and the proposed amendment to the law as submitted to the government by the Prime Minister and the Minister of Finance," Press release: Amendment to the Bank of Israel Law, 10 March 2002.

13 Ministry of Finance, "Explanation to the proposed amendment to the Bank of Israel Law," 14 March 2002.

14 Bank of Israel, Office of the Spokesperson and Economic Information, "The Bank of Israel's response to the proposed amendment to the Bank of Israel Law as submitted today by the Ministry of Finance to the government," 10 March 2002.

15 His comments were published as Transcript of Press Briefing, IMF, 13 February 2002, and were widely quoted by the local press (for example, Atted, 2002a).

16 Bank of Israel, Office of the Spokesperson and Economic Information, "Update for the monetary program June 2002," 9 June 2002; Bank of Israel, Office of the Spokesperson and Economic Information, "Inflation report for the first half of 2002," 1 August 2002.

17 David Klein, "The required policy for achieving the economy's objectives: situation report for mid-2002," 4 July 2002.

18 The report also indicated that it was desirable to add a general ruling in the law that would anchor the Bank of Israel's independence (European Central Bank, "First assessment of the new draft Law of the Bank of Israel against the requirements of legal independence as laid down in the Treaty establishing the European Community," n.d.).

19 A few days before the draft law was set for its first reading in the Knesset, the MoF's Accountant General, Nir Gilad, was sent to London to persuade the analysts from the international rating agencies to give Israel an extension before dropping its credit rating. The press suggested that Gilad was warned by the analysts that, should the amendment pass into law, they would have no choice but to reduce Israel's credit rating (Atted, 2002c).

References

Atted, A. (2002a, 15 March). A council of governors is the main actors' doomsday weapon, *Ynet Economy* (in Hebrew). Retrieved 1 February 2013 from www.ynet.co.il/articles/1,7340,L-1766568,00.html.

Atted, A. (2002b, 14 March1). Klein warns: The public's savings are at risk, *Ynet Economy* (in Hebrew). Retrieved 1 February 2013 from www.ynet.co.il/articles/1,7340,L-1765289,00.html.

Atted, A. (2002c, 18 May). Where has the governors' council law gone?, *Ynet Economy* (in Hebrew). Retrieved 1 February 2013 from www.ynet.co.il/articles/1,7340,L-1897988,00.html.

Bank of Israel (2003). *Bank of Israel Report, 2002*. Jerusalem: Bank of Israel (in Hebrew).

Bank of Israel Law (2010). Retrieved 15 August 2013 from www.bankisrael.gov.il/dept-data/pikuah/bank_hakika/eng/new_law_2010_eng.pdf?

Bank of Israel Law (1954). Retrieved 11 August 2013 from www.boi.org.il/en/News-AndPublications/LegislationAndRegulations/Documents/102.pdf.

Barnett, M. and Finnemore, M. (2004). *Rules for the World: International Organizations in Global Politics*. Ithaca, NY: Cornell University Press.

Bassock, M. (2010, 10 March). Senior official in Netanyahu's bureau: The Prime Minister decided to nominate Fischer for a second term, *The Marker*, p. 37 (in Hebrew).

Bell, S. (2004). *Australia's Money Mandarins: The Reserve Bank and the Politics of Money*. Cambridge: Cambridge University Press.

Carruthers, B., Babb, S., and Halliday, T. (2001). Institutionalizing markets, or the market for institutions? Central Banks, bankruptcy law, and the globalization of financial markets. In J. Campbell and O. Pedersen (eds), *The Rise of Neoliberalism and Institutional Analysis* (pp. 94–126). Princeton, NJ: Princeton University Press.

Cukierman, A. (1992). *Central Bank Strategy, Credibility, and Independence: Theory and Evidence*. Cambridge, MA: MIT Press.

Dobbin, F., Simmons, B., and Garret, G. (2007). The global diffusion of public policies: Social construction, coercion, competition, or learning? *Annual Review of Sociology, 33*, 449–472.

Hall, R. (2008). *Central Banking as Global Governance: Constructing Financial Credibility*. Cambridge: Cambridge University Press.

IMF (1997). World Economic Outlook. Washington, D.C.: International Monetary Fund.

Kahler, M. (1992). External influence, conditionality, and the politics of adjustment. In S. Haggard and R. Kaufman (eds), *The Politics of Economic Adjustment: International Constraints, Distributive Conflicts, and the State* (pp. 89–138). Princeton, NJ: Princeton University Press.

King, M. (2005). Epistemic communities and the diffusion of ideas: Central bank reform in the United Kingdom. *West European Politics, 28*(1), 94–123.

Maman, D. and Rosenhek, Z. (2011). *The Israeli Central Bank: Political Economy, Global Logics and Local Actors*. London: Routledge.

Marcussen, M. (2005). Central Banks on the move. *Journal of European Public Policy, 12*(5), 903–923.

Marcussen, M. (2006). Institutional transformation? The scientization of Central Banking as a case study. In T. Christensen and P. Laegreid (eds), *Autonomy and Regulation: Coping with Agencies in the Modern State* (pp. 81–109). Cheltenham: Edward Elgar.

Maxfield, S. (1997). *Gatekeepers of Growth—The International Political Economy of Central Banking in Developing Countries*. Princeton, NJ: Princeton University Press.

Meyer, J., Boli, J., Thomas, G., and Ramirez, F. (1997). World society and the nation-state. *American Journal of Sociology, 103*(1), 144–181.

Polillo, S. and Guillen, M.F. (2005). Globalization pressures and the state: The worldwide spread of Central Bank independence. *American Journal of Sociology, 110*(6), 1764–1802.

Sharel, M. (2002, 13 March). Open market: Price stability—the Bank of Israel's only objective, *Haaretz*, p. 2 (in Hebrew).

Weiss, L. (2003). Introduction: Bringing domestic institutions back in. In L. Weiss (ed.), *States in the Global Economy: Bringing Domestic Institutions Back In* (pp. 1–33). Cambridge: Cambridge University Press.

8 Global "diffusion," banal nationalism, and the politics of policy legitimation

A genealogical study of "zest for living" in Japanese education policy discourse

Keita Takayama

Introduction

In recent years, education policy scholars have documented the considerable influence that supranational organizations such as the Organization for Economic Cooperation and Development (OECD) and the United Nations Educational, Scientific and Cultural Organization (UNESCO) exert on national education policy-making (Bieber and Martens, 2011; Lingard and Rawolle, 2011; Martens, 2007). In particular, OECD's Programme for International Student Assessment (PISA) has become a powerful policy reference for advanced industrial nations. Through "soft tools"—the production and dissemination of comparative indicators and expert advices—these organizations have "become one of the most significant players in matters of education" (Martens, 2007, p. 44), "clearing the way for greater convergence and commitment amongst states to uniform models of best practices" (p. 54). Though whether or not the increasing presence of such supranational organizations results in the global convergence in education policy is unclear (see Rappleye, 2012; Takayama, 2012), there is no question that national–global interactions have become more intensified in today's national education policy-making (Lingard and Rawolle, 2011).

Just as elsewhere, the international education policy discourse disseminated via the supranational organizations has considerably influenced the recent education reform discourse in Japan. Throughout the 1990s, the Japanese Ministry of Education, Culture, Sports, Science and Technology (MEXT) actively incorporated the lifelong learning policy discourse promoted by the OECD and UNESCO into the school curricular reform pursued under the slogan *ikiru chikara* (hereinafter referred to as "zest for living") (see Takayama 2013). Furthermore, the PISA 2003 results, which indicated the declining international standing of Japanese students, generated a major impact on Japanese education reform discourse. The disappointing results were utilized by reform-minded political figures to manufacture a "crisis," and then to legitimize a set of contested reform plans including national academic testing (see Takayama, 2008). The PISA 2003 "shock" has firmly established OECD's education work as the "global standard" against which the performance of the Japanese education system is to be assessed and new reform ideas justified. Though MEXT's interpretation of the international policy discourse involves a degree of recontextualization (see Matsushita, 2010) and thus we cannot assume its straightfoward "impact" on Japanese education policies, the OECD has undoubtedly become a powerful source of external influence for Japanese education policy-making.

While MEXT's acknowledgement of the international influence on its national education policies is a relevantly recent phenomenon (only after the PISA 2003 "shock"), the Ministry has been well integrated into the global networks of educational policy-makers, as evidenced by its well-established relationship with UNESCO and the OECD going as far back as the early 1970s and the 1990s respectively (see NIER, 2009; Saitō, 2009). The Ministry and its research institute—the National Institute for Educational Policy Research (NIER), which has been amalgamated into MEXT since 2001[1]—have played an important role in UNESCO's educational work in Asia Pacific, cosponsoring a series of UNESCO conferences and workshops, though their involvement with UNESCO has somehow diminished since the 1990s (Saitō, 2009). Likewise, the Ministry and NIER were involved in the initial development of OECD's PISA in the mid-1990s, and continue to play a prominent role with a NIER senior researcher serving as the chair of the PISA Governing Board (as of 2007) and with another NIER researcher listed as part of the PISA expert group (OECD, 2009, p. 291). NIER is one of the research institutes that constitute the international consortium responsible for the design and implementation of the PISA assessment and survey (OECD, 2009, p. 17). Furthermore, it is well known that MEXT regularly dispatches its officials to OECD's Education Department for a one- to two-year "internship," while top ministry bureaucrats frequently visit its Paris headquarters (Rappleye, 2012).

Given this history of close relationship between Japanese education policy-makers and the two supranational organizations, it is hardly surprising that Japanese education policy discourse over the last two decades has been consistently influenced by the international education policy discourse. In fact, as I am going to demonstrate in this chapter, there is unmistakable resemblance between Japanese education reform discourse that has emerged since the 1990s and that of these two supranational organizations. Curiously, however, MEXT did not explicitly acknowledge their influence on its education policy prior to the 2003 PISA "shock," from which point on the OECD and its PISA have achieved virtually uncontested referential authority in the Japanese education policy discourse. This fact renders the question of "why now?" a particularly interesting question to explore for the present study.

Hence, this study attempts to answer why MEXT chose to keep unannounced the international policy influence on their reform ideas in the 1990s, and yet made it explicit from the mid 2000s onwards. To this aim, I trace the shifting articulations of one particular policy keyword, *ikiru chikara* ("zest for living"), which has been consistently and extensively used by MEXT from 1996 to the present (see OECD, 2012). Since the mid-1990s, MEXT has used several catchy keywords such as *kosei* ("individuality"), *yutori* ("allowing more room for growth, relaxation"), and *ikiru chikara* ("zest for living") to mark the overall policy directions (Takayama, 2009). The much-criticized ambiguity of these keywords (see Satō, 2000, p. 33) has served to designate no clear referent but condense into them "a host of different meanings and connotations which might diverge if more specific referents were attempted" (Zarefsky as cited in Jasinski, 2001, p. 98). As Stone (2000) argues, ambiguity constitutes the art of politics, as it allows the government to speak to competing political interests simultaneously. With close attention to the politics of ambiguity, hence, this chapter examines the shifting articulation of "zest for living" in a series of reports prepared by MEXT and the Central Council of Education (CCE, *chūō kyōiku shingikai*), the Ministry's formal deliberative body for its policy development.[2] It illuminates how MEXT selectively appropriates the "internationality" of reform ideas, that is, either to declare or silence international influence on its reform ideas and programs (Waldow, 2009).

Conceptually, this study tests and nuances the conceptual tools (for example, "silent borrowing," "externalization," "indigenization," and "banal nationalism") that have been developed by other scholars—namely Alasuutari (2013), Waldow (2009) and Steiner-Khamsi (2002)—to be explored in the following section of the chapter. These scholars have critically engaged with neoinstitutionalist world culture theory (WCT) and attempted to conceptualize the process and mechanism of global policy "diffusion," which they claim to have been under-recognized in WCT. In conclusion, I put the findings of this study in a critical dialogue with these scholars' earlier conceptual work, and articulate the significance of the present study with the wider literature on global policy "isomorphism," banal localism/nationalism and domestication in education policy studies, and comparative education.

Theorizing the "black box"

In a nutshell, the neoinstitutionalist account of WCT defines globalization as "a cultural and institutional process" (Meyer, 2007, p. 263) and stresses "the common and rationalized identities of nation-states" as one of the key driving forces of global isomorphism in education policy (Meyer and Ramirez, 2000; Meyer, 2007). It explains the increasing convergence of education policy around the world in terms of the emergence of global institutional culture, or "the global model" of curriculum and educational governance disseminated through a network of policy professionals who act as the "carrier." Global isomorphism in education policy is a manifestation of nation-states' identity work; the nation-states "enact" the prescribed global policy models, because the source of their political legitimacy lies entirely in their incorporation into the global polity and its modernist world cultural scripts of "progress" and "justice" (Ramirez, 2003).

In the last decade or so, however, the WCT-inspired studies have been criticized for their relative lack of attention to the actual process and mechanism of global "diffusion" and the recontextualization of "global models," which might occur in the course of diffusion (see Alasuutari 2013; Dale, 2000; Rappleye, 2012; Steiner-Khamsi, 2000, 2002). As Rautalin and Alasuutari (2009), among many others, rightly maintain, WCT under-theorizes the "black box" of global isomorphism: "the actual mechanism by which the global cultural script becomes integrated with the process in which national education policy takes its shape" (Rautalin and Alasuutari, 2009, p. 541). These scholars hence call for a methodological shift from the empirical verification of institutional isomorphism in various aspects of state institutions to a close investigation of how the transnationally circulated values and models are processed in the specific local and national context of adaptation.

To advance a conceptual understanding of the domesticating process and mechanism, Alasuutari (2013) examines the newspaper coverage on the report of the development plan for Finnish cities' cultural activities.[3] He focuses on the media discourses around the report in order to examine the mechanism through which the transnationally circulated ideas about the "competitive and creative city" (or the notion of cities as "strategic actors") become domesticated into specific Finnish localities so that they are reconstituted as "our" strategies. Alasuutari (2013) identifies two factors that induced the process of media domestication. The first is what he calls the "cultural framework of competition" (p. 5) evoked by comparative league tables of cities' cultural activities, which was included in the report and extensively reported by the local newspapers. The sense of competition serves to "construct the citizens of the state or other regional entity as a team with shared interests" (p. 5). Hence, the league tables ranking Finnish cities in terms of their cultural activities powerfully generate a strong sense of localism, leading to the assertion of "our" unique strategies for cultural development in various cities. The second factor Alasuutari (2013) identifies is local political contestation. As exogenous policy ideas are inserted into a local area of political contestation, local actors of divergent views and interests tailor them to the specificity of local conditions, hence rearticulating them as "our" ideas and policies.

In sum, Alasuutari demonstrates that global policy models are widely diffused and yet barely recognized as such due to the cultural framework of "banal localism/nationalism" (after Michael Billig), which promotes the view that "nations are unique cultural entities, decisions about changes are made locally, and each nation-state or local government follows its own developmental path" (p. 1). Alasuutari further argues that the diffusion of global policy models and their domestication through banal localism/nationalism are simultaneous and intertwined, with the process of domestication necessarily invoking banal localism/ nationalism.

Whether or not extraneous models are reconstituted as "ours," however, also depends on the particular political context at a particular point in time. Waldow (2009) develops the notion of "silent (or undeclared) borrowing" in his analysis of the contrasting responses of the Swedish government to OECD's education policy ideas in different time periods. He maintains that when Sweden's education policy followed OECD's education policy recommendations closely in the 1960s and the 1970s, the government chose not to make explicit the international origin of its education policies. In Sweden, Waldow goes on to explain, an explicit reference to its borrowing of international policy was politically unwise in the context of the Swedish belief in its educational supremacy and its self-image of engaging in rational policy-making. Hence, the borrowed ideas and policies needed to be constructed as "ours" for policy legitimization purposes: what he terms "silent borrowing." However, this national self-sufficiency could no longer persist, he concludes, when international comparative assessments such as PISA gain powerful referential authority as "a surrogate measure of the potential international competitiveness of the national economy," and the scientific rationality of its policy ideas gains considerable political purchase in many countries, including Sweden (Lingard and Rawolle, 2011, p. 493).

The above discussion has highlighted two key differences between Alasuutari's and Waldow's findings, which will be taken up in my subsequent analysis of Japanese education policy discourse. First, Waldow predicts that the international competition generated by the PISA league tables is one of the key factors, if not the only one, that has led the Swedish government to make explicit its borrowing of the OECD and PISA's policy discourse. This contrasts with Alasuutari's discussion of the "cultural framework of competition" as one of the key factors driving the localized rearticulation of global policy ideas as "ours." Second, Waldow's study draws more attention to the temporal specificity of the context, showing how the logic of policy legitimation formed at a given point in time shapes the government's political choice of whether to declare or silence the extraneous "origin" of reform ideas.

Resonating with Waldow's thesis but drawing more attention to the specific role of policy actors in the process of policy domestication, Steiner-Khamsi (2002) further advances the conceptualization of external referencing in national education policy discourses. Drawing partly on Niklas Luhmann's System Theory, she maintains that policy actors use external references to international reform ideas (externalization) to "signal a rupture from the past and promise a new (political) future" (p. 80). Externalization is more likely to be utilized at a time of radical political, economic, or social transformation, when a nation-state's internal references to tradition, beliefs, and organizations lose their efficacy. Policy actors quickly "indigenize," or domesticate, references to the "international consensus" or "foreign examples," however, once they are incorporated into domestic political contestation (Steiner-Khamsi, 2002). To illustrate her point, Steiner-Khamsi discusses how policy actors in Zurich initially stressed the US origin of the quasi-market education governance reform that they pursued in the 1990s, in order to mark a clear break from the detested past and promise a new policy direction. But once faced with opposition, they began stressing the characteristics of the reform that were supposedly unique to the "Zurich model," so as to deflect criticism. She concludes that externalization is a "transitionary policy strategy that is eventually replaced by self-referentiality" (p. 74), with the effect of the former largely limited to the policy discourse level only.

Two notable observations can be drawn about the similarities and differences between Alasuutari's and Steiner-Khamsi's findings. First, both studies recognize domestic political contestation as the key factor driving the invocation of banal localism/nationalism. The "domestication" (Alasuutari) or the "indigenization" (Steiner-Khamsi) of extraneous policy ideas is driven by domestic political struggle, wherein the extraneous ideas become the source of contestation and transformative possibilities of new ideas are quickly tamed as they are reconstituted as "ours." Second, while Alasuutari recognizes the global diffusion and the domestication through localism or nationalism as a simultaneous process, Steiner-Khamsi sees them as sequential, with the former eventually leading to the latter. Third, they differ in the extent to which the diffusion of global policy models is recognized as "real." While Alasuutari (and Waldow), focusing on the process of domestication (or silencing), recognizes the diffusion of global models, Steiner-Khamsi is less inclined to do so. Instead, she stresses the gap between the diffusion of global ideas at the policy discourse level and what gets to be implemented "on the ground," hence implying the diffusion of global models as "imagined."

Despite the notable differences among these scholars, Alasuutari, Waldow, and Steiner-Khamsi commonly recognize the complex interactions between the global and the domestic in the process of policy "diffusion," and attempt to identify the mechanism and process through which global ideas become domesticated. They are guided, by and large, by the clear acknowledgment that global "diffusion" is an internally driven process with domestic actors and factors considerably shaping what gets to be diffused and how. They draw attention to the importance of understanding the particular context of domestic polity and political contestation into which extraneous policy models are inserted and subsequently recontextualized. The set of conceptual tools advanced by these scholars—"banal nationalism," "silent borrowing," "externalization," and "indigenization"—will be explored in the subsequent discussion of "zest for living" in the context of Japanese education.

The rise of the "humanizing" policy discourse

The policy keyword "zest for living" emerged out of the humanizing policy discourse actively promoted by MEXT from the late 1980s. At this time a policy consensus was formed that Japan had completed its "catch-up" with advanced Western economies, and policy actors started recognizing the social "cost" of rapid postwar economic growth (Rappleye and Kariya, 2011). In search of a new direction for the nation appropriate to the twenty-first century, policy actors engaged in a reflexive reconsideration of the postwar social, political, and economic systems, calling for a shift from materialistic (quantitative) expansion to spiritual (qualitative) enrichment in life. They identified children in particular as the primary victim of the postwar pursuit of materialistic prosperity; so-called "today's children" were deemed morally, emotionally, physically, and socially "deficient." The series of education reform proposals made during this time therefore called for individualizing and humanizing the bureaucratic and competitive education system, which was organized around efficiency and rationality.

Reflecting this humanizing policy discourse, the CCE reports and MEXT policy documents in the 1990s extensively used two policy keywords of the explained above: *yutori* and *kosei*. They were utilized to justify a set of reform measures aimed supposedly at nurturing children's emotional and social well-being (Takayama, 2009). More concretely, the "humanizing" effort was translated into reducing the curricular content and number of schooling days and introducing moral teaching, integrated learning opportunities, and the child-centric pedagogic approach. It is out of this policy discourse that "zest for living" first appeared in the 1996 CCE draft report. The report closely articulated the term with *yutori*, as indicated in the subtitle of the report: "we shall give our children *ikiru chikara* and *yutori*" (CCE, 1996, Section I).

Underpinning this humanizing policy discourse was the dismal representation of the social and educational conditions under which children allegedly lived. According to the CCE's 1996 draft report, children today spend a large portion of the day studying at school or *juku* ("cramming school"), leaving little time for sleep. In addition, extended exposure to the electronic media (such as TV and computer games) leaves little time for their authentic experience in nature or rich socializing experiences. Growing up in families of few children, the report further argues, today's children are deprived of opportunities to learn social skills and moral values, and they suffer from superficial social relations. These descriptions resonated with the rising number of media reports on children's "pathological" problems including *ijime* ("bullying"), *tōkōkyohi* ("school refusal"), *hikikomori* ("youth social withdrawal"), and *gakkyūhōkai* ("unruly classroom behavior"). Hence, by the 1990s, the "salvation" of children's *chi* ("knowledge"), *toku* ("morality"), and *tai* ("physical health") through humanizing and moralizing interventions was firmly established as MEXT's master policy narrative (Honda, 2005; Takayama, 2009).

Driving the deficit construction of "today's children" was the desocializing discourse of moral conservativism, which became prominent in the second half of the 1990s when conservative political forces gained popular support against the backdrop of the prolonged economic recession (Takayama, 2010). The desocialized discussion of "youth problems" became abundant, with considerable media attention given to the aforementioned "educational pathologies." It bracketed out the socio-cultural and economic transformations of the time that had contributed to the rise of such school-related problems. The MEXT policy documents in the late 1990s subscribes to this deficit construction of children, calling for *kokoro no kyōiku* ("education for a rich mind," often translated into moral and patriotic education) and tougher disciplinary measures (see Chichibu, 2003). Moralizing language about sympathy with others, self-discipline, cooperation, and respect for adults and the nation were now fully integrated into the "humanizing" policy discourse.

The rise of the humanizing policy discourse also mirrors the particular shift in the nation's capital accumulation strategies in the 1990s. This was the period when the Japanese political economy underwent a "regime shift" (Pempel, 1998); the postwar economic, social, and political settlements, central to the nation's stability since the end of the Second World War, were recognized as "out of sync" with the fast-changing reality of advanced globalized capitalism. Corporate sectors demanded the radical restructuring of the nation's economic, political, and social institutions to revitalize its global economic competiveness. In so doing, they drew on the humanizing discourse in their proposals for education reform with "humanization" redefined as the "liberation" of children from government regulations, thus rearticulating it into their preferred neoliberal discourse of deregulation and the minimalist state. By the late 1990s, therefore, "humanization" came to be articulated into three competing languages: (1) the liberal, humanist language of children's rights, creativity, individuality, and competition-free education; (2) the culturally and socially conservative language of morality, ethics, self-discipline, and patriotism; and (3) the neoliberal language of choice, deregulation, and the market. As will be demonstrated shortly, these somehow contradictory and yet overlapping policy discourses constitute the domestic education policy field, shaping the way international policy ideas around lifelong learning are translated into "zest for living."

International "origin" of "zest for living"

Actively promoted by such intergovernmental organizations as UNESCO, the European Commission, and the OECD, the notion of lifelong learning achieved a global policy consensus by the 1990s and was enthusiastically endorsed by advanced industrial nations thereafter, though the extent to which the idea was actually implemented varied from country to country (Field, 2006). Echoing this international trend, Japanese MEXT began drawing on the same international policy discourse and, unlike some of the nations where lifelong learning remained merely political rhetoric, implemented a series of relevant policy measures to promote this new concept of learning (Field, 2006). According to Okumoto (2008), this was partly due to the appeal that the notion of lifelong learning presented to MEXT, which was searching at the time for a "humanizing" solution to the institutional and operational rigidity and uniformity of its education system.

"Zest for living" emerged in the mid 1990s when MEXT attempted to incorporate the international policy discourse of lifelong learning into its domestic policy discourse. Though the term sounds like a uniquely Japanese concept, (see Satō, 2000, p. 33), its underlying concept clearly parallels the international policy discourse of "the learning society" and "lifelong learning." Ikuo Arai (2001), a former NIER researcher, locates the origin of part of the keyword, *"ikiru"* (to live), in the UNESCO's so-called Fall Report, *Learning to Be* (UNESCO, 1972).[4] Drawing on Robert Hutchins' (1968) *The Learning Society* and the 1972 UNESCO Fall Report, Arai (1993, 2001) maintains that in a lifelong learning society, schooling must encourage children to "learn to be" (one must learn to be self-motivated to achieve one's goal and lead a fulfilling life); and that education systems need to be flexible enough to encourage such individual volitions "to be." In Arai's mind, many of the reforms undertaken by

MEXT throughout the 1990s under the name of "zest for living" and *yutori* represent the shift towards the twenty-first century model of *gakushū shakai* ("the learning society") (see UNESCO, 1996). In this model, public education shifts its focus from *chiiku* (teaching facts based on subject disciplines) to teaching "skills and knowledge for life" with teachers acting as the "facilitator" for their self-motivated learning, the idea clearly materialized in MEXT's *atarashii gakuryoku kan* ("new conceptualization of academic ability"), which was introduced in the mid 1990s (see also Yamada 2011).

From the late 1990s, the OECD has become the key advocate of "lifelong learning" and "the learning society," initially promoted by UNESCO (see Rychen, 2004). Unlike UNESCO, however, the OECD discusses lifelong learning more explicitly within the sphere of formal schooling and in terms of its contribution to nations' human capital development strategies (Field, 2006; Takayama, 2013). In the late 1990s, the OECD proposed school curricular reform that promotes new forms of knowledge: "know-why, know-how, and know-who" kinds of knowledge rather than "know-what" or "factual knowledge/ recall" (OECD, 2000, p. 3). Reflecting this conceptualization of new schooling, the OECD designed PISA to assess "young people's capacity to use their knowledge and skills in order to meet real-life challenges," hence "knowledge and skills for life" (OECD, 2001, p. 1). Later, the OECD further elaborated on its conceptualization of what the PISA assesses with the notion of "key competencies," which refers to the ability to meet complex demands using "cognitive and practical skills, creative abilities and *other psychosocial resources such as attitudes, motivation and values*" (OECD, 2005, p. 8, emphasis added).

The Japanese term "zest for living" clearly reflects this international discourse of lifelong learning, whereby the focus of pedagogic intervention and assessment is placed on individual learners' "psychosocial resources,"—their desire, interest, attitude, and motivation—what is internal to them (Honda, 2005; Yamada, 2011). The 1996 CCE report defines "zest for living" as composed of the following three domains: (1) an "ability to identify problems, learn and think independently, make an autonomous judgment and act accordingly, and solve problems;" (2) "self-discipline, cooperation with others, empathy for others, emotion, and rich humanity;" and (3) "health and stamina for robust living" (CCE, 1996; see also Chichibu, 2003). The report argues that these are the key attributes and capabilities that children must acquire in the emerging life-long learning society. Clearly, the first domain of "zest for living"—"an ability to identify problems, learn and think independently, make an autonomous judgment and act accordingly"—resembles UNESCO and OECD's international policy discourse of twenty-first century schooling. Despite this clear resemblance, the MEXT and CCE documents published at that time make no reference to any international influence on "zest for living."[5]

However, "zest for living" was not simply the Japanese "silent borrowing" of the international policy discourse, either. As Honda (2005) argues, when the term appeared for the first time in the 1996 CCE document, Japanese business sectors demanded, as part of their new human resource strategies, that schools shift their curricular focus from passive acquisition of knowledge to problem-solving skills, independent thinking, and creativity. In such proposals, they drew on the deficit representation of "today's youth," who were supposedly incapable of thinking independently and creatively or applying newly acquired knowledge and skills in problem-solving situations. These "deficiencies" were attributed to the specific problems of Japanese education, its traditional focus on memorization and recall, testing, and the lack of flexibility and choice (see Honda, 2005).

Furthermore, the last two domains in the definition—(2) "self-discipline, cooperation with others, empathy for others, emotion, and rich humanity" and (3) "health and stamina for robust living"—not only resonate with the increasing international recognition of learners' "psychosocial resources" as central to the development of key competencies. They also draw explicitly on the domestic discourse of moral conservativism discussed earlier. It is also important to note that the triad-domain framework in the definition of "zest for living" derives from *chi, toku,* and *tai* (explained above), a popular pedagogic expression that has been used in Japan to signify a well-rounded learning experience. Therefore the 1996 CCE report embeds the international policy discourse of "the learning society" and "learning competencies" within the domestic policy discourse of "humanization" as well as the "Japanese" conceptualization of quality learning.[6] In so doing, it allows for a particular representation of the policies under "zest for living": They are "our" (Japanese) solutions to "our" unique problems.

"Crisis" in the humanizing policy discourse

Soon after the 1997 release of the CCE final report, MEXT publicized the new National Course of Study to be implemented in 2002, featuring *yutori* as the overarching keyword of the reform. The reform involved a 30 percent reduction in curricular content, the introduction of complete five-day schooling (as opposed to six-day schooling), a new definition of teachers as learning "facilitators," and a new cross-curricular subject (*sōgō gakushū no jikan*). Soon after, the so-called debate over declining academic standards took place wherein the *yutori* reform became the focus of intense public criticism (see Takayama 2007). Cultural conservatives and other social critics perceived the "relaxing" reform as undermining the nation's moral, economic, and cultural foundations. With the release of the PISA 2003 results, which registered a drop in Japanese students' international ranking in many tested areas, a public consensus was formed that the academic "crisis" was "real" and that the *yutori* reform was to blame (see Takayama, 2007, 2008). In the course of the debate, the term *yutori* and the humanizing policy discourse that encompassed it quickly lost political legitimacy. Many critics interchanged *yutori* with a similar-sounding and yet derogatory term *yurumi* ("slack," or "lazy"), making it impossible for the Ministry to salvage the term as its policy keyword.

The backlash against the "humanizing" policy caused a subtle and yet notable shift in the articulation of *ikiru chikara* ("zest for living"). After the PISA 2003 "shock," MEXT and CCE dropped *yutori* and instead featured "zest for living" much more explicitly in its presentation of reform measures (e.g. CCE, 2002, 2003). However, given the widespread public concern about declining academic standards and the view that the humanizing (now seen as "slacking") policy measures were the culprit, the Ministry could not continue with the same articulation of "zest for living." A closer look at the CCE reports in 2002 and 2003 reveals an expansion of the definition of the term; now it includes as its key domains *tashikana gakuryoku* ("solid academic abilities"), alongside "rich humanity" and "heath and stamina," with "problem-solving" tucked under "solid academic abilities." "Solid academic abilities," which embodies the idea of academic basics and rigors, was announced in 2002 by then Education Minister Atsuko Tōyama in response to mounting criticism of the *yutori* reform (MEXT, 2002), and this was quickly integrated into the definition of "zest for living."

This slight shift of emphasis in the direction of MEXT's curricular reform direction was quickly mirrored in the 2005 CCE report on structural education reform. The report defines one of the missions of compulsory education as fostering children's "zest for living" and explains that the concept encompasses the following three domains: *tashikana gakuryoku* ("solid academic abilities"), *yutakana kokoro* ("rich humanity"), and *sukoyakana karada* ("health and stamina"). Under "solid academic abilities," the report stresses the compatibility of teaching basics on the one hand and fostering creativity, problem-solving skills, and autonomous thinking on the other, which are now all subsumed under "zest for living" (CCE, 2005a, Section II, Chapter 1). Likewise, the report's executive summary (CCE, 2005b) stresses in its definition of "zest for living" a "thorough teaching of basic knowledge and skills" along with an "ability to learn and think on their own" (p. 4); this was an explicit discursive move to disarticulate "zest for living" from the now unpopular humanizing/slacking policy discourse.

International and national simultaneously

The MEXT and CCE documents, published after the PISA 2003 "shock," register a clear shift in the articulation of "zest for living." By this point, the OECD and PISA had gained powerful referential status in the Japanese education policy discourse with the triennial publications of the PISA results and the ranking rise and fall of Japanese students becoming a major media event. Accordingly, Education Ministers and bureaucrats started explicitly referring to the PISA reports and other OECD publications in characterizing and legitimizing policies (see MEXT, 2007, 2010), while featuring "zest for living" as the key feature of the policy direction. For instance, the two CCE reports published in 2008 (CCE 2008a, 2008b) prominently feature "zest for living" and OECD's terminology, "knowledge-based society" and "key competencies," throughout the document. It is noteworthy that these reports provide a description of "key competencies" immediately after discussing "zest for living" (CCE 2008a, p. 10; 2008b, p. 6), though at the time these reports were published they were not explicitly linked with each other.

The subsequent CCE and MEXT documents related to the new National Course of Study, scheduled to be implemented in 2011, reveal a more explicit re-embedding of "zest for living" within the international policy discourse. For instance, the 2009 CCE report (CCE 2009) regarding the new Course of Study, along with the associated promotional pamphlets that are also titled "zest for living" (MEXT, 2008), explicitly includes OECD's "knowledge-based society" and "key competencies" as part of the definition of "zest for living." Furthermore, these documents go as far as to assert that "zest for living" actually precedes OECD's development of these terminologies (see also CCE, 2008b, p. 6; MEXT, 2008, p. 2). Hence, the set of reforms pursued under the slogan of "zest for living" are now internationalized without erasing their nationally specific origin. MEXT asserts the Japanese "origin" of this direction in policy, while at the same time validating its "originality" by stressing that it now leads a global trend.

Discussion

The above genealogical review of "zest for living" has shown a series of shifts in the way MEXT has articulated the keyword in response to changing political conditions surrounding its education policy. The initial appearance of the term in the CCE and MEXT documents of the mid 1990s closely paralleled the international policy trend of lifelong learning set by the supranational organizations. And yet, in its earlier articulation, the international influence on "zest for living" was kept "undeclared" (Waldow, 2009); MEXT presented it as a purely domestic response to a set of educational issues at the time. MEXT eclectically drew on the three dominant domestic discourses of the time: humanistic, moralistic, and human capital discourses, in articulating the term, while erasing any trace of the international origin of the idea.

This makes perfect strategic sense to MEXT. At that time, the dominant discourse of education reform was construed around the emotional, moral, and social "suffering" of children caused by a set of "uniquely Japanese" problems; namely, didactic teaching, rote-memorization, excessive academic competition, MEXT's bureaucratic control, and mindless entrance exam preparation. OECD and UNESCO's lifelong learning policy discourse was actively integrated into Japanese education policy as a solution to the set of "our" problems. But the de-nationalized and de-contextualized international policy discourse was not well suited to the particular domestic discursive context of the time. Hence, MEXT chose "uniquely Japanese" policy keywords (such as *yutori, kosei,* and *ikiru chikara*) to domesticate the reform ideas, which drew considerably on the international policy discourse in the first place. It was a strategy to "indigenize" (Steiner-Khamsi, 2002) the global policy discourse so that it would speak directly to the particular domestic construction of the policy "problem": the "pathological" state of Japanese children, to which only the "humanizing" language of "salvation" was deemed appropriate.

The "undeclared" borrowing of the international policy discourse became less politically viable, however, after the serious legitimacy crisis of MEXT's reform discourse in the aftermath of the PISA 2003 "shock." As the humanizing policy discourse lost its political legitimacy, MEXT was forced to drop *yutori* as its central policy keyword and instead featured "zest for living"—which it had used continuously since the mid 1990s but never privileged over *yutori*—to achieve a public perception of its policy "consistency." Then, MEXT added, to its original definition, "solid academic abilities" to mark its departure from the now defunct partner, *yutori.* Once OECD's policy discourse became recognized as the "global benchmark" by the mid 2000s, the Ministry started closely re-embedding "zest for living" within the international policy discourse. But this re-internationalizing effort was pursued simultaneously with an attempt to assert the Japanese "origin" of "zest for living," with MEXT claiming that it had preceded OECD's key terminologies. Therefore, "zest for living" has become a polysemic keyword encompassing competing domestic policy discourses, while either nationalized or internationalized according to MEXT's policy legitimization needs.

This finding illuminates the complex processes through which a given international policy idea and discourse becomes integrated into the national policy context. It shows that the reception of the "extraneous" policy ideas and models is subject to the particular domestic policy context and the agency of political actors at a given moment in time, a point stressed by aforementioned Steiner-Khamsi and Waldow's studies. Though the Japanese case clearly indicates the considerable alignment of its curricular policy to the "global model," this does not mean that the OECD and its PISA exert powerful converging effects on nations' curricular policies. To be more accurate, these global policy "actors" gain their political agency *only when* domestic policy actors activate their agentive capacity by domesticating their ideas and models to the particular policy exigencies arising under a given political circumstance (Rautalin and Alasuutari, 2009).

Furthermore, the findings of the study challenge the state-centric epistemology, or methodological nationalism that has guided much education policy scholarship (Dale 2000). As demonstrated in the study, Japanese national policy discourse has been integrated into global policy discourse to such an extent that there are always elements of "international" in policies and programs that are commonly perceived as "uniquely Japanese." MEXT bureaucrats and NIER researchers are part of the globally linked networks of policy actors through which a particular "consensus" about educational reform is generated and circulated transnationally. They constantly draw upon, often partially, the de-territorialized policy discourses of the international policy community and embed them within the nationalized policy language. Whether the international "origin" of the extraneous ideas and models is declared or undeclared depends largely on the needs for policy legitimation, which are shaped by the constantly shifting political circumstances.

Lastly, the present study offers useful insights to the existing conceptual work around banal nationalism, indigenization, externalization, and silent borrowing in education policy studies. Turning to the three studies (those of Alasuutari, Waldow, and Steiner-Khamsi) discussed earlier, one of the key insights of Alasuutari's study concerns how the construction of comparative indicators (e.g. league tables) generates competition among political entities (cities, states, and nations). It is this sense of competition, he argues, that leads them to assert their ideas and policies, which are drawn from the international policy discourse, as "ours." In the Japanese case that I have examined, however, international competition was less clearly linked to MEXT's decision to silence the international origin of "zest for living." Quite contrary to Alasuutari's thesis, MEXT chose to keep it undeclared when it was faced with less competition (before the PISA 2003 "shock") and declared it after the "shock" when it was faced with much greater international competitive pressure generated by the declining PISA rankings of Japanese students. In the case of Japan, therefore, it was the shifting logic of policy legitimation rather than the cultural framework of competition that predominantly influenced the domesticating process of the international policy discourse.

On the other hand, the present study confirms Alasuutari and Steiner-Khamsi's identification of domestic political contestation as one of the key factors driving the nationalization of global policy models. As highlighted earlier, "zest for living" continues to be defined within the explicitly national policy framing, despite increasing acknowledgement of international influence. The international policy discourse of lifelong learning has been reconstituted within the conventional "Japanese" way of defining balanced learning experience (*chi, toku*, and *tai*). Furthermore, "zest for living" is now defined as "preceding" OECD's "key competencies", hence MEXT asserting its uniquely Japanese characteristics. These attempts to frame globally circulated policy models in the nationally specific language are undoubtedly influenced by domestic political contestation over education policies. They reflect MEXT's attempt to endow the set of highly contested reform programs under "zest for living" with much-needed political legitimacy. Alternatively, these nationalizing efforts could be argued to have resulted from the intense international competition in the post-PISA 2003 "shock" era. The global "horse race" in education might have generated a strong sense of "us" and "them" and thus the re-articulation of "zest for living" within a more explicitly national policy discourse to present it as "ours." These findings therefore do not necessarily refute Alasuutari's explanation but suggest a need to contextualize carefully the discussion of competition and political contestation as an inducement for banal localism/nationalism.

The synchronic nature of the global and national referencing highlighted in the present study confirms the central point that Alasuutari makes, that the domestication of global models necessarily invokes the simultaneous response of banal localism/nationalism. This stress on simultaneousness complicates Steiner-Khamsi's (2002) rather linear, sequential description of the shift from externalization to indigenization, best represented by her definition of externalization as "a transitionary policy strategy that is eventually replaced by self-referentiality" (p. 74). The Japanese case has shown that "zest for living" was initially articulated largely within the domestic policy discourse (indigenization), and then its extraneous origin was highlighted in later years (externalization). Furthermore, it has shown that externality and internality are asserted simultaneously in the most recent articulation of "zest for living," with the international policy discourse of lifelong learning deeply embedded within the explicitly nationalized policy language. Hence, the finding draws attention to the more complicated process of external and internal referencing. Political decisions as to whether to foreground the externality or internality of reform ideas or to hybridize them is shaped by the constantly shifting domestic political context and corresponding changes in the logic of policy legitimation. This thesis should be further tested and nuanced by case studies of international policy "diffusion" in divergent socio-political, economic, and temporal contexts.

Notes

1 After the amalgamation, NIER became the National Institute for Educational Policy Research but continues to use "NIER" as its institutional acronym.
2 MEXT established the CCE in 1958 to add democratic legitimacy to its policy decision-making. It is well known, however, that the Ministry maintains its control over CCE deliberation by handpicking the members and having its own bureaucrats serve as "observers" and secretaries at CCE meetings (see Ichikawa, 2003). MEXT develops its policy documents based on CCE's recommendations.
3 The report concerns the research and development project launched by the Association of Finnish Local and Regional Authorities whose aim was to "create a statistical standard about how to calculate the costs and profits of cultural activities in Finnish towns and cities) (Alasuutari, 2013, p. 8).
4 Another former NIER researcher, Eiichi Kajita (1997), one of the longest-serving CCE members, also makes the same point.
5 This contrasts with the fact that the aforementioned NIER researchers such as Arai (1993, 2001) and Kajita (1997) trace the origin of "zest for living" to UNESCO's lifelong learning policy discourse. It is noteworthy that these views were published after their departure from NIER.
6 Here, I place "Japanese" in quotation marks to indicate that the triad expression is drawn from a Chinese expression.

References

Alasuutari, P. (2013). Spreading global models and enhancing banal localism: the case of local government cultural policy development, *International Journal of Cultural Policy, 19*(1), 103–119.

Arai, I. (1993). *"Ikikata" wo kaeru gakkōjidai no taiken: raifukōsu no shakaigaku* [Schooling experience in a time of life-changing schooling: Sociology of life course]. Tokyo: Gyōsei.

Arai, I. (2001). *yutori no manabi yutori no bunka: 21 seiki no gakushū shakai* [Low pressure learning and low pressure culture: 21st-century learning society]. Tokyo: Kyōiku shuppan.

Bieber, T. and K Martens (2011). The OECD PISA study as a soft power in education?: Lessons from Switzerland and the US. *European Journal of Education,* 46(1), 101–116.

CCE (1996). *Nijyūissēki wo tenbōshita wagakuni no kyōiku no arikata ni tsuite (daiichiji tōshin)* [The new vision of our education towards the 21st century (the first report)]. Tokyo: MEXT.

CCE (2002). *Atarashī jidai ni okeru kyōyōkyōiku no arikata ni tsuite* [On the foundation education in the new era]. Tokyo: MEXT.

CCE (2003). *Shotō chūtō kyōiku ni okeru tōmen no kyōiku kadai oyobi shidō no jūjitsu kaizen hōsaku ni tsuite* [On the educational agenda and strategies for improvement in primary and secondary education]. Tokyo: MEXT.

CCE (2005a). *Atarashii jidai no gimu kyōiku o sōzō suru* [Imagining compulsory education for the new era]. Tokyo: MEXT.

CCE (2005b). *gimu kyōiku no kōzō kaikaku chuō kyōiku shingikai tōshin no gaiyō* [Summary of the CCE report on structural reform of compulsory education]. Tokyo: MEXT.

CCE (2008a). *kyōiku shinkō keikaku ni tsuite: kyōiku rikkoku no jitsugen ni mukete* [On the education promotion plan: towards the realization of education nation]. Tokyo: MEXT.

CCE (2008b). *atarashī jidai o kirihiraku shōgai gakushū no shinkōhōsaku ni tsuite* [Policies to promote lifelong learning, which pioneers the new era]. Tokyo: MEXT.

CCE (2009). *yōchien, shōgakkō, kōtōgakkō oyobi tokubetsu shien gakkō no gakushū shidō yōryō tō no kaizen ni tsuite* [On the revision to the National Course of Study for kindergarten, primary, secondary and special schools]. Tokyo: MEXT.

Chichibu, T. (2003). *kokoro wo sodateru kyōiku sesaku* [Education policies for nurturing children's mind]. Ningen kyōiku kenkyū kyōgikai ed. *Kyōiku fōramu 32*. Tokyo: Kaneko shobō.

Dale, R. (2000). Globalization and education: Demonstrating a "common world educational culture" or locating a "globally structured educational agenda"? *Educational Theory*, 50(4), 427–448.

Field, J. (2006). *Lifelong Learning and the New Educational Order*. Staffordshire, UK: Trentham Books.

Honda, Y. (2005). Tagenka suru 'nōryoku' to nihonshakai [Multifaceted 'ability' and Japanese society]. Tokyo: NTT shuppan.

Hutchins, R.M. (1968). *The Learning Society*. New York: Praeger.

Ichikawa, S. (2003). *Kyōiku kihonhō o kangaeru* [A thought on the Fundamental Law of Education]. Tokyo: kyōiku kaihatsu kenkyūjo.

Jasinski, J. (2001). *Sourcebook on Rhetoric: Key Concepts in Contemporary Rhetorical Studies*. London: Sage Publications.

Kajita, E. (1997). *"ichiru chikara" no ningen kyōiku wo* [Towards human education, "zest for living"]. Tokyo: Kaneko shobō.

Lingard, R. and Rawolle, S. (2011). New scalar politics: implications for education policy. *Comparative Education*, 47(4), 489–502.

Martens, K. (2007). How to become an influential actor: The "comparative turn" in OECD education policy. In K. Martens, A. Rusconi, and K. Leuze (eds), *New Arenas of Education Governance* (pp. 40–56). New York: Palgrave.

Matsushita, K. (2010). *PISA de kyōiku no naniga kawattaka: nihon no bāi* [What has PISA changed in education?: the Japanese case]. Tokyo: kyōiku tesuto kenkyū sentā.

MEXT (2002). *tashikana gakuryoku no kōjō no tameno 2002 apīru* [2002 appeal for improvement of solid academic abilities]. Tokyo: MEXT.

MEXT (2007). *PISA 2006 no kekka o uketa koNGO no torikumi* [The Cabinet responses to PISA 2006 results]. Tokyo: MEXT.

MEXT (2008). *ikiru chikara* [Zest for living]. Tokyo: MEXT.

MEXT (2010). *gakuryoku kōjō ni kansuru koremade no seisaku to PISA 2009 no kekka* [Existing strategies for improving academic standards and the results of PISA 2009]. Tokyo: MEXT.

Meyer, J.W. (2007). Globalization: Theory and trends. *International Journal of Comparative Sociology*, 48, 261–273.

Meyer, J.W. and Ramirez, F.O. (2000). The world institutionalization of education. In J. Schriewer (ed.), *Discourse Formation in Comparative Education* (pp. 111–132). Frankfurt a.M.: Peter Lang.

NIER (2009). *kokuritsu kyōiku seisaku kenkyūjo no 60 nen* [60 years of NIER]. Tokyo: NIER.

OECD (2000). Schooling for Tomorrow: OECD Scenarios, Paris: OECD.

OECD (2001). Knowledge and Skills for Life: First Results from PISA 2000: Executive Summary. Paris: OECD.

OECD (2005). The Definition and Selection of Key Competencies: Executive Summary. Paris: OECD.

OECD (2009). Pisa 2009 Assessment Framework. Paris: OECD.

OECD (2012). Lessons from PISA for Japan, Strong performers and successful reformers in education. Paris: OECD. Retrieved 12 January 2013 from http://dx.doi.org/10.1787/9789264118539-en.

Okumoto, K. (2008). Lifelong learning in England and Japan: three translations. *Compare*, 38(2), 173–188.

Pempel, T.J. (1998). *Regime Shift: Comparative Dynamics of the Japanese Political Economy*. Ithaca, NY: Cornell University Press.

Ramirez, O.F. (2003). Toward a cultural anthropology of the world? In K. Anderson-Levitt (ed.), *Local Meanings, Global Schooling: Anthropology and World Culture Theory* (pp. 239–254). New York: Palgrave.

Rappleye, J. (2012). *Educational Policy Transfer in an Era of Globalization*. Frankfurt a.M.: Peter Lang.

Rappleye, J. and Kariya, T. (2011). Reimagining self/other: 'catch-up' across Japan's three great education reforms. In D.B. Willis and J. Rappleye (eds), *Reimagining Japanese Education* (pp. 51–83). Oxford: Symposium Books.

Rautalin, M. and Alasuutari, P. (2009). The uses of the national PISA results by Finnish officials in central government. *Journal of Education Policy*, 24(5), 539–556.

Rychen, D. (2004). Key competencies for all: An overarching conceptual frame of reference. In D.S. Rychen and A. Tiana (eds), *Developing Key Competencies in Education: Some Lessons from International and National Experience* (pp. 5–34). Paris: UNESCO International Bureau of Education.

Saitō, Y. (2009). *wagakuni no kokusai kyōiku kyōryoku ni kansuru kenkyū* [Study of Japan's international education cooperation]. Tokyo: NIER.

Satō, M. (2000). *"manabi" kara tōsōsuru kodomotachi* [Children running away from learning]. Tokyo: Iwanami shoten.

Steiner-Khamsi, G. (2000). Transferring education, displaing reforms. In J. Schriewer (ed.), *Discourse Formation in Comparative Education* (pp. 155–187). Frankfurt a.M.: Peter Lang.

Steiner-Khamsi, G. (2002). Reterritorializing Educational Import: Explorations into the Politics of Educational Borrowing. In A. Novoa and M. Lawn (eds), *Fabricating Europe: The Formation of an Education Space* (pp. 69–86). Boston: Kluwer.

Stone, S. (2000). *Policy Paradox* [Revised ed.]. W.W. Norton & Company.

Takayama, K. (2007). *A Nation at Risk* crosses the Pacific: Transnational borrowing of the U.S. crisis discourse in the debate on education reform in Japan. *Comparative Education Review*, 51(4), 423–446.

Takayama, K. (2008). The politics of international league tables: PISA in Japan's achievement crisis debate. *Comparative Education*, 44(4), 387–407.

Takayama, K. (2009). Is Japanese education the 'exception'?: Examining the situated articulation of neoliberalism through the analysis of policy keywords. *Asia Pacific Journal of Education*, 29(2), 125–142.

Takayama, K. (2010). From the Rightist 'coup' to the new beginning of progressive politics in Japanese education. In M.W. Apple (ed.), *Global Crises, Social Justice, and Education* (pp. 61–111). New York: Routledge.

Takayama, K. (2012). Exploring the interweaving of contrary currents: transnational policy enactment and path-dependent policy implementation in Australia and Japan. *Comparative Education*, 48(4), 505–523.

Takayama, K. (2013). OECD, "Key competencies" and the new challenges of educational inequality. *Journal of Curriculum Studies*, 45(1), 67–80.

UNESCO (1972). *Learning to Be*. Paris: UNESCO.

UNESCO (1996). *Learning: The Treasure Within*. Paris: UNESCO.

Waldow, F. (2009). Undeclared imports: silent borrowing in educational policy-making and research in Sweden. *Comparative Education*, 45(4), 477–494.

Yamada, T. (2011). *Hyōka/senbatsu* [Assessment/selection]. In N. Ishido and S. Imai (eds), *shisutemu toshite no kyōiku o saguru* [Exploring education as a system] (pp. 97–117). Tokyo: Keisōshobō.

9 Culture and history in the domestication of global trends of higher education in Pakistan

Ali Qadir

Introduction

The rise and rise of higher education across less industrialized nations in recent times has been the subject of much scholarship, seeking to explain the growth even in unexpected circumstances. Enrolment rates almost everywhere have increased steadily, disparities have reduced, and policy directions are converging.

This is also the case in Pakistan, where one of the most remarkable developments since 2002 is in higher education. Gross tertiary enrolment ratios—having hovered between 2 and 3 percent from 1965 to 1995 (TFHES, 2000, p. 106)—went up by 168 percent between 2002 and 2008 (HEC, 2009, p. 66). This growth includes a narrowing gender gap, with women's participation in higher education moving from 37 to 46 percent in the same period. Pakistan inherited only two universities upon independence in 1947; the number increased to 74 degree-awarding institutions by 2002. In the next six years, between 2002 and 2008, that number almost doubled, moving the total number of degree-granting institutions to 132 by 2008 (HEC, 2010, p. 4). From 274 doctorates produced in the year 2002, Pakistani universities conferred 616 doctoral degrees in 2008, while the number of full-time faculty increased by 127 percent (HEC, 2010, p. 79). Many of these developments accelerated after the seminal reform in the sector in 2001 and 2002.

This unprecedented growth has been analyzed in Pakistan, as in many other countries, mostly with recourse to functional, political, or actor-centered theories. However, such approaches tend to overlook certain important aspects. Functional perspectives, for instance, cannot explain why higher education enrolment has expanded so rapidly in Pakistan despite persistent poverty and high income inequality, low employment rates, and low secondary school enrolments and attainments. Meanwhile, political systems theories fail to account for the rapid increase in women's proportionate enrolment (despite their continuing politico-cultural suppression), as well as huge increases in higher education funding in the face of other pressing demands on a very limited state purse. Theories according a high degree of agency to potential students, families, and university administrators cannot explain enrolment that leads away from (often rural) jobs and towards continuing unemployment, or the way in which local universities ignore local conditions and aspire to universal standards and formats that are often misaligned with local needs.

Many of these objections are countered by a range of globalist approaches, which most often seek to explain developments in individual countries, especially in economically weak ones like Pakistan, by pointing to a diffusion of models from powerful centers such as international agencies and some industrialized countries. World polity theory, in particular, is one strand of world-level theorizing that builds consistent accounts of higher education expansion across the world by referring to a national enactment of worldwide models (Meyer, Ramirez, Frank, and Schofer, 2007; Schofer and Meyer, 2005). This approach is useful in explaining otherwise puzzling trends in Pakistan, such as the remarkable increase worldwide in female enrolment in universities (Bradley and Ramirez, 1996; Meyer, Ramirez, and Soysal, 1992). This theory's perspective that national developments aim to seek external legitimacy in the world's system of nation-states (e.g. Barrett and Tsui, 1999), rather than internal legitimacy in the field of national actors, provides a reasonable explanation for Pakistan's continuous reform of higher education. In the case of the Pakistani reform in 2001–2002 this is especially relevant, since reform followed immediately after the launch in 2000 of a report by the global Task Force on Higher Education and Society (TFHES), convened by the United Nations Educational, Scientific and Cultural Organization (UNESCO) and the World Bank (TFHES, 2000). The Pakistani reform report published in 2002 (hereafter "Pakistani report") acknowledged that this national reform was "triggered" and "encouraged" by the UNESCO/World Bank task force report (hereafter "UNESCO report").

While a number of convergences between the UNESCO and Pakistani reports are evident, and I will discuss them at length below, it is also clear that this was not simply a matter of a national "enactment" of a global policy model. First, the UNESCO report never prescribed formal structures or directly applicable procedures, but rather emphasized principles for national action. Second, not all (and perhaps not even what might be interpreted as the "central" spirit) of the recommendations were brought into the Pakistani report, let alone into subsequent policy actions. Third, the Pakistani report justified its recommendations not by referring to global models or even the UNESCO report, but rather as an entirely "national" development related to apparently natural functional needs. It is, therefore, not immediately clear how or to what extent the two reports may be said to be related, and even less clear how to justify world polity theory perspectives on the national report being an enactment of a global model.

In fact, closer readings of these reform reports show a more complex and thoroughly nationally driven process of policy-making at work. On the one hand, it is clear that this process is already embedded in the world's system of states and what others are doing. On the other hand, the actual process of national uptake reflects national constructions of local, historicized particularity. How do such national policy uptakes of global models happen in ways that make them appear naturally local? What is and what is not adopted in cases of local mimesis of global policy models? And by what devices is it possible for a reform that is obviously foreign in inspiration to be made to appear so national in its justification?

I seek to address these general questions in this chapter by examining the case of the 2001–2002 policy reform of higher education in Pakistan, using the UNESCO report of 2000 as a reference point for global policy models. In order to do so, I draw on the framework of domestication discussed throughout this volume.

Many of the insights from world polity theory are useful in setting the stage for such an analysis, beginning with the recognition of a world polity comprising structurally isomorphic nation-states (Meyer, Boli, Thomas, and Ramirez, 1997) and the view that "the world is much more cultural than functional, political-economic, systems, and actor-centered theories acknowledge" (Thomas, 2009, p. 116). However, as outlined in the introduction to this volume, world polity theory tends to ignore the local field battles that tame and nationalize global policy models, while at the same time distinguishing their application from global proposals. It does not help (or seek) to explain how these patterns are presented and accepted as thoroughly national developments. Furthermore, while giving undeniable evidence for world-wide isomorphism in higher education, world polity theory does not aim to describe the actual processes that lead to the uptake of global models in some aspects but not in others, what factors inform that selective choice, and what its implications are.

Domestication offers a more bottom-up perspective, which builds from world polity accounts but emphasizes the national processes of policy-making. Relevant to the case at hand, this framework stresses nationalization as naturalization to be a key step in seeing national policy-making as the domestication of global policy models. However, domestication is an evolving framework, and conceptual details still need to be added to make it a more thorough explanatory frame. International comparisons are, indeed, important in justifying reforms, and help to bring a worldwide perspective to national policies, and local field battles do indeed promote "banal nationalism." All of these may be read also in the case of the Pakistani reform of 2001–2002. But my focus here is on the step of naturalization as nationalization: the processes by which a worldwide model is made to appear local, and the factors that inform this process. At the risk of letting the cat out of the bag, my intention in this chapter is to contribute to this conception of nationalization in policy reform by foregrounding the importance of the weight of history (or, more accurately, of the weight of constructions of national history) in the process of naturalization. In the course of the argument I will also propose the aspects of global policy model expression that lend to such nationalized naturalization.

In order to do so, I will set the stage with a brief context description, and then move immediately to outlining the thematic convergences between the UNESCO and Pakistani reports. I then present an interpretive analysis of the naturalizing effect of history and, finally, discuss what this means for nationalization in domestication.

Higher education in Pakistan

Higher education in Pakistan refers to formal education after Grade 12, the Faculty of Arts (equivalent to the North American high school or the British Advanced Level). Institutionally, higher education is completed through colleges or universities, the primary differences between the two being that colleges typically do not engage in any substantive research, typically do not award their own degrees but instead are affiliated with or constituent parts of universities that do, and typically do not offer doctorate training. As such, the determination of higher education is by universities, notably through examinations, admissions, and curricula. As the 2001–2002 report states, "the public universities control the quality of higher education provided for a very large proportion of the students ... [universities] are the chief determinants of the quality of higher education" (TFIHE, 2002, pp. 11, 18).

The story of higher education in Pakistan is, inevitably, tied to the events that mark it most evidently: eight efforts at policy reform (1947, 1959, 1970, 1972, 1977, 1992, 1998, and 2001–2002). The 2001–2002 reforms were only the last of a series of attempts at "modernization" of the sector. While all governments and development actors have considered higher education of vital importance, they have likewise agreed on the poor condition in which they find the sector. The first is difficult to reconcile with the second, and makes successive reform efforts all the more remarkable.

In fact, the reforms have almost invariably occurred immediately after a change of government or regime. Political theory might point to a solution in terms of weak states seeking legitimacy (Rees, 1994), but this is suspect since it doesn't account for the political climate of a general lack of accountability in Pakistan and the far fewer reforms in more popular areas of health care or infrastructure. I have argued elsewhere that education has a colonial history of association with modernization, which explains some of this reform impulse (Qadir, 2011).

Throughout the reforms, three key concerns in Pakistani higher education have remained constant. The 2002 report notes that "many of the generic faults were identified more than 40 years ago [by the 1959 Commission]" (TFIHE, 2002, p. 16). These "generic" faults are generally classified in terms of (1) access—less than 5 percent of the post-secondary age cohort; (2) teaching and research quality—Pakistan's proportionate research output remains low compared with similar countries; and (3) governance and management—confusion between governance and management roles, and a high degree of political interference on campuses. Consequently, reforms have followed a techno-managerial approach to higher education to "solve" these faults.

This is the case also for the 2001–2002 reform, which led to the remarkable outcomes listed above. In addition, state financing of higher education grew from 3.4 billion Pakistan rupees (US$59 million) in fiscal year 2001/2002 to 32 billion (US$469 million) in fiscal year 2008/2009, the 850 percent increase more than covering rises in real costs. The growth in financing is especially remarkable given the condition of Pakistan's economy. For instance, although higher education, along with all development sector programs in Pakistan, suffered from the financial crisis between 2007 and 2009, the proportion of higher education budgetary allocation grew steadily and rapidly. Between 2000 and 2006 budgetary allocation to higher education had already increased by over 270 percent (EAD, 2009, p. 164), far outstripping any other development sector. Even in the high-deficit budget for the fiscal year 2009–2010, higher education once again received an increase. In this budget, education as a whole received 31.6 billion rupees (equivalent to US$388 million in February 2010), out of which 23.4 billion rupees (about US$287 million) was reserved for tertiary education alone. In addition, the Government allocated another 22.7 billion rupees (US$279 million) for development projects by the Higher Education Commission (HEC) (*Dawn*, 2009). In October 2009, Pakistan's President declared that the budget for higher education would be further enhanced by 20 percent of GDP over the next five years (*Chronicle*, 2009). To put this emphasis in perspective, the Government of Pakistan allocated 23.2 billion rupees (about US$285 million) for the entire health sector (*Nation*, 2009) in a country with poor health indicators (for instance in the top ten highest number of maternity-related deaths in the world).

Much of this increase is justified in the words of the Higher Education Commission (HEC), the central regulatory and support agency constituted in 2002 after the reforms:

> Considering the entire issue of development in a holistic manner, it thus becomes apparent that "Higher Education" serves as the engine of change that not only impacts economic development, but also serves to strengthen the entire system of education. The higher education system produces the teachers that are the most critical component of the entire education system, the graduates who power the "knowledge economy," and the researchers who unleash the power of Critical Thinking. The products of this system then catalyze the development of new products and processes, an imperative in today's highly competitive industrial world.
>
> (HEC, 2005, p. 1)

The significance of the steps taken for higher education in Pakistan, led by the HEC and stemming from the recommendations of the 2002 report, is undeniable. However, these reforms have never been critically analyzed, and there has been no comment on how to understand this development in the backdrop of the UNESCO report of 2000.

The UNESCO/World Bank task force on higher education and society

Concern for higher education in Pakistan in 2000 on the part of the new military government of President Musharraf was complemented by a renewal of interest in higher education for economic development globally. In 1999, UNESCO and the World Bank had convened a Task Force on Higher Education and Society led by eminent educationists from 13 countries to examine and give guideline recommendations for higher education in developing countries. Their report, entitled "Higher Education in Developing Countries: Peril and Promise" was launched globally in 2000. Two of the leading members, both from Harvard University, USA, were invited to launch the report in Pakistan. The invitation was led by the Pro-Chancellor of one of Pakistan's leading universities and a member of the global Task Force.

The report was launched in Pakistan in February 2001, in Karachi and in Lahore. Following the launches, the Federal Minister of Education established a Task Force on Improvement of Higher Education in Pakistan (TFIHE) in April 2001, co-chaired by the executive heads of the two leading private universities where the global report had been launched. The Pakistani Task Force report noted that the UNESCO report had "triggered the process that led to the establishment of this [Pakistani] Task Force, and *often served as a guide to its deliberations*" (TFIHE, 2002, viii, emphasis added), and acknowledged the "stimulus" and "encouragement" of the UNESCO/World Bank Task Force (TFIHE, 2002, viii, xi, xiii, 1, 5). The Pakistani Task Force, comprising 17 eminent educationists and educational administrators, presented its recommendations in January 2002 to the President of Pakistan, who accepted them.

The Pakistani task force was also minimally financed by the World Bank, which supported its meetings and organization of consultative seminars across the country (although the 17 members all contributed voluntarily), as well as the publication of the report. However, beyond this limited financing, there was no other involvement by the World Bank or by members of the global UNESCO/World Bank Task Force. Neither the World Bank nor UNESCO or any other multilateral agency made any statement of support for the reform or commitment to future financing. Eventually, no multilateral financing was forthcoming for Pakistani higher education from the World Bank until 2009, seven years after the publication of the report. The project document approving this 2009 financing of US$100 million makes no mention of the 2002 report, and hinges instead on the apparent effectiveness and commitment demonstrated by the HEC. This support signaled other donors, such as the United States Agency for International Development, whose first support to higher education of US$40 million, also in 2009, refers only to the HEC.

As such, the apparent correlation between the contents of the global Task Force and the Pakistan TFIHE reports cannot be explained by coercion or incentive. The causality appears limited to "stimulation" and "trigger[ing]" of the process and general "guide to deliberations." The Pakistani report makes no further specific mention of the UNESCO report. In fact, the UNESCO report did not give any explicit recommendations for governance structures, management procedures, admissions or examination criteria, or other academic affairs. In its own words, the UNESCO report "does not offer a universal blueprint for reforming higher education systems, but it does provide a starting point for action;" this was done through clearly delineated "qualities" that higher education systems must develop in *all* developing countries in certain focus areas, such as financing, governance, and academic affairs especially in science and technology (TFHES, 2000, pp. 11, 14). Despite this, there is a remarkable convergence of principles and approaches in the two reports, yet with some curious divergences.

Thematic convergences: worldwide models and national invocations

Four outstanding thematic convergences between the UNESCO and Pakistani reports are presented here, based on close readings of these texts: massification, the knowledge-based economy, a systemic view of higher education, and the culture of resistance. At first sight, and in view of the timing of the respective reports, it appears that the Pakistani report (2002) mimicked the model presented by the UNESCO report (2000). However, on closer analysis, it is evident that each policy recommendation in the Pakistani case is built so as to develop a national argument referring to specific constructions of national history.

Massification

The first finding regards what has been termed the "massification" of higher education, or attention given to enhancing tertiary enrolment ratios in national higher education. The UNESCO report terms this phenomenon "expansion," and refers to the increase in numbers of students since the 1950s as both a reality to be faced and a reality to be desired. That is, on the one hand, the report considers *expansion* of higher education (primarily evident in increased numbers of students demanding higher education) to be a given *fact*, including in developing countries, part of a (unexplained) "dramatic shift from class to mass" (TFHES, 2000, p. 16). On the other hand, the TFHES report is clear that expansion is also to be *desired*, since developing countries need "more and better higher education" (TFHES, 2000, p. 9). The starting point for the report is that "[a]lthough developing countries contain more than 80 percent of the world's population, they account for just half of its higher education students, and for a far smaller proportion of those with access to high-quality higher education. Overcoming these gaps is a daunting challenge" (TFHES, 2000, p. 91). This double emphasis establishes the first challenge that the report addresses: access to higher education by more and more youth in all countries, irrespective of the country's unique condition or history. One implication of this emphasis, taken for granted in the TFHES report, is that student enrolment will take place on the basis of "merit" rather than identity classifications, such as gender, race, ethnicity, religious belonging or even economic status. This emphasis supports independent findings by world polity theorists on the significant increase in worldwide tertiary enrolment, especially since the 1950s (Schofer and Meyer, 2005).

The same emphasis on enhancing access to higher education is clearly evident as the first significant challenge identified in the Pakistan TFIHE report. This report begins (TFIHE, 2002, p. 9) with a situation analysis of tertiary enrolment figures, and continues with an understanding that massification of higher education in Pakistan is essential, irrespective of the individual classification of students. Two key justifications are presented for this: (1) that Pakistan's peer group (South Asian and other neighboring countries) are outperforming Pakistan in enrolment trends, and (2) that national economic development requires more and more highly qualified individuals (although no evidence is offered for this). The field within which the anticipated reform is to be conducted, therefore, is outlined as national need (referring to abstract economic indicators like GDP) in comparison with a peer group (referring to regional neighbors). This emphasis has found its way beyond the reform statement of 2002 into the HEC's overwhelming stress on establishing new universities.

The knowledge-based economy

The UNESCO report links the desire for higher tertiary enrolment to the "new reality" of the knowledge revolution: "The economy is changing as knowledge supplants physical capital as the source of present (and future) wealth. Technology is driving much of this process" (TFHES, 2000, p. 9). This knowledge revolution is described in terms of an increase in the rate of scientific publishing and patent applications, and access to information technology. The report relates this revolution to developing country needs by noting that, "Countries that are only weakly connected to the rapidly emerging global knowledge system will find themselves increasingly at a disadvantage" (TFHES, 2000, p. 34). The rationale for greater attention to, and investment in, national higher education is therefore largely (albeit, not exclusively) defined in terms of national economic goals: higher productivity in the contemporary global reality of knowledge-based capital. The report claims that these "new realities" are distinct from the "traditional 'nation-building' goals" of higher education in most developing countries after decolonization (TFHES, 2000, p. 16). These, it suggests, also emphasized economic growth, but through raising individual standards of living rather than relying on the inherent value of knowledge capital.

Likewise, the Pakistani report also justifies a call for greater tertiary enrolment, driven by enhanced state financing, with an economic argument: "Of all the economic growth initiatives of the Government of Pakistan, perhaps none holds more promise and the possibility of large scale and sustainable returns than effectiveness and expansion of the Higher Education infrastructure in Pakistan" (TFIHE, 2002, p. 1). Other "non-economic goals of higher education" are also stated as being consistent with the principles that flow from the knowledge-based economic argument but this is not elaborated on anywhere. The Pakistani report then relates the same economic argument from the earlier landmark Commission on National Education (1959).

While the principle of higher education expansion in the Pakistani report of 2000 draws on the "new" knowledge economy realities as outlined by the UNESCO report, it translates this into the same economic argument of national planning used more than 40 years ago as part of an explicit nation-building attempt (Qadir, 2009b; Saigol, 2003). This is especially evident in the more detailed recommendations of the Pakistani report, which do not refer to the global knowledge economy or revolution even once in discussing the structural changes to be introduced. By contrast, the earlier national Commission report of 1959 becomes a growing reference point for national recommendations in 2002.

The system of higher education

The UNESCO report does not prescribe any specific structural features for higher education institutions in developing countries. Instead, the focus is on "the web of public and private education institutions, governing bodies, and individuals that form a higher education system" (TFHES, 2000, p. 46). The report stresses that academics and policy-makers had not adopted a systems perspective when dealing with higher education in the past, making this report unique. The "desirable features of a higher education system" are presented in detail (TFHES, 2000, pp. 50–52): stratification (the separation of higher education institutions that focus on research from those that educate large numbers of students); long-term funding to institutions and diverse resources for the system as a whole; "more intense competition" indicated by faculty mobility; flexibility to "significant external changes" (especially in the labor market); clear institutional performance standards; no political manipulation; linkages with other sectors (primarily industry); and a supportive regulatory structure.

Such a systems approach naturally enables a bird's eye view of higher education within national state boundaries. It also encourages an emphasis on governance, "the formal and informal arrangements that allow higher education institutions to make decisions and take action ... [including] relations between individual institutions and their supervisors" (TFHES, 2000, p. 59). The UNESCO report lays out principles for good governance, leading to management, or the "tools for achieving good governance." These management structures (TFHES, 2000, pp. 64–67) include powers to faculty representative councils (Senates); independent governing councils to "act as a buffer between a higher education institution and the external bodies to which the institution is accountable, such as the state"; "transparent, logical and well-understood set of rules for budgeting and accounting"; a "plethora of data" for decision-making; merit-based, peer-reviewed procedures for faculty appointment and promotion; "long-term [faculty appointment] contracts, though not necessarily indefinite ones"; faculty engagement in external markets; external monitoring by visiting committees; and institutional charters that define the university missions. The conclusion points out that "[g]ood governance promotes educational quality," and that the principles and management tools outlined could enhance quality "across a wide variety of situations" (TFHES, 2000, p. 68).

This same emphasis on structure and governance within (broadly) a systems perspective is striking within the Pakistani report, whose first substantial section is "The System of Higher Education" (TFIHE, 2002, pp. 9–11). After a year-long consultative process (involving its own meetings and consultations with more than 400 stakeholders), the Pakistani report lists the following "most prominent amongst the issues identified" in the higher education system in the country: "ineffective governance and management structures and practices; inefficient use of available resources; inadequate funding; poor recruitment practices and inadequate development of faculty and staff; inadequate support for research; politicization; and strong scepticism about the realisation of reforms" (TFIHE, 2002, p. xiii). Leaving aside the last (addressed below), the list is almost a direct copy (inversely) of the UNESCO list of "desirable features of a higher education system." Among other aspects, the primary attention to governance and management structures is notable, with this being the lead recommendation to enhance quality: "to improve the performance of universities substantially ... the Task Force concentrated its attention on systems that would enable efficient governance" (TFIHE, 2002, p. 19). The key recommendations for improved governance and management, mirroring precisely the UNESCO report, are: independent governing boards; executive and academic councils with faculty representation; merit-based (but not peer-reviewed) faculty appointment and promotion procedures; time-bound appointments of faculty renewable upon performance evaluation; and clear university mission statements. These recommendations were subsequently formalized by the follow-up Steering Committee on Higher Education (2002) in a Model University Ordinance to (re-)charter universities.

In addition, a key recommendation of the Pakistani report is a new central body for "supporting the improvement of the quality of academic programmes" (TFIHE, 2002, p. 26). The proposed Higher Education Commission again mirrors the recommendation of the UNESCO report for "active oversight by the state" to ensure an "effective system of higher education" (TFHES, 2000, p. 53). However, the global model of a central body is refracted through (the construction of) a national lens: "political interference." Much of the global model for a national system of higher education is simply ignored (including the aspects about accountability, educational quality, faculty appointment and mobility procedures, accounting practices, and fundraising requirements). Instead the emphasis is on a single aspect: professionalization by way of de-politicizing academic governance. Of course, this is part of a worldwide, rationalized model of higher education governance (Meyer and Ramirez, 2000; Ramirez, 2006). However, the Pakistani report presents it as the primary problem for higher education, selectively invoking only one aspect of the worldwide model of higher education reform that is linked to a national narrative of resistance.

Culture of resistance

Political interference on campuses in Pakistan has been considered an outstanding problem since the Commission on National Education (1959). The 1959 Commission's key apprehension was the prevalent attitude of the population of the newly independent nation, "the attitudes of a subject people rather than of free men." It diagnosed this problem as relating to colonial history, which on the one hand fostered indifference and passivity, and on the other hand meant that "non-cooperation became the badge of patriotism" in resistance to all steps by the (colonial) government (CNE, 1959, pp. 5–6).

This same belief, that actions of government may be intrinsically good or bad but are resisted by people for unprofessional reasons, is voiced by the 2001 Pakistan Task Force: "seemingly unreasonable resistance to change is a natural phenomenon and ours can be classified as a normal experience" (TFIHE, 2002, p. 11). Reviewing past educational policies, it notes that, "If some of the reasonable policy recommendations had been implemented with the requisite earnestness, the situation of higher education in Pakistan would have improved and evolved over time" (implying that the earlier recommendations were not implemented and the sector has not "evolved") (TFIHE, 2002, p. 4). The concern is that "many of the attitudes mentioned [in a long quotation from the CNE 1959] are strongly manifest today," and so the Task Force report emphasizes a change in "the central importance of attitudes that condition the performance of individuals" (TFIHE, 2002, p. 40). This conclusion at the end of the Pakistani report, coming after a three-paragraph direct quote from the CNE report (1959) is obviously significant. Even earlier, the Pakistani report identifies the problem with higher education in Pakistan as: "strong scepticism about the realisation of reform" (TFIHE, 2002, p. xiii). The fundamental problem, therefore, is seen as a culture of resistance—to reforms in general and to professionalizing reforms in particular.

This concern finds broad resonance in the UNESCO report, where a key issue is the "chaotic and unplanned" evolution of higher education in developing countries (TFHES, 2000, p. 11). The report outlines issues of poor governance, including a brief mention of political interference and activism, along with lack of accountability. Again, the issue appears to be one of a culture of resistance in developing countries—resistance to excellence in quality and professionalism. However, the Pakistani report of 2002 overlooks many of the recommendations (such as accountability), and invokes this problem with exclusive reference to the Commission on National Education of 1959. That Commission, in turn, was dealing with a very specific context: recent decolonization from British rule (in 1947). The invocation of politicization in that context lends a particular tone to the generic issue of "political interference," discussed below.

The weight of history: interpreting worldwide principles of higher education reform

In each case of thematic convergence between the Pakistani reform report of 2002 and the UNESCO report of 2000 there is a double movement embedding the Pakistani recommendation into the worldwide system, but at the same time relating it to cultural constructions of national history. In this section I explore three such invocations of history, and the implications of such historicized nationalization of a worldwide model of higher education.

The secularization problem

Implicit in the feature of massification is a desire to make existential classifications (such as gender, ethnicity, and religious beliefs) irrelevant. One of the implications of this rational desire has been to secularize higher education in Pakistan in order to make it religiously neutral and hence accessible (theoretically) to all, as well as stimulating tolerance. This has been an attempt nominally pursued since colonial policy first officially introduced "modern" higher education in the form in which it exists today in Pakistan. However, the secularization of higher education concomitant with massification has not been a straightforward enactment, as evident by the escalating extremism on campuses and in the Pakistan academia. Furthermore, it soon becomes clear that due to the peculiar colonial history of Pakistan, what is meant by secularization in the country is not the same as what is meant by the term in Western Europe or the USA, for instance (Qadir, 2012). Not only are the curricula and subjects deeply informed by modern Islamic beliefs, but also religious groups and parties remain very active in campus politics, in public no less than in private universities. In the perspective of the Pakistani reform report of 2002, the peculiar notion of secularization has to do with its statement that modern reforms must conform to the constitutionally "Islamic" character of Pakistan, but nowhere is this expanded upon. It is entirely unclear what this statement actually means for the reforms, and it remains more as lip service in the report than anything substantial. The national enrolment statistics presented in the Pakistani report are not religiously disaggregated, and elide the fact that the country's religious minorities (mostly Christians, Hindus, and Sikhs) stand at a tremendous disadvantage in higher education.

Of course such part-silence is, itself, loaded. The secularization impulse so integrally a part (even a "central" principle) of the rational global model is not operationalized in the Pakistani report. In fact, by paying lip service to the "Islamic character" of Pakistan, the national report of 2002 de-prioritizes this impulse. Instead, it invokes and supports the mainstream narrative of Pakistan as an "Islamic" country, with a history of Muslim activism against Christian colonists as well as Hindu Indians. The problems generated by this tension or ambivalence are obvious in events across Pakistani campuses: religiously motivated (often legitimized) violence and even structural exclusion of minorities. This is no straightforward issue of "decoupling" between formal statements and informal practices, but rather a sign of ambiguity at the weld points where global models are fused with self-evident, natural, "national" history. The very act of making the reform national by invoking history disturbs the fault line of secularism in the global model.

The English problem

A second norm is the orientation of higher education to global competitiveness, closely related to utilitarian justifications of higher education (Calhoun, 2006; Qadir, 2011, pp. 169–215; Readings, 1997; Young, 1996). The Pakistani report of 2002 relates this to global economic competitiveness. For instance, when describing the poor quality of higher education in the country, the report notes that graduates are ill prepared to "participate effectively in ... the competitive global economy," a task presented as demanding even more quality than for competition nation-wide. Global competitiveness is also the notion prescribed by the UNESCO report in its underlining the knowledge economy and the need for developing countries to participate effectively by recognizing the "new realities." One aspect of this competitiveness in the Pakistani report, notable by its lack of explicit mention, is the not-quite-stated assumption of English as the medium of instruction, an assumption with a long-standing history again related to colonialism (Qadir, 2009a). The Pakistani report never mentions the issue of medium of instruction. However, the emphasis on economic utility and global competitiveness leaves little room for speculation. The fact that the Pakistani report does not mention this issue through all its deliberations is as telling as if it had made a statement, since the issue of medium of instruction has been at the heart of long-standing polemics in Pakistani education (Rahman, 1996), beginning with the language movement that led (at least in part) to the creation of Bangladesh in 1972 from its earlier identity as East Pakistan.

The Task Force report was never translated into the national language, Urdu, or other prevalent regional languages. Again, this is not a direct emulation of global norms, as in most non-Anglophonic countries considerable resources are devoted to developing higher education in national languages. Even in Pakistan, a number of campuses rely de facto on Urdu or other regional languages, and the entire body of "traditional" institutions known as *madrassahs* (religious seminaries) is devoted to Urdu and Arabic instruction. By setting these issues aside, the Pakistani report's authors relate themselves to the history of colonial origins of modern higher education in the subcontinent.

The resistance problem

Just as the 1959 report noted that people have "unreasonably" resisted reforms by the colonial government only for the sake of resistance, the Pakistani report of 2002 cites this earlier report at length and ends its recommendations with the same complaint. Both mention the willingness of faculty, staff, students, and administrators for reform as a prerequisite for the sector to "improve and evolve over time," yet both point out that this has been the single biggest hurdle in that improvement. For the Commission on National Education (CNE 1959, pp. 5–6), resistance was primarily a result of people's leftover attitudes from subjection to colonial rule. In the report of 2002, one can also add "skepticism" about reform, failure of previous efforts, and entrenched interests against professionalization (TFIHE, 2002, xiii, 4, 13, 40).

The reliance of the authorities on unchangeable attitudes is, perhaps, symptomatic of techno-managerial reforms typical of higher education in Pakistan. In this specific case, by invoking the earlier Commission report of 1959, the authors of the 2002 Pakistani report (maybe unwittingly) relate their own reforms under "new" global dispensations to earlier reforms under colonial dispensations. In any case, what the report ends up reinforcing is an "us" and "them" relationship between governors and governed. Furthermore by suggesting that what could have been a culture of cooperation is instead a culture of resistance, the authors of the 2002 report assume that individuals (with their inevitable interests) determine the nature of their own culture and how they put it to use. This is a rather odd notion of culture, which acts precisely to de-legitimate opposition to reforms by constructing them as "vested interest."

There is no consideration in the Pakistani report of the possibility that, as Marshall Sahlins (1999) points out in another context, the issue may not be a culture of resistance but rather a resistance of culture. By positioning themselves at the vanguard of globally competitive change, the authors of the 2002 report devalue the resistance of culture, or of a reaction by a historicized cultural matrix to new, foreign models.

Discussion

This is a necessarily brief window into what is obviously a complex field of education in Pakistan and a complex process of national policy-making. However, with my limited focus on emphasizing the role of history in the domestication of global policy models I can tentatively put forward a few proposals in response to my initial questions.

The comparative readings of the UNESCO report of 2000 and the Pakistani report of 2002 indicate that while the former did "trigger" the process of Pakistan reforms, its recommendations were not directly taken up in Pakistan. Rather, a more nuanced understanding of causality is called for, one that relies on closer unpacking of national processes. Naturally, local politics and interests were important in this process of domesticating a global model of higher education policy, but the focus here has been on how that was done to make the reform appear naturally national. A key strategy that emerges is reference to, and further construction of, national historical narratives. Such narratives, in turn, inform *what* is and is not taken up selectively as well *how* it is put into play. Rhetorical embedding serves to naturalize the model thoroughly in the local field. Overarching features thus appear isomorphic, such as massification, global competitiveness in a knowledge economy, system-oriented views of national higher education, and references to a culture of resistance to professionalization. However, the invocation of local history embeds these in a national field, and the particular selections of historical narrative give distinct impulses to that domestication.

My aim here is not to imply that the authors of the Pakistani report of 2002 somehow created these narratives. However, the report does indeed reflect the way in which particular constructions of history inform the cultural matrix in which such global models are domesticated. As pointed out in the introduction to this volume, this is the case with domestication generally—it is best seen not as an intentional step-wise process but rather as the natural way in which national policy-making is done, especially during reform.

I also do not intend to suggest that there is some form of unique national history that exists *an sich*, and thus necessarily causes variations in national uptakes of global models. Rather, it is the way in which history is implicitly or explicitly invoked to support the process of domestication that adds explanatory power to the domestication framework. Such an invocation of history is phenomenological in that there is no fixed period of relevance but rather a subjective reliance on the "longue durée" of eventual history.

In the case of Pakistani higher education, this eventual history goes back through the various reform efforts (principally the Commission report of 1959) to the independence of Pakistan (in 1947), and further to the various instances of British colonial higher education policies in India. A consequence of this point is that institutional isomorphism driven by cognitive schema is not a post-1950 phenomenon (as is often depicted in world polity theory) but a far longer one.

Another point that emerges from this analysis about domestication by way of naturalization is the importance of abstract principles that can be legitimately "applied" to a local situation. The very nature of abstractions in worldwide models—for instance of "economic development"—allows them to be nationalized in particular contexts as perfectly natural applications. Abstractions in worldwide models (or local constructions of abstractions in some cases) function as what Ernesto Laclau calls "floating signifiers," whose "radical ambiguity, which subverts the fixity of the sign, is precisely what gives the context its openness" (Laclau, 1989, p. 71). In the process, global or foreign origins are elided. In the case here, this was particularly straightforward for the Pakistani report of 2002 since the UNESCO report of 2000 deals anyway in abstract "principles."

Finally, my reading of the reports highlights the national use of inter-textuality as a rhetorical strategy in the domestication of a foreign policy model. In this case, the Pakistani report of 2002 refers continuously to the Commission report of 1959 to convey the sense of continuity of challenges and perils to higher education development in the country. Not only does this bring along a historicized baggage (for example, the colonial origins of higher education in Pakistan) but it also consistently builds a sense of "our" national system facing "our" own problems in a perceived national trajectory. The ongoing construction of national history in policy-making—particularly by way of inter-textual references—appears to be a key component in establishing the myth of national culture, including "our" political culture. One effect of this aspect of national policy-making is to elide the foreign origins of a policy model, even in a case with such intimate connections as this one, and make it appear thoroughly natural.

However, the narratives of continuous national history invoked in policy-making have a crucially ambivalent effect. On the one hand, national history construction appears to be a mechanism that is deeply coupled with the interpretation of a global policy model in the "domus." On the other hand, this very invocation also sets up fault lines in what the global model *means* in national policy-making, resulting in this case in renewed problems of secularism, medium of instruction, and de-legitimizing opposition as a postcolonial culture of resistance.

References

Barrett, D. and Tsui, A.O. (1999). Policy as Symbolic Statement: International Response to National Population Policies. *Social Forces, 78*(1), 213–233.

Bradley, K. and Ramirez, F.O. (1996). World Polity Promotion of Gender Parity: Women's Share of Higher Education, 1965–1985. *Research in Sociology of Education and Socialization, 11*, 63–91.

Calhoun, C. (2006). The University and Public Good. *Thesis Eleven, 84*(7), 7–43.

Chronicle (2009, 17 October). Pakistan Will Increase Higher-Education Budget by 20 Percent of GDP, President Says, *Chronicle of Higher Education.* Retrieved 16 August 2013 from http://chronicle.com/blogs/ticker/pakistan-will-increase-higher-education-budget-by-20-percent-of-gdp-president-says.

CNE (1959). Report of the Commission on National Education. Karachi: Commisson on National Education, Government of Pakistan.

Dawn (2009, 20 June). Deoband Ulema term all Taliban actions un-Islamic, Staff Report, *Dawn Pakistan.* Retrieved 10 February 2010 from http://archives.dawn.com/archives/41418.

EAD (2009). Pakistan Economic Survey 2008–09. Islamabad: Economic Affairs Division, Government of Pakistan.

HEC (2005). Medium-Term Development Framework. Islamabad: Higher Education Commission, Government of Pakistan.

HEC (2009). Higher Education Commission Report 2002–08. Islamabad: Higher Education Commission, Government of Pakistan.

HEC (2010). Higher Education Statistics Update 30 June 2010. Islamabad: Higher Education Commission, Government of Pakistan.

Laclau, E. (1989). Politics and the limits of modernity. *Social Text, 21*(Special issue—the politics of postmodernism), 63–82.

Meyer, J.W. and Ramirez, F.O. (2000). The World Institutionalization of Education. In J. Schriewer (ed.), *Discourse Formation in Comparative Education* (pp. 111–132). New York: Peter Lang.

Meyer, J.W., Boli, J., Thomas, G.M., and Ramirez, F.O. (1997). World Society and the Nation-State. *American Journal of Sociology, 103*(1), 144–181.

Meyer, J.W., Ramirez, F.O., Frank, D.J., and Schofer, E. (2007). Higher Education as an Institution. In P.J. Gumport (ed.), *Sociology of Higher Education: Contributions and Their Contexts* (pp. 187–221). Baltimore, MD: Johns Hopkins University Press.

Meyer, J.W., Ramirez, F.O., and Soysal, Y. (1992). World expansion of mass education. *Sociology of Education, 65*(2), 128–149.

Nation (2009, 14 June). Text of budget speech, *The Nation.* Retrieved from www.nation.com.pk/pakistan-news-newspaper-daily-english-online/Business/14-Jun-2009/Text-of-budget-speech.

Qadir, A. (2009a). Good Subjects: Sir Sayyid Ahmad Khan, English and the Punjab University. *Pakistan Journal of History and Culture, 30*(2), 43–66.

Qadir, A. (2009b). Hired Education: The Commission on National Education and Modernity in Pakistan. *International Journal of Humanities, 6*(10), 105–114.

Qadir, A. (2011). *Tangential Modernity: Culture of Higher Education Reform in Pakistan.* DSocSc Monograph, University of Tampere, Tampere.

Qadir, A. (2012). Between Secularism/s: Islam and the Institutionalisation of Modern Higher Education in mid-19th century British India. *British Journal of Religious Education (iFirst)*, 1–15. doi:10.1080/01416200.2012.717065.

Rahman, T. (1996). *Language and Politics in Pakistan.* Karachi: Oxford University Press.

Ramirez, F.O. (2006). The rationalization of universities. In M.-L. Djelic and K. Sahlin-Andersson (eds), *Transnational Governance* (pp. 225–244). Cambridge: Cambridge University Press.

Readings, B. (1997). *The University in Ruins.* Cambridge, MA: Harvard University Press.

Rees, H. (1994). Legitimation, Higher Education and the Postcolonial State in a Comparative Study of India and Kenya. *Comparative Education, 30*(3), 193–204.

Sahlins, M. (1999). What is Anthropological Enlightenment? Some Lessons of the Twentieth Century. *Annual Review of Anthropology, 28*, i–xxiii.

Saigol, R. (2003). *Becoming a Modern Nation: Educational Discourse in the Early Years of Ayub Khan.* Islamabad: Council of Social Sciences.

Schofer, E. and Meyer, J.W. (2005). Worldwide Expansion of Higher Education in the 20th Century. *American Sociological Review, 70*, 898–920.

TFHES (2000). Higher Education in Developing Countries: Peril and Promise. Washington, D.C.: World Bank.

TFIHE (2002). Challenges and Opportunities: Report of the Task Force on Improvement of Higher Education in Pakistan. Islamabad.

Thomas, G.M. (2009). World Polity, World Culture, World Society. *International Political Sociology, 3*(1), 115–119.

Young, R.J.C. (1996). The Idea of a Chrestomathic University *Torn Halves: Political Conflict in Literary and Cultural Theory* (pp. 290–351): Manchester University Press.

10 Converging national with stakeholder interests

Establishing a national bioethics committee in Finland

Jukka Syväterä and Pertti Alasuutari

Introduction

Expert policy advice continues its expansion worldwide and across all possible policy fields. Over the last few decades, the proliferation of all kinds of expert panels, councils, committees, and advisory boards has been dramatic. The question to be explained is why policy solutions of this particular type, taking the form of an advisory board, diffuse so efficiently throughout the world.

National bioethics committees (NBCs) can be considered to supply a specific type of expert policy advice (Bogner and Menz, 2010). Among the purposes of these bodies is to give policy advice concerning health care, biomedical advances, and biotechnology, and to stimulate public discussion on these issues (Dodds and Thomson, 2006; Fuchs, 2005; Jasanoff, 2007). Earlier research has offered mainly two kinds of explanations for the upsurge of NBCs. First, the functional role of NBCs in responding to the challenges that modern societies confront due to developments in life sciences has been pointed out (Gottweis, 2008; Kelly, 2003; Salter and Jones, 2005; Salter and Salter, 2007). Second, it is argued that NBCs are devices mainly used for legitimating political decisions in the governance of health care and to protect biomedical sciences from closer scrutiny (Galloux et al., 2002, p. 146; Rose, 2007, p. 256).

NBCs have emerged as a global phenomenon. Practically all developed countries have established such a body within a rather short time frame. Most of them were set up during a period of less than 15 years: as many as 27 OECD member states founded a NBC between 1988 and 2002. Later, an increasing number of developing countries have founded such bodies.

However, the functional explanations briefly described above are insufficient in explaining all the cases. In an earlier study (Syväterä and Alasuutari, 2013) on establishing the Finnish version of the NBC, the National Advisory Board on Health Care Ethics (ETENE), we have argued that these explanations are insufficient in explaining the phenomenon in its whole global magnitude. In Finland, for example, the NBC was not established as a response to preceding public opposition towards biotechnology or to new medical technologies. There had been no remarkable conflicts or public discussion around these issues, since medical science (and science in general) has always been highly trusted by the public. Thus the global proliferation of NBCs within such a short period of time, without any external coercion to act uniformly, could actually be presented as a typical example of the explanatory power of world polity theory (Meyer, 2009; Meyer, Boli, Thomas, and Ramirez, 1997). World polity theory points out that the standardization of institutional structures and the convergence of policies is a result of the tendency of nation-states to enact global models spreading throughout the world, and argues that such isomorphic behavior is caused by emulation. Within this theory, nation-states and other individual or institutional actors are viewed as conformists who are culturally tamed by rationalistic world culture (Meyer, 2004).

However, in our earlier study we pointed out that policy-makers were motivated to adopt the worldwide model by world cultural ideas about the national interest and modernization. In other words, within the national context, establishing a bioethics committee was not justified by simply following the example of other countries, but rather by evoking the nation as a self-evident imagined community and by serving the common good. The argument that the national interest required the advisory body was justified by saying that founding such bodies is part of modernization and that failing to establish it would mean that the nation was "lagging behind" other countries.

Thus, in our previous research we showed how instituting the bioethics committee was seen as a "rational" decision to make when viewed from the viewpoint of the national interest. That does not, however, provide a sufficient explanation for the fact that the reform was carried through by a change in the law without any real opposition during the parliamentary process. Although decisions made in national politics are always justified by the national interest, and although most politicians defend their claims as being in the interest of the whole nation, this does not mean that politicians would not also defend their group or stakeholder interests. Besides, had the policy-makers come to the conclusion that no bioethics advisory body is needed in Finland, this would have also been justified by the national interest. Considering the outcome, the decision-makers had to see benefits in establishing the bioethics committee from the viewpoint of their interests.

Although the proposal to establish the NBC in Finland met no opposition, it would be mistaken to suppose that it did not trigger a political struggle. Political battles are not necessarily about taking sides for or against a given reform. Rather, a struggle may also take place about the ways in which the reform can be articulated with different interests and ideas. Thus the acceptance of a reform has to be explained by its potential advantages for the different stakeholders that form the domestic political field (Bourdieu, 1991; Wacquant, 2004). For a law to be passed, enough decision-makers need to consider it potentially advantageous for their interests or from the viewpoint of the ideals they promote, or at least they need to regard opposing it as more harmful. In the domestic field battle (as outlined in the introduction to this volume), different parties and stakeholders will thus try to influence the form the new law will assume so that it best suits their views.

By talking about individual or group views or interests as decisive in determining whether a political decision such as adopting a global model is made within local politics, we do not imply that actors can be reduced to their objective interests stemming from, say, class positions. Nor do we imply that decision-making comprises a battle, the outcome of which can be predicted by a calculus that takes into account clashing interests and forces behind them, as rational choice theory would have it. Rather, constructing groups with which to identify and articulating their "objective" interests is also part of the rhetoric of political battles (Alasuutari, 2004, pp. 121–139). Some of the stakeholder groups involved are older and more organized than others. In any case, as also mentioned in the introduction to this book, the ideas of different parties or stakeholder groups typically have a transnational origin and character as part of world culture. Yet any claim made in the political field can be seen both as a means to defend a group's predefined interests and as a move to define the group in question as a community with shared interests. Thus, in this chapter we focus on a better understanding of how national interests and stakeholder interests were reconciled when the NBC was established in Finland by analyzing how the interests of different actors were articulated in the parliamentary process.

The case study

The domestication of transnational models always entails potential changes in established practices and relative positions between different actors in the national political field. Hence it is typical that various local groups of actors view it either as a threat or as an opportunity for their position. In the case of establishing the NBC in Finland, the reform itself was not opposed by anyone participating in the discussion. On the contrary, it was justified on many different grounds. It was, for instance, seen as a necessary aid in decision-making concerning the allocation of resources to public health care, in solving problems related to certain methods of medical treatment and those created by new medical technology, in ensuring the fairness of the health care system, in helping medical and nursing staff with ethical guidelines, and in generating discussions on ethics in society. Over and above these and other purposes invented on the way, the government justified the reform using the language of modernization: establishing the NBC was seen as a necessary part of the development of advanced societies (Syväterä and Alasuutari, 2013). Yet a political field battle was triggered by the suggestion to establish the NBC.

From the viewpoint of domestication it can be expected that the taming of an exogenous model (like the NBC), or idea (for example, the idea of ethical policy advice), triggers a field battle in which actors aim to protect or strengthen their positions depending on whether they assume the reform to be a threat or an opportunity (Alasuutari, 2013). Local field battles actually have an important role in the process in which global trends are domesticated. Exogenous models are used as ammunition in the domestic power games in which different groups of actors do their best to turn the suggested reforms into justifications for their own aspirations. In this way the global origins of a model are often forgotten, since the process of reform is viewed as a domestic political struggle.

The empirical analysis presented in this chapter focuses on the parliamentary discussion and relevant government documents related to the reform by which ETENE was established in 1998. The data consists of 23 policy documents and 82 speeches given by Members of Parliament (MPs). All the addresses are comments on the Government Bill (1998) proposing that Parliament add a decree to the existing Law on the Rights of the Patient. We also analyze the draft and the final versions of the Government Bill, reports of parliamentary committees, and expert statements commenting on or proposing revisions to the draft Bill.

Our methodological orientation can be described as discursive policy analysis (e.g. Howarth and Torfing, 2005). This means that we pay attention to the discursive practices through which policies are made and political struggles are organized. In practice we focus on the ways in which participants of the analyzed discussion articulate the reform in question with their interests and aspirations. Our analysis aims to tease out different interest-based rationales underlying the arguments by which the reform is justified by discussants.

The results of the analysis are presented in the following two sections. First we focus on highlighting the speakers' interests by analyzing whom or what groups they suggest to be members of the future advisory body and how these demands are justified. After that we focus on revealing the underlying stakeholder interests by analyzing how the speakers propose to define the tasks of the committee in relation to the roles and expertise of existing institutions and professions. Speaking on behalf of those stakeholders, related to their constituency as MPs, the speakers are hence engaged in defending or strengthening their positions in the new circumstances.

The struggle over representation

Arguing which kind of individuals or groups should have a seat in the advisory body on bioethics was one of the two ways in which actors articulated their interests in the process. Such articulation, through the idea of representation, was already an essential part of the draft Government Bill, which set the agenda for the discussion. The composition and qualifications expected of the members are described as follows:

> The members have to be persons who are well versed in the ethical questions of health care. They have to represent the point of view of the users and organizers of health services, the professionals of health care, legal science, health science and the ethical study concerning the human being and the society. *In the choice of the members who represent the users of services, different cultural and convictional factors and age structure of the population have to be taken into consideration.* At least four members of the consultative committee are nominated from the members of the parliament.
>
> (Government Bill, 1998, emphasis added)[1]

The Government Bill emphasizes diversity in the membership structure. Most of the members are to be experts in different fields, but stakeholder groups and different views amongst citizens are also to be taken into account. As the first sentence of the above quote illustrates, all members are expected to possess some kind of *ethical expertise* in addition to expertise derived either from individuals' professional or disciplinary background.

While the discussants shared the view that there is a need for a body responsible for giving "ethical policy advice," the meaning of "ethical policy advice" and "ethical expertise" was left open.[2] The vagueness of the idea of ethical expertise created a space for a political field battle. In this particular case it meant that the MPs taking part in the discussion spoke on behalf of different groups of people constructed as essential stakeholder groups regarding bioethics and bioethical expertise. On that basis the MPs and experts argued about what groups should have a representative on the committee. In the discussion, physicians, nurses, "service users" (such as disabled people) and those representing religious convictions are among these groups. Each speaker makes an effort to convince the audience (including decision-makers and citizens) that the strong position of a given group on the advisory body is a condition for the legitimacy of its expertise.

Instituting a national committee on bioethics naturally touches on the work and social standing of physicians and nurses. Thus it is not surprising that the position of these health care professions was one of the points around which the struggle was organized. While it was taken for granted by all sides that the physicians would be represented in the body, there was much more uncertainty about the position of nurses and the relation of nursing ethics to medical ethics. Some discussants related the dispute about the committee members' backgrounds to the nurses' fight for professional appreciation. Some MPs who rose to defend the social standing of the nurses demanded that a sub-committee on nursing ethics should be formed as a part of ETENE, in addition to the Sub-Committee on Medical Research,[3] suggested by the Government Bill:

> A stand on the order of importance of [medical] research and nursing is taken here [in the Government Bill] ... It is proposed that a sub-committee on medical research is established ... this means being on the side of medicine, and I do not consider it necessary because I see that the sub-committee on nursing ethics is important as well.
>
> (Parliament of Finland (PoF), 1998: MP Rask, Social Democratic Party)

Thus the demand to include representatives of nurses to the advisory body is justified by framing the issue as a question about the proper relation between nursing ethics and medical ethics. In the previous and other addresses demanding the founding of a sub-committee on nursing ethics alongside the sub-committee on medical research, it is argued that it would be important to balance the influence of the medical authority of doctors by creating an equivalent body of nursing ethics where nurses and an understanding of nursing ethics would be represented. This is justified by stating that nurses confront ethical issues on a regular basis in their everyday working practices. In the background is the idea that different kinds of ethical expertise are needed in tackling different issues. The recommendation to establish a sub-committee on nursing ethics was also made in a statement by the Hospital District of Central Finland (1998), which states that more attention should be given to urgent ethical issues faced in everyday health care. Instead of focusing mainly on the ethics of medical research, it expresses the hope that national guidance would be given to the current ethical challenges of health care. However, the idea of establishing a sub-committee on nursing ethics was ultimately rejected in the parliamentary proceedings, a decision justified mainly by the argument that taking the ethics of care into account is to be the duty of ETENE as a whole and thus a specific sub-committee would be unnecessary.

The idea hinted at in the draft version of the Government Bill (1998), according to which clients should have representatives, was also utilized in the law-making process. The sentence in question says that "in the choice of the members who represent the users of services, different cultural and convictional factors … have to be taken into consideration." That sentence, which was omitted from the accepted decree, opened up the possibility of speculating on and making claims about how "the users of healthcare" should be represented, and how different convictions and cultural backgrounds should be taken into account in the criteria applied for appointing committee members.

Hence, the National Council on Disability presented the stance that representatives of users of health care should be persons who are actual users, such as the disabled themselves. The Council demanded that the users should be represented equally with the health care profession:

> It is desirable that the representatives of users of services are the users of services themselves. It is important that the disabled people have sufficient representation in the advisory board because manifold ethical questions in the public health care are connected with disability … I indeed propose that establishing a sub-committee within the advisory board is considered. This sub-committee could consist of the representatives of disabled and the other users of services.
>
> (National Council for Disability, 1998)

The suggestion to establish a sub-committee for users of health care was not well received by medical experts. The chair of the National Council on Disability expressed disappointment about it, anticipating that the suggestion would not be taken up: "The professionals seldom want to include patients or customers in real interaction" (Könkkölä, 1998).

Another claim made in the discussion was that the four members of ETENE who are also MPs should represent the users of health care on the advisory body. This suggestion was challenged in the following address:

> There [in the Parliament] are also many kinds of ethical expertise here as it has already been seen in this discussion but if this kind of playful continuation is allowed, it would seem that certain members of Parliament, Kokkonen and Kautto, have already reserved seats for themselves on this advisory board ... but I would consider the representativeness of research on values, of the religious viewpoint and of Christian values, as much more important than that politicians are sharing these seats among themselves.
>
> (PoF, 1998: MP Alaranta, Centre Party)

The same MP justifies his opinion by referring to public opinion or world views that he believes to be widely shared within the Finnish population:

> From us, the Finns, the majority surely believes that in these matters of life and death, it is God who is the lord of life and death; not a doctor, not a cleric, nor the police nor any human being but the power which is above all of us. This is a point of view that should also be connected some way to this discussion.
>
> (PoF, 1998: MP Alaranta, Centre Party)

The inclusion of religious viewpoints was taken up when MPs discussed who would represent the users of health care on ETENE. Thus there was similar ambiguity concerning both questions: who are the representatives of health care users, and how broadly should the views of the public be included in the body? Some MPs expressed the hope that ETENE could bring religion back into politics. These MPs referred to the examples of other countries, and then stated that that in Finland the religious viewpoints are "for some strange reason" marginalized from political discussion:

> For some strange reason, it is extremely difficult for us in Finland to use the word "religious," for example. Yes, I am surprised about that. In my opinion, this could be put right, and in this case it is desirable that there are people representing religious and philosophical views on the advisory board.
>
> (PoF, 1998: MP Vehkaoja, Social Democratic Party)

In spite of the fact that several addresses aspired to include the religious viewpoint, it is not visible in the revisions to the Government Bill. The field battle over including or excluding religious viewpoints remained one-sided, in that in the parliamentary discussion nobody was explicitly against it. Those who were against the inclusion of religious viewpoints simply did not comment on the issue. Yet, the viewpoint remained excluded. The quote above also illustrates a demand for the inclusion of philosophical views, or of experts who have formal education in philosophy. Yet this issue too did not receive much more attention in the discussion, and philosophers were not given any special position on the Finnish version of the NBC.[4]

In conclusion, the arguments made for reserving quotas for particular groups or public views to be represented on ETENE were not successful. Instead, the MPs ended up concluding that the general public, with its different views on ethical issues, is sufficiently or best represented by MPs themselves. In that sense the power of deciding about these "lay" members of the advisory board was handed over to the political parties and to the parliament. That is, instead of instituting particular stakeholders groups regarding bioethics, the parties retained their role as general stakeholders.

When considering expertise and authority in bioethical issues, medical doctors as a group were considered the most significant candidate. This is surprising in light of the fact that medical practice forms a major part of the field that the prospective advisory body was to monitor. Although critical voices considering the role of the medical profession in the committee were also heard, relatively few addresses constructed the prospective ETENE as a kind of jury in which ordinary sensible citizens reflect on what is right or wrong, thus controlling the ethics of medical doctors. Rather, many addresses expressed the wish that ETENE could help citizens learn how to discuss difficult issues regarding the ethics of health care. One medical doctor, an "elder" in the profession, was mentioned as a potential candidate for the chair of ETENE:

> It came to my mind that archiatre[5] Risto Pelkonen has guided public discussion clearly on many occasions in such a way that it has been possible to understand it easily. Obviously, we would need this kind of public discussion and guiding of the discussion in the questions connected to health care.
>
> (PoF, 1998: MP Väistö, Centre Party)

As a whole, the reform clearly did not pose a threat to the established institutional order of health care. The discussion reproduced a hierarchical order in which politicians and expert knowledge were elevated above the views of the public. The demands for the inclusion of religious viewpoints or for a symmetrical representation for the users of health care in relation to representatives of science-based expertise remained marginalized. It is hence striking that even the discussants taking a stand on behalf of the marginalized viewpoints supported the reform. It is possible that they anticipated that the advisory body might serve as a medium for bringing forward their views in the future.

The role of key professions and institutions

Participants' interests in the discussion on instituting ETENE can also be seen in the way the speakers proposed to define the tasks of the committee in relation to the roles and expertise of key institutions and professions. Foreclosing what they deemed the harmful definitions of the position of an institution or profession and instead promoting beneficial ones, the actors in question advanced their views or interests. In this respect the key stakeholders, especially the medical profession, aimed to make their voices heard. In addition, several participants voiced their views on how to define the role of the advisory body in relation to politics, particularly economic policy.

When debating the role of the advisory body in relation to key stakeholder groups, medical science attracted much attention. While its central position was often taken for granted in the discussion, the ethical expertise of physicians was called into question by some MPs:

> I think it is extremely important that these ethics advisory boards will not be mere playgrounds of the medical doctors. I respect doctors, thanks to their professional skills, but for example in these ethical questions, in profound moral matters, the profession has not necessarily trained doctors to this kind of discussion that is now going on here and what above all is needed.
>
> (PoF, 1998: MP Kekkonen, Social Democratic Party)

Although acknowledging the physicians' expertise regarding their professional skills, the speaker points out that medical doctors are not trained to be experts in ethical questions. On this basis he demands that other kind of expertise—in other words, expertise in ethics—is also needed on ETENE. Although the address is critical of a large representation of medical science on the advisory body, it does not entirely denounce the representation of medical doctors.

For medical doctors and the Finnish Medical Association (FMA), on the other hand, ensuring a wide representation of medical science on the committee was the main objective. In defending the profession's significant role on the new advisory body, the FMA promoted the view that experts from many special fields of medicine have to be represented. In its statement concerning the draft of the Government Bill, the association does not openly argue that medical doctors are also experts on ethical questions, but stresses that a wide range of medical expertise is needed on the committee, complemented with lay members with experience in ethical questions.

> A wide range of medical expertise has to be secured in the composition ... Concerning the members it is stated [in the draft of the Government Bill] that they have to be experts or laymen who are interested in ethical questions. According to the view of the Finnish Medical Association, the proportion of experts on the advisory board must be guaranteed, and laymen cannot replace experts. Naturally, the presence of both is desirable. It is also important that when members are chosen, a sufficient number will be persons who have worked already earlier with ethical questions.
>
> (FMA, 1998)

By establishing a dichotomy between experts and laymen, in which the epithet "expert" refers only to medical experts, the statement excludes the possibility of talking about the expertise of those who operate in other fields such as ethics. It is implied that ethics is an area where there can be no expertise, only personal interest and prior experience. Hence the FMA statement constructs medical doctors as the only group of experts, whose wide representation they deem necessary, but they also gracefully welcome laymen interested in ethical questions.

In the parliamentary discussion, the medical profession's right to wide representation was justified also by the claim that the profession has acquired much ethical expertise and that especially Finnish physicians are responsible in their professional approach. For example, an MP who was active in promoting the founding of an NBC in Finland years before the Government Bill, says:

> In my opinion, we can give quite a big credit to the Finnish Medical Association, the medical profession and also to the pharmaceutical industry. Because the Finnish pharmaceutical industry has, broadly speaking, been the first on the globe to make their own ethical rules ... Of course in some small workshops something unethical might be going on, but when it comes to the pharmaceutical side, it seems that the matters are under control.
>
> (PoF, 1998: MP Kokkonen, National Coalition Party)

In contrast with the idea that the new committee's central task is to oversee the ethics of the pharmaceutical industry or the medical profession, the statement makes it clear that the purpose of the new body is not meant to act "against" those stakeholders. Rather, the address praises the pharmaceutical industry for its early recognition of ethical issues.

The same line of argumentation can be found in the FMA's statement on the draft of the Government Bill. To demonstrate that the medical profession has solid experience and expertise in coming to terms with ethical questions, the statement lists its own bodies, principles, and declarations and those of the World Medical Association. Commenting on the claim made in the Bill that there is no national body in Finland that focuses on ethical matters in the field of medical science and health care, the FMA mentions its own ethics committee as an already existing body. However, the association endorses the instituting of the NBC in Finland in order to get other groups than the medical profession to engage themselves in a discussion of ethics. Instead of presenting the reform as a threat, the association's statement thus presents the view that establishing ETENE is an opportunity to strengthen the legitimacy of the medical profession and a means to influence future policy-making concerning health care and medical practices. By this kind of framing the FMA preempts the view that the purpose of establishing the NBC is to control the medical profession.

In addition the new advisory board on bioethics might be either a threat to or an opportunity for the medical profession, the pharmaceutical industry, and others responsible for political or administrative decisions related to ethics. It is no surprise, then, that the relation of this new subfield to the established ways of policy-making became an issue in the law-making process. For instance, the statement of the Hospital District of Uusimaa concerning the draft of the Government Bill (Hospital District of Uusimaa, 1998) states that if politicians are incapable of establishing clear guidelines for prioritization within public health care then the new advisory body could help in this task. The politicians, for their part, avoided defining any clear order of prioritization, although in the parliamentary discussion several MPs stressed that ethics should be discussed within economic realities. One MP, for instance, presented the view that ethics would be an easy matter if there weren't any economic constraints: "A wide mutual understanding is found in our midst about these ethical viewpoints, but unfortunately the financial matters lag behind" (PoF 1998, MP Vihriälä, Centre Party). Another MP presented a contrary view of the relation between the economy and ethics, underlining the incongruity of economic and ethical questions:

> The statement talks about the importance of the economy and about the fact that it must be taken into consideration. It sounds very good but, in my opinion, it is not relevant due to the fact that this advisory board deals with ethical questions. One cannot think that when we now are in a bad situation financially, we have different ethical norms. When the economy improves, it will make little difference to our ethical view. Ethical opinions do not change in this way ... ethical questions are ethical questions. They must be above economic questions.
>
> (PoF, 1998: MP Rask, Social Democratic Party)

These two views on the relation between ethics and the economy imply different ideas about the tasks of the NBC. While the statement of the Hospital District of Uusimaa and the address of MP Vihriälä promote the idea that the NBC could help policy-makers or administrators in making tough decisions of prioritization in changing economic conditions, or in making those decisions for them, the address of Rask maintains that ethics and the economy must be kept separate. In that sense it implies that the task of the NBC would be to define general ethical guidelines or universal rights.

As the prospective body was planned to consist mainly of specialized experts, the view that the reform might contribute to depoliticizing political issues haunted the discussion. The Minister of Social Affairs responded to such presuppositions by arguing that the political dimension should not be sidelined. In that way she justified the proposal in the draft of the Government Bill to include four MPs in the membership:

> When we nominate the members to the advisory board on healthcare ethics, there must also be experts other than those in healthcare and medicine. There must be a strong political dimension. Our politicians must raise these matters in debate, define policies and guide the public discussion. Therefore it is stated in the decree that also four members of the Parliament are to be nominated for the ethical advisory body. The intention is to get a political dimension included that way. I myself consider it extremely important that

different fields will be represented on the advisory body, for example theologians, lawyers, etc. It must be as broad-based as possible because of the complexity of these problems.

(PoF, 1998: Minister of Social Affairs and Health Huttu-Juntunen,
Left Alliance)

Thus the consensus formed in the law-making process had elements that appealed to several viewpoints and interests. The expertise of the medical profession was acknowledged and medical doctors' heavy representation was accepted, but experience and expertise in ethics was also acknowledged. Political control over the new body was also guaranteed by securing a quota for MPs.

For the legitimacy of ethical policy advice, it thus seemed to be vital that the advisory body be independent enough of the political and administrative system to be seen as capable of objectivity in its advice. On the other hand, it was in the interest of decision-makers that the advisory body be sufficiently under political control, because it would be, in the end, a tool meant to help in legislation as well as in creating and guiding public discussion. It is important to note that establishing ETENE did not replace any existing structures of policy-making. Instead, it added one new element to policy-making in health care. Thus, from the viewpoint of those who participated in the discussion, the reform did not constitute much threat to existing hierarchies or actor positions. Another reason the reform was not opposed even when it was seen as a potential threat for one's interests is the fact that the model of NBC embraces many aspects of what is taken as virtuous in the modern world culture (see Boli, 2006): rational progress, greater participation for citizens and the protection of humanity and civil rights, for example. Taking a stand against such a reform would not look good and hence might actually work against one's interests. Hence the safer way to avoid expected problems is to strive for a definition of a reform that does not conflict with stakeholder interests in the question.

Discussion

In this chapter we addressed the puzzle as to how it was possible that the proposal to institute a bioethics committee in Finland was accepted in the Parliament without any opposing arguments presented, although it was generally agreed that there had been no such public controversies over bioethical questions that such an institution would reconcile. In that sense the Finnish example shows that the typical functional explanations (e.g. Galloux et al., 2002; Gottweis, 2008; Kelly, 2003; Salter and Salter, 2007) are not sufficient in all cases. In an earlier article dealing with the same question (Syväterä and Alasuutari, 2013) we pointed out that the Finnish case fits better in the remit of world society theory, which stresses emulation as the reason why nation-states enact global models. However, we also showed that for the actors involved, the rationale was not simply to imitate, but rather to act in the interest of the nation. In this chapter we have pursued actors' views and interests further by asking how the politically correct motive of the national interest also converged with their stakeholder interests, making it possible for the law to be passed without opposition.

The results of the analysis show how the struggle over the advisory body was entangled with the interests of different groups. These could be seen for instance in the discussion on the composition of the future body. The participants made suggestions about several groups that should be represented. The representation of the medical profession was taken for granted, although there was controversy about how strong their position should be. The positions of other groups such as nurses, users of health care, and those representing religious views were much more contested. In any case, the reform acquired much of its legitimacy from the way it was defined in the Government Bill, as a body in which many different stakeholders are included.

Stakeholder interests could also be seen in the proposals about the role of key professions and institutions in the future bioethics committee. This discussion dealt particularly with the role and expertise of the medical profession and the pharmaceutical industry in ethical issues on the one hand, and the relation of bioethical advisory committee to political decision-making on the other. The spokespersons of the medical doctors defended their positions by appealing to science and by obscuring the difference between scientific and ethical expertise. In the discussion of the relationship between ethics and politics, some participants greeted with delight the possibility that the bioethics committee would make difficult decisions about prioritization for politicians and civil servants, whereas a majority of the MPs wanted to retain political control over the advisory body.

In all, revisions made to the original draft of the Government Bill as a consequence of the law-making process were marginal. ETENE was not meant to replace any earlier bodies or practices, and thus it was not a direct threat to any group or institution. Rather it was seen as an opportunity for pursuing different interests. Several interest groups aimed to define the tasks of the bioethics committee so that it would support their interests and objectives in the best possible way. Although many of these objectives were not officially recorded as the aims or tasks of ETENE, the discussion served as a platform for articulating them. At least it was possible for different groups to consider ETENE as a way to advance their interests or to become a forum in which to get publicity for their ambitions. It was also justified by many virtues such as rationality, citizens' participation, and human rights, cherished in world culture (see Boli, 2006), which is why taking a stand against such a reform was probably seen as risky, and as something that might work against one's interests. Hence a safer way to avoid potential problems was to influence the definition of the reform in such a manner that it would not contradict an actor's interests in the question.

We can conclude that to understand how transnational models are enacted in national policy-making, local power games and the interest-based rationales of local actors should not be dismissed. What might look like unthinking conformity from the viewpoint of world polity theory (Meyer, 2004) is actually often, we argue, an outcome of a political field battle in which domestic actors articulate a transnational idea or model with prevailing conceptions concerning the common good and the national interest. The participants' success in a political field battle depends on their ability to present their stakeholder interests *as* the national interest.

The enacting of NBCs has not been such a consensual process everywhere as it was in Finland. In Austria, for example, the founding of the Austrian Bioethics Commission in 2001 instantly triggered a heated political debate (Bogner and Menz, 2005, pp. 25–26). Critics of the commission criticized it for being a purely expert body instead of engaging the public in decision-making. The members of the Commission were chosen on the grounds of their specialized knowledge (that was the criterion officially stated), but critics pointed to a lack of transparency in the process through which the members were nominated. The debate culminated soon in the founding of a "counter-commission" by organizations of the disabled. Although the political struggle was milder in Finland, it is interesting to note that the debate was organized around a similar set of issues in both countries: how "ethical expertise" should be defined, who should be represented on the advisory body, the nature of proper ethical expertise, and the relation between expert knowledge and the people affected by political decisions. Obviously, ethics is a field in which the definition of expertise is even more contested than, for instance, in the case of scientific advisory bodies (see Bijker, Bal, and Hendriks, 2009; Jasanoff, 1994). While the authority of scientific advisors is fundamentally epistemic, it is commonly understood—especially in the context of pluralistic democracies—that it is questionable to insist that one's better knowledge could make one's ethical standpoint more viable than that of those who possess less knowledge of the substance in question. The very idea that there could be expertise in ethical matters is a controversial issue (e.g. Bogner and Menz, 2005; Varelius, 2008). The case analyzed in this chapter shows that the struggles around the construction of expertise are an important part of the domestication of policy models, especially when new actor positions (like that of ethical policy advisor) are created. The case discussed in this chapter also exemplifies how ideas or models domesticated by nation-states already include the discourses that may be used to oppose or demand a reformulation of the model. Political field battles contribute to the synchronization of political discourses and upcoming struggles between different nation-states. Emerging local struggles triggered by global trends are thus already framed by global scripts.

We suggest that this example also contributes to explaining more generally why committee-type policy solutions—e.g. advisory boards and expert panels—proliferate and spread so successfully everywhere in the world. One aspect is the relation of advisory bodies to already existing institutionalized hierarchical structures. An advisory board is a rather light organizational form, and normally it does not replace anything that already exists within the institutional structure. In other words, it only adds a new element to the organizational structure of policy-making without interfering with established practices or hierarchical positions between actors. Of course this does not need to mean that establishing bodies of this kind would not have any real influence on policy-making. Yet, founding such a body does not appear to threaten anyone's position directly. The second aspect is that advisory bodies are seen as easy responses to diverse problems. They do not usually use formal power but produce opinions and suggestions that can be used and interpreted by decision makers in various ways. Thus, in the political imagination of the actual users of formal power, they serve as a rich resource for legitimation that can be tapped when a political situation calls for additional support in making decisions on difficult matters.

Notes

1 The emphasized sentence in the quotation was cut out of the final version. The accepted decree (Statutes of Finland, 1998) restricts the number of members to 20, including the chair and the vice chair. The members are to be nominated by the Council of State for four years at a time. Here and throughout, the translations from Finnish to English are our own.
2 The Government Bill does not elaborate where the intended ethical expertise is to come from. Formal training in ethics is not required from all the members. Rather, it is thought that suitable ethical expertise is derived from inclination and personal experience.
3 The role of the Sub-Committee on Medical Research is not so much in dispensing national policy advice, but principally in issuing ethics reviews on clinical drug trials, and supporting and coordinating the activities of local-level ethics committees (National Committee on Medical Research Ethics, 2011). The members are mostly experts from the fields of medical science (such as pharmaceutical research, genetics and medical genetics, and epidemiology) but also include people with expertise on law and ethics acquired by formal training. In addition, at least one member represents the interests of patients.
4 It was only afterwards that this decision led to a debate in which the outcome has been both questioned and defended (e.g. Rydman, 2002; Takala, 2002).
5 Archiatre is the honorary title always given to one medical doctor who serves as the elder of the profession. The title stems from French, and originally it depicted "doctor to the King."

References

Alasuutari, P. (2004). *Social Theory and Human Reality*. London: Sage.
Alasuutari, P. (2013). Spreading global models and enhancing banal localism: The case of local government cultural policy development. *International Journal of Cultural Policy, 19*(1), 103–119.
Bijker, W.E., Bal, R., and Hendriks, R. (2009). *The Paradox of Scientific Authority. The Role of Scientific Advice in Democracies*. London: MIT Press.
Bogner, A. and Menz, W. (2005). Bioethical controversies and policy advice: The production of ethical expertise and its role in the substantion of political decision-making. In S. Maasen and P. Weingart (eds), *Democratization of Expertise? Exploring Novel Forms of Scientific Advice in Political Decision-Making* (pp. 21–40). New York: Springer.
Bogner, A. and Menz, W. (2010). How politics deals with expert dissent: the case of ethics councils. *Science, Technology and Human Values, 35*(6), pp. 888–914.
Boli, J. (2006). The rationalization of virtue and virtuosity in world society. In M.-L. Djelic and K. Sahlin-Andersson (eds), *Transanational governance. Institutional dynamics of regulation* (pp. 95–118). Cambridge: Cambridge University Press.

Bourdieu, P. (1991). Political Representation: Elements for a theory of the Political Field. In J.B. Thompson (ed.), *Language and Symbolic Power* (pp. 171–202). Cambridge: Polity Press.

Dodds, S. and Thomson, C. (2006). Bioethics and democracy: Compteing roles of national bioethics organizations. *Bioethics, 20*(6), 326–338.

FMA (Finnish Medical Association) (1998). Statement of Finnish Medical Association on the Government Bill to Parliament on adding a decree to Law on the Rights of the Patient. Unpublished letter included in the record of Social Affairs and Health Committee (StV:n ptk 19/1998).

Fuchs, M. (2005). *National Ethics Councils: Their Backgrounds, Functions and Modes of Operation Compared*. Berlin: Nationaler Ethikrat.

Galloux, J.-C., Mortensen, A.T., De Cheveigné, S., Allansdottir, A., Chatjouli, A., and Sakellaris, G. (2002). The institutions of bioethics. In M.W. Bauer and G. Gaskell (eds), *Biotechnology. The Making of Global Controversy* (pp. 129–148). Cambridge: Cambridge University Press.

Gottweis, H. (2008). Participation and the new governance of life. *BioSocieties, 3*(3), 265–286.

Government Bill (1998). *HE 19/989*, Hallituksen esitys Eduskunnalle laiksi potilaan asemasta ja oikeuksista [Government bill to Parliament on adding a decree to Law on the rights of the patient]. Retrieved 3 February 2013 from http://217.71.145.20/TRIPviewer/show.asp?tunniste=HE+19/1998&base=erhe&palvelin=www.eduskunta.fi&f=WP.

Hospital District of Central Finland (1998). Statement of Hospital District of Central Finland on the Government Bill to Parliament on adding a decree to Law on the Rights of the Patient. Unpublished letter included in the record of Social Affairs and Health Committee (StV:n ptk 19/1998).

Hospital District of Uusimaa (1998). Statement of Hospital District of Uusimaa on the Government Bill to Parliament on adding a decree to Law on the Rights of the Patient. Unpublished letter included in the record of Social Affairs and Health Committee (StV:n ptk 19/1998).

Howarth, D. and Torfing, J. (eds) (2005). *Discourse Theory in European Politics: Identity, Policy and Governance*: Basingstoke: Palgrave Macmillan.

Jasanoff, S. (1994). *The Fifth Branch: Science Advisers as Policy-makers*. Cambridge, MA: Harvard University Press.

Jasanoff, S. (2007). *Designs on Nature: Science and Democracy in Europe and the United States*. Princeton, NJ: Princeton University Press.

Kelly, S.E. (2003). Public Bioethics and Publics: Consensus, Boundaries, and Participation in Biomedical Science Policy. *Science, Technology and Human Values, 28*(3), 339–364.

Könkkölä, K. (1998). *Letter to Social Affairs and Health Committee*. Unpublished letter included in the record of Social Affairs and Health Committee (StV:n ptk 19/1998).

Meyer, J.W. (2004). The Nation as Babbitt: How Countries Conform. *Contexts, 3*(3), 42–47.

Meyer, J.W. (2009). Reflections: institutional theory and world society. In G. Krücken and G.S. Drori (eds), *World Society: the Writings of John W. Meyer* (pp. 36–63). Oxford: Oxford University Press.

Meyer, J.W., Boli, J., Thomas, G.M., and Ramirez, F.O. (1997). World Society and the Nation-State. *American Journal of Sociology, 103*(1), 144–181.

National Committee on Medical Research Ethics (2011). Operating procedures of the National Committee on Medical Research Ethics (TUKIJA) Retrieved 20 December

2012 from: www.tukija.fi/c/document_library/get_file?folderId=68389&name=DLFE-1603.pdf.

National Council on Disability (1998). The statement of National Council on Disability on the Government Bill to Parliament on adding a decree to Law on the Rights of the Patient.

PoF (Parliament of Finland) (1998). *Records of parliamentary proceedings on Government Bill 19/1998 on adding a decree to the Law on the Rights of the Patient*. Retrieved 3 February 2013 from www.eduskunta.fi/valtiopaivaasiat/he+19/998.

Rose, N. (2007). *The Politics of Life Itself. Biomedicine, Power, and Subjectivity in the Twenty-First Century*. Princeton, NJ: Princeton University Press.

Rydman, J. (2002). Etiikka ei kuulu muille kuin filosofeille? *Tieteessä tapahtuu, 21*(1), pp. 48–49.

Salter, B. and Jones, M. (2005). Biobanks and Bioethics: The Politics of Legitimation. *Journal of European Public Policy, 12*(4), 710–732.

Salter, B. and Salter, C. (2007). Bioethics and Global Moral Economy. The Cultural Politics of Human Embryonic Stem Cell Science. *Science, Technology & Human Values, 32*(5), 544–581.

Statutes of Finland (1998). *Asetus valtakunnallisesta terveydenhuollon eettisestä neuvottelukunnasta* [Decree on the national advisory board on health care] (494/1998).

Syväterä, J. and Alasuutari, P. (2013). Conforming to Global Policy Trends: Legitimating Narratives in the Case of Ethical Policy Advice. *Critical Policy Studies, 7*(1), 37–52.

Takala, T. (2002). Kuka päättää etiikasta? Eikö sitä saa kysyä? *Tieteessä tapahtuu, 21*(1), p. 58.

Wacquant, L. (2004). Pointers on Pierre Bourdieu and Democratic Politics. *Constellations, 11*(1), 3–15.

Varelius, J. (2008). Is Ethical Expertise Possible? *Medicine Health Care and Philosophy, 11*(2), 127–132.

11 Cleansing our hands of the "dirty war"

The Colombian domestication of human rights

Selina Gallo-Cruz

Introduction

The world polity perspective steers global analysis clear of some of the snares of a functional approach to human rights: the grand oversights of human rights as deeply culturally embedded in particular—not universal—views of social actors and their assumed entitlements, and thus—often extensively—socially constructed; that human rights therefore necessarily impose hierarchies of some social categories over others; and that rights are not spontaneously advocated for by free-floating agents of social change but develop through highly rationalized social networks and institutions (Boli, 1998; Boyle, 2006; Cole, 2006; Elliott, 2008; Finnemore, 1996; Koenig, 2008; Soysal, 1994; Wotipka and Tsutsui, 2008). Nevertheless this growing body of world polity research (and on human rights specifically) tends to maintain a "bird's eye view" of how the global expansion of rights as a cultural model occurs at the state level through a "black box" of enactment, largely reiterating that global expansion occurs as states emulate the most legitimate global cultural authorities.

Refracting its analytical lens to the national level, the concept of domestication offers a new view of enactment that problematizes how legitimate global models are deemed as such and the process by which they become institutionalized into national policy. It makes two particular contributions to world polity theory: it offers a more comprehensive understanding of the varieties of actors driving local enactment, and it underscores that the process by which this happens is often a highly conflictual battle of competing and contradictory interest groups. It both affirms that these groups' very ontologies and their interests (to be bracketed as such in a deeply cultural understanding of how interests have been historically and socially constructed) emanate from a complex world society, as they also emerge out of a nation's unique local, historical engagement with that world society. Here I will unpack how this process has shaped the Colombian response to its "dirty war," as a battle of global–local forces evolved into a new Colombian constitution that set out to enshrine human rights—at once endogenous and indigenous in their origins—as uniquely Colombian. I add to both the world polity and domestication perspectives a nuanced consideration of how global and local non-state actors fold into the fray of the local polity, providing a vital non-state conduit for global forces to impact the reorganization of the local polity culminating in (as opposed to emanating from) state changes.

Global and local tensions in Colombia

The Colombian conflict that has come to be known as the "dirty war" emerged out of a complex layering of weak social structures and seemingly intractable social problems. The fourth largest and third most populous country in South America, Colombia, has historically been characterized by extreme economic disparities. Today, roughly half the population lives below the poverty line. And yet, being rich in natural resources, Colombia adds an important link to global markets. This global positioning provides Colombia with its mainstay cash crops and industries that have directly fed its economic development. The dynamics of how these are organized exasperate the local strife. Like other "peripheral" resource hubs producing globally demanded products, Colombia faces the typical gamut of industrialization and social welfare problems and environmental degradation as it has also become home to a variety of social movements making human rights claims on the state. There are four dimensions of social problems that have particularly fed into the conflict now known as the dirty war.

First, Colombia's land distribution issues grew out of its colonial and postcolonial history. Concentrated land ownership was inherited from Spanish colonizers and worsened after independence in 1818 as landowners continuously pushed poorer campesinos (farm workers) out to peripheral rural areas. Today the top 3 percent of Colombian landed elite own over 70 percent of arable land. Fifty-seven percent of the poorest farmers live on less than 3 percent of the land. Colombia's land situation sits in stark contrast to other Latin American countries that implemented some forms of land redistribution earlier in the twentieth century. Colombia has experimented with serious land retribution laws only recently in the 2000s, and still land redistribution remains the number one agenda item on activists' lists of demands for socio-economic rights. The United Nations High Commissioner for Refugees (UNHCR) has noted Colombia as having one of the world's highest numbers of internally displaced persons, due largely to continuing "land grabs" from rural peasant communities (UNHCR, 2013). The issue of land redistribution among poor farmers has been a central one whenever peace talks are held between the government and rebel forces (Agence France-Presse, 2013). As Colombia's President recently said of the issue, land distribution efforts will be a cornerstone in efforts to "seed peace" among principal opponents in the conflict (Kaplan and Albertus, 2012).

Second, Colombia's experimentation with democracy has been tenuous at best and has only recently gained widespread momentum in the development of new, formal institutional structures for democratic participation. The country has gone through several passes of heightened tensions and violence in the early twentieth century, including a decades-long period known as *La Violencia* ("The Violence", in which over 200,000 people were killed in the cross-fire. Feuding

Liberals and Conservatives then banded together in a decades-long political power sharing-pact, known as *La Frente Nacional* ("The National Front"), which effectively marginalized all others from participation. This pact lasted formally until 1974, but in practice until the late 1980s.

Third, the expansion of the global economy in Colombia added new complexities to these tensions. The early twentieth century elites' hoped-for modernization eventually took off mid-century, and the predominantly rural, agricultural Colombia of the 1950s soon became an increasingly urbanized and industrialized country, consolidating rural products into several key cash crops (coffee, sugar, and later marijuana and cocaine). By 1972 Colombia was said to be "nudging Brazil in economic leadership" in the region (Maidenberg, 1972), and by 1974 Colombia had begun to refuse all foreign aid packages, boldly declaring to the international community that "foreign aid breeds an unhealthy economic dependency and delays or undermines economic measures that should be taken for development" (Lopez in Maidenberg, 1975). Between 1970 and 1979 GDP grew annually by 7 percent and the electrical capacity of the country by a factor of 13 (Americas Watch, 1986).

Then, a global economic crisis in the 1970s led to unprecedented inflation in Colombia, as elsewhere, although Colombia was the last to be affected among its Latin American neighbors. Unemployment by the early 1980s was as high as 20 percent and the 21 percent foreign debt of 1981 climbed to 41 percent by 1983 (Americas Watch, 1986). Drug trafficking was already offering competition to the other cash crops, and with the crisis of global coffee inflation, drug markets offered one of the most stable links to the global economy (Coates, 1978). The local crime industry linked to that market (based largely on exports to the US) made Colombia's crime rate the world's highest (Belnap, 1977). The drastic decline in coca production in Bolivia and Peru was then followed by a monumental expansion in Colombian coca production—helping to diversify the already successful marijuana market. The poorer, rural regions of the country provided fertile land in which to produce the crops and an equally fertile system of unincorporated local polities where drug cartels could build a base of social power (Gonzalez, 2010). Enter the drug war, and a new entanglement of relations between regional political and economic actors, the state, the military, and the insurgency.

While drug cartels sometimes launched all-out attacks on the central government, they also helped to fund the creation of paramilitary groups later connected to squeezing peasants off coveted lands. It was not long before paramilitaries were regularly found to be closely tied to the military resources of the state. Guerilla-resisters also gained a foothold in the drug industry, realizing what was to be gained in this now highly lucrative market for poor campesinos with few other economic prospects. By the 1980s, some guerilla groups, like the Revolutionary Armed Forces of Colombia (FARC), had gained new financial autonomy through formal control over drug production and trafficking. Drug violence became a means of routine security for the now institutionalized insurgency (Gonzalez, 2010).

Paramilitary violence occupies the fourth pillar of Colombian social strife and paramilitaries have "dirtied" the internal conflict in at least two respects. First, paramilitaries have muddied the waters of the conflict, making it less clear who the perpetrators of the violence really are. Paramilitaries act not only as the strong-arm for drug cartels, but also historically for the ultra-right. They repeatedly target mobilization efforts on the left. It is argued, for example, that "being a trade unionist in Colombia is one of the most dangerous occupations in the world" (Gill, 2004, p. 1). They are found to be highly integrated into formal politics and business. "Parapolitics" scandals have been brought into formal trials, with more than 120 elected officials investigated and more than 40 convicted of collusion with paramilitaries (Human Rights Watch, 2001). Mining, farming, and other transnational industries are repeatedly found to have direct ties with paramilitaries (Grajales, 2011; Lopez-Gamundi, 2011; Ortega, 2008).

Second, they have gained a significant level of autonomy at the nexus of conflictual social forces. They are not dependent on one corrupt social body but now mediate relationships between the state and military, guerilla and civil resistance, narco-traffickers, and the local and international business community. They meet with international diplomats and heads of state and provide interviews to the international news media. This autonomy and global–local social power means they are able to defend and deepen the inequalities that lie at the heart of widespread grievances and of the social justice movement, all while speaking a language much outside the lexicon of international human rights law that other key Colombian actors must contend with: the language of terror and violence. Paramilitaries are cited as causing two-thirds of all violence against the civilian population in the country (Joxe and Junqua, 2004).

Given this complex intermingling of the global and local in Colombia's social sufferings, am I arguing, then, that the dirty war is a product of the expansion of the world polity? Well, that's where domestication comes in. What has been noted by globalization scholars about the Colombian conflict is that the use of transnational networks to quell the conflict is stronger than ever, and yet these networks have been ineffective for two reasons attributable to the local idiosyncrasies of the conflict: (1) morally, the paramilitaries cannot be shamed and they do not care about their bad international reputation; and (2) materially, paramilitaries are too well situated among active global–local economic networks and resources to be shaken by shaming and blaming (Sikkink, 2009). In other words, the Colombian domestication of international human rights at the state level will only be really effective if their de jure authority ceases to be over-ridden by an oppositional de facto authority. Through the lens of domestication, the local field battles in the Colombian conflict necessarily involve de facto forms of social power, and competing and contradictory local interests rooted in competing and contradictory global social forces.

The Colombian domestication of human rights

The essence of the domestication framework is the study of how idealized principles organized into a particular model, policy, or framework are brought to a local political agenda, and how through field conflicts or deliberation, they come to be wholly local (Alasuutari, 2009; Alasuutari and Qadir, this volume). Where world polity theory may suggest a weakening of nationalism, through domestication, globalization is found to strengthen banal nationalism in several steps: (1) the initial process of national competition over valued global (cultural) resources (such as legitimate policies and institutional structures), (2) the cross-national comparisons that ensue in local debates and deliberation, (3) the creation of new local actors (who can be seen as authentic, local specialists) ontologically created in addressing debated-upon issues, and (4) the final stage of naturalization, when countries come to embrace policy practices as their own (taking the intricate process of diffusion and social construction that brought such practices to institutionalization for granted).

From a historical perspective, so many of the forces at play in the Colombian conflict are "global in origin," from the legacy of colonization, to the push for modernization of the economy, to the drug markets and networks; it is hard to pinpoint one channel through which world society has shaped Colombia. Although not explicitly positioned within the emerging literature on "domestication," Neve Gordon and Nitza Berkovitch's work (especially 2007) has helped to challenge the oversimplification of global diffusion of cultural models of human rights by emphasizing the importance of providing a more differentiated view of the local–global interaction. Here I follow the role of civil society in promulgating a local precedence and support for human rights (defining civil society as those actors that do not, and could not, work through formal political parties or interest groups). I track human rights as a global-in-origin cultural product, as outlined in the world polity literature cited above—but my concern is with how human rights have become domesticated as indigenously Colombian in scope, organization, and implementation. And I point to the varied important cultural connections made outside of the formal institutions of government, connections that have ushered in new models for thinking about how to overcome the conflict of the dirty war and how to build a better Colombian state through a commitment to human rights.

Civil society networks have played a crucial role, foremost because just as the problems outlined above grew and developed, so too did civil society grow and domesticate ideas of how to use human rights to solve these problems—from the outside of Colombian institutional politics in.[1] The number of non-violent peace initiatives—violently repressed through the 1970s—began to spike dramatically in the 1980s. This can be attributed in part to the strengthening of the student movement ans also the strengthening of ties to new globally influential social movement organizations. International Non-Governmental Organizations (INGOs) like Amnesty International had begun to make contacts with and globally publicize local organizations' experience of repression in a first wave of global human rights shaming (Hopgood, 2006). But the local mobilization of these claims on the state had been long developing.

Rights as a global local resource

Colombia's experimentation in institutionalizing human rights dates back to its early independence struggle (Fox, Gallon-Giraldo, and Stetson, 2010) and marginalized groups have been experimenting with efforts to institutionalize human rights ever since. In Colombia the movement for human rights gained significant momentum in the late 1970s when the state's interactions with global others drove it to define and defend its human rights position. Despite Colombia's extensive internal struggles and the extreme political marginalization imposed through the *Frente*, before this time, it was not yet listed among notable human rights abusers in the region, such as Guatemala, Chile, Argentina, and El Salvador (McBee, 1977). But the increasing disenchantment of the marginalized non-state actors, and state actors' disinterest in civil liberties, finally came to a head in 1979 when Amnesty International (after collecting information from various local groups and organizations) began to list Colombia among the world's worst human rights abusers (Diuguid, 1980). In a first defensive act against this charge that human rights was something the Colombian state lacked, the President at the time, Julio Cesar Turbay Ayala, invited Amnesty International to come to the country and see the human rights situation for themselves. Much to Turbay's dismay, the trip worked against his ambitions of keeping Colombia out of the international spotlight of shame, and Amnesty International immediately published secret documents regarding the abusive treatment of political prisoners, documents that were in fact willingly offered them by Turbay!

Turbay's missing the mark on how best to impress the international NGO was indicative of two important internal contextual factors that illustrate how domestication works in this first stage. First, Turbay was only the latest of a long line of leaders who had operated in a system characterized by corruption, back-door deals, and the systemic collusion among elites used to achieve such pressing goals as maintaining the "public order." Second, his focus was understandably elsewhere, the intense confrontation in which his administration had become embroiled as the guerillas had just recently launched a historical offensive on the state. He had inherited a coalescing of internal conflict of civil unrest, guerilla and paramilitary violence, and drug trafficking from the end of the preceding administration. In response, he had instituted a "security statute" that curtailed the already small margins of civil liberties, restricted press coverage, and dragged all those accused of acts of terror through military trials. With the international shaming of his efforts, however, Turbay's political sensibilities were then wedged between the Scylla and Charybdis of doing things the Colombian way or the way of the global (local) human rights regime.

For local human rights advocates, this international shaming importantly signaled that, in Colombia, the defense of the national as opposed to the transnational position came only from a small group of elites that had historically maintained a stronghold on institutional politics. And advocates' efforts were both shaped by and actively relied on new global authorities to delegitimize historically local authorities, insisting that such political inequalities had to be untied to make real changes in the social and economic inequalities that afflicted the country.

In 1981 the Second National Human Rights Forum was organized by a diverse political and civil constituency with the aim of reintegrating marginalized voices into the polity. To appease Liberal claims for expanded rights, in September of 1982, Conservative Party President Betancur established a Peace Commission to negotiate with rebels and instituted a number of positive economic reforms and amnesty programs throughout the Colombian countryside to this end (Diehl, 1983). The process broke down, however, and Betancur was blamed for the heightened rebel–army–paramilitary tensions that followed (Onis, 1985). The violence only worsened, and Colombia frequented international news headlines as a nation wrought by internal violence. In 1984 Rodrigo Lara, then Minister of Justice, was assassinated following his launching of an aggressive campaign to stamp out drug trafficking. He was the first of a laundry list of political killings that stained the 1980s, including later the Attorney General, 12 Justices of the Supreme Court, hundreds of judges, lawyers, and journalists, not to mention thousands of anonymous peasants caught in the fire between the army and the guerillas (Banks and Alvarez, 1992). Between 1987 and 1990, four presidential candidates were assassinated. People began to organize because the entanglement of violence, corruption, and fear and its ensuing repression became so bad. At the head of this organizing activity were those most embedded in global thinking about the institutionalization of human rights, the university law students (Colprensa, 2011).

In 1987 a National Assembly, which incorporated broad participation through a series of working groups, was created to develop a series of proposed reforms. It was a development driven by a complex internal "field battle" (the term used here as defined in the Introduction to this volume) over whether or not it was in the state's interests to follow the path of human rights to stamp out the problems of the dirty war. These field battlers debated not just the appropriate and most effective methods for controlling the conflict but also who the perpetrators of the conflict were and what social problems lie at its roots. It was the unceasing claim of the popular movement that the first real solution to the dirty war was to open political participation and begin to extend human rights to those whose had long been dispossessed of those rights. Then the initiative failed.[2]

The students continued to organize through the violence and set up a series of *mesas del trabajo* (working groups) that analyzed the possibility of judicial reform (Fox et al., 2010). Although resistance from the Congress was strong, in 1989 the students published a manifesto in another national newspaper, *El Tiempo*, calling on the president to hold a plebiscite for a National Constitutional Assembly declaring, "We Can Still Save Colombia." The popularity of this effort gained them 35,000 voluntary mail-in signatures to a petition, but the effort was soon eclipsed by other pressing issues (Dugas, 2001). In 1989 Barco endorsed the establishment of a Commission of Institutional Readjustment to draft amendments. At the year's end this effort also fell through, as the Council of the State suspended all deliberation (Banks and Alvarez, 1992).

Mobilized students urged the public to cast a seventh ballot (after which the movement was called *la septima papeleta*) for constitutional reform. Approximately 2 million voters cast extra ballots in favor of the reform (Cárdenas, Junguito, and Pachón, 2006). The President then held an official election with the following presidential election, and 88 percent of the voters voted in favor of establishing an Assembly for Constitutional Reform. By the end of 1990 elections were held, and the Assembly for Constitutional Reform was organized. Having moved through the first stage of the domestication of human rights, that is, the development of a local Colombian commitment to institutionalizing human rights, it was believed that constitutional reform would also be the beginning of an end to the dirty war.

Globalizing democracy and domesticating diversity

The second stage of domestication is defined by a concerted effort at making cross-national comparisons, and the third stage by the concordant recognition of new types of social actors. Through both of these general ideal-typical phases in domestication, the global cultural object becomes localized in a field battle over competing local standpoints and conflicting global and local interests. In the Colombian Constitutional Reform process, these next two stages unfolded in tandem through the iterative development of a national understanding of how Colombian rights could be both globally legitimate and nationally authentic and then, a process of deciding which actors could best address and embody these ideals. The way the reform initiative was structured enhanced the emergence of those identified as the socially and politically disenfranchised.[3] This diverse nexus of newly recognized actors converged on the formal invitation of the state into the proposal effort, which then proceeded through a dynamic and iterative effort at global mimicry and local innovation.

The Constitutional Reform Assembly (a democratically elected body) was explicitly committed to enhancing participatory democracy in the reform process and this was perhaps its greatest innovation (although not without some global orchestration, which I will elaborate on below). It was strategically comprised of elected representatives from the various Liberal and Conservative factions, former guerillas, a party known as the Democratic Alliance, Indigenous communities, an independent party called the Patriotic Union, different Christian parties (Catholic and non), and labor unions. There was also an effort to include the FARC (Fuerzas Armadas Revolucionarias de Colombia, "Revolutionary Forces of Colombia"), but the FARC staunchly rejected any participation in the formal state-led process. To further expand participation, the government set up 1,580 working groups throughout the country. These working groups were to facilitate the drafting of proposals that reflected diverse social perspectives, from academics and lawyers to laborers and farmers. In the end 131 official and 28 non-official proposals were submitted and brought before the Assembly for debate and formal deliberation. And in this process, a host of formerly politically excluded claimants were accorded a new ontological status as the diverse societal constellation that would comprise the Colombian polity (Fox et al., 2010).

Of the formally organized Assembly five Commissions were established. The First Commission was tasked with the study of principles, rights, obligations, guarantees and liberties, mechanisms and institutions of democratic participation, the electoral system, political parties and the status of opposition, and the process of constitutional reform. The Second Commission studied territorial and regional governance. The Third Commission studied the reform structures of the state, Congress, police, states of emergency, and international relations. The Fourth Commission studied the principles and offices of criminal law and due process. The Fifth Commission studied economic, social, ecological, fiscal, and other public services. That is, these Commissions were formally organized to compare the Colombian constitution's treatment on these matters with that of other countries (as is characteristic of second stage domestication), which in turn lent them to a bit of borrowing of others' constitutional formulations of human rights. And borrow they did.

In the end product, the new Colombian bill of rights was heavily based on the US and French bills. Article 88's articulation of citizen rights and collective interests was fitted together from the Brazilian, Spanish, and Portuguese constitutions. A Human Rights Ombudsman was developed after the Scandinavian model. The formerly European model of inquisitorial justice now followed the more American prosecutorial form of justice. Following the example of France and Spain a separate Constitutional Court was established.

Overall, the concept of universal human rights was given great status in the new constitution. Article 93 mandated that all ratified treaties must recognize universal human rights. Article 86 established the *tutela* system, offering writ of protection for every citizen fearing their rights threatened by a public authority (a mechanism now since widely used). Article 103 placed high requirements on the adoption of human rights legislation. Article 152 placed much stricter controls on states of exception, as Article 377 placed stringent parameters around amendments. That is, constitutional laws could no longer easily be suspended in a declared "state of war" (foreign or internal) without passing through new channels of legislative approval, which imposed a new system of checks and balances on presidential authority. The new constitution also innovatively established peace-making as a mandate of the state and the "right and duty of society" in its Preamble and Articles 2 and 22. Most significant among these stipulations was that the state was to pursue and advance peace talks between the different political factions. And Article 30 formally extended amnesty and pardons to all those who had been involved in guerilla activities before the new constitution went into effect.

At the heart of the document was the spirit of equality and rights for all, which drew heavily from a number of documents of international law articulating concepts of "popular sovereignty" and "democratic participation." In this spirit, a number of new actors were given special status in particular rights, foremost among them women, children and adolescents, an array of minorities, persons of different sexual orientations as well as transgender individuals and indigenous communities (Delaney, 2008). Significant aspects of central state power were also heavily curbed, as new checks and balances were instituted over the representative election of mayors and governors, the Congressional enactment of decrees and power to veto presidential vetoes, broadened representation in the House and Senate, and the limiting of state-of-emergency powers (Cárdenas et al., 2006). The global cultural script for universal human rights was instituted into a Colombian constitution, born of decades of conflict, grievances, and the conflictual process that brought it to and across the table of deliberation.

With all the dynamism of the Reform process there is yet one final and important layer to the global dimensions of domesticating human rights and diversity rights in Colombia. And that is that although scholars downplay the political role of the international community in this process (arguing, for example, that the UN did not formally participate through Assembly representation or mediation), the international community did play a significant cultural and structural role in expanding and facilitating civil society networks and frameworks for action. Structurally, the United Nations and numerous NGO and INGO corollaries provided financial support to a number of civil groups and coalitions. The UN and other international bodies sent technical advisers to the President and the Assembly and contributed to the elaboration of drafts for deliberation. Inside Colombia, these international agencies publicly promoted the new constitution to the legal communities and other government agencies, disseminated drafts among the population and provided education about constitutional rights and guarantees and training in the use of new mechanisms like the *tutelas*. And internationally the UN helped to publicize the Assembly's debates and progress, enhancing the global spotlight on the process, in turn ontologically bolstering the Colombian Constitutional Reform as a major international event (Fox et al., 2010).

A number of NGOs remained actively networked with—and some of them were directly supported by—European agencies. A large pool of NGOs in particular was organized around an initiative called *Viva la Ciudadania* ("In support of our citizenship"), which provided a bridge between the Assembly and a host of other social and political organizations. This coalition formally organized debates throughout the country and published a monthly newsletter on constitutional reform. They channeled local proposals to the Assembly, updated the population on Assembly progress, and educated the population on the meaning of the changes. Furthermore, several international NGOs played an important part in representing the voice of international law, they participated in debates, and some of them even directed the Assembly with their own views on how best to institute a modern human rights framework and checks on public security violations.

Cleansing our hands of the dirty war

The final stage of domestication is naturalization, characterized by the state's embracing of new policies as their own. In the broader scheme of world culture theories, naturalization is much like Robertson's (1992) concept of "the universalization of the particular" and the "particularization of the universal," in which he explains that global forces spread both homogeneous practices, beliefs, and behaviors throughout the world and, in response to the expansion of global culture, local cultures bolster their particular and authentic identities, beliefs, practices, etc. Boli and Elliott (2008) later expand on the world-polity emphasis on the expansion of homogeneous structures explaining that such local efforts at particularization in fact create "façade" forms of "diversity."

In the Colombian case, a strong sense of national identity was born through the 1991 Reform and you can see this in the wording of Article 70, which praises the essential contribution of distinctive local identities into the distinctive national identity.

> Culture in its diverse manifestations is the basis of nationality. The state recognizes the equality and dignity of all those who live together in the country. The state will promote research, science, development, and the diffusion of the nation's cultural values.
>
> (Colombia, National Constitution, Article 70)

Furthermore, the global left has loudly praised the Colombian constitutional process as exemplifying the power of indigenous organizing, speaking to the taken-for-grantedness of its global–local origins.

But Colombia also remains a country marred by a poor human rights record and is continuously castigated by international organizations for its human rights abuses. And both world polity theory and the domestication framework are careful not to confuse the deeply cultural nature of the construction of human rights with the often highly fragmented actual outcome in terms of implementation. This, for world polity theorists in particular, is where the concept of the "loose coupling" or "decoupling" between initiative and outcome becomes crucial. Colombia remains a country where the decoupling between practice and policy is extreme. Constitutional analysts find that representation is, on the one hand, more equal and participation in government much more fair than before 1991. On the other hand, they note how the rigorous tenets for political consensus make bringing persistent factions into agreement an arduously difficult task (Cárdenas et al., 2006). Human rights lawyers are formally operating in ways previously not possible. And yet they are consistently targeted and often violently attacked for their work against corruption. The number of civil society groups has grown immensely in the years following the reform. But they remain highly limited in their ability to stop the ill effects of the drug war, which rages on. The state now prosecutes and convicts the leaders of paramilitary groups and corrupt government officials, as it never did before 1991. Meanwhile, community raids and massacres still frequently grace the headlines. The US has invested billions of dollars in supporting Colombia's fight against the drug war. And narco-trafficking remains a multi-billion dollar industry for Colombia. These paradoxes remain a constant problem for Colombia's national identity and international relations. No matter how indigenously Colombian the rights process has been, the state has not yet been able to cleanse its hands of the dirty war. All this is to state that the "naturalization" of "universal" human rights in Colombia does not mean it has become fully institutionalized in practice; rather rights have come to characterize new ways of organizing—even corrupt—politics and the culture of civil society.

Ultimately, the naturalization of human rights as a tool for solving the conflict has retained saliency in the state, Colombian society at large, and in Colombia's international relations, as it has also thus far failed to be fully and effectively implemented. A series of peace talks between the government and the guerillas were organized following the Constitutional Reform of 1991. The state extended a demilitarized zone to the rebels, who in turn released hundreds of political prisoners. They negotiated a ceasefire in 2002, but the talks eventually failed, and soon after the FARC launched an attack on Bogota. The government and FARC have since attempted to reach agreements on various occasions and many high-profile and other hostages have been released by the rebels over the years. But efforts taken against the group involving cross-border negotiations in Venezuela and Ecuador have met with mixed tensions. And the government remains at loggerheads with the rebels.

Recent efforts to demobilize paramilitaries saw the public surrendering of 30,000, who claimed to have been involved in such violent groups (although the percentage of them that were not actively involved is debated). In 2011 the Victims Land and Retribution Act sought to redistribute some of the prime rural farmlands to displaced peasants (although the offered retributions were far outnumbered by the registered claims for land lost), thereby offering an olive branch to guerillas who maintain that land distribution is at the top of their concerns. Several widespread protests have erupted throughout the country over the course of the 2000s, against the violence of the paramilitaries and the rebels as well as about the instability of economic opportunities.

Conversely, the persistence and continued globalization of Colombia's social problems have also ironically aided the growth and globalization of its human rights movement. In many respects, Colombia has become an international rights activist hotspot. While human rights lawyers and union leaders remain highly threatened in their activities, they are some of the most globally networked activists in the world and have been quite successful in publicizing abuses, which keeps the spotlight of shame on the state, paramilitaries, and guerillas. And just as its networks of violence continue to permeate the countryside, so too has Colombia become inundated with global peace efforts. Colombia now has the concerted, active investment of more international third-party non-violence organizations (which place international peacekeeping volunteers directly into conflict zones to deter the outbreak of violence) than any other country!

Conclusion

The domestication framework, which aims to shed light on the conditions under which the enactment of world polity scripts unfolds at the national level, helps to elucidate how human rights was institutionalized in Colombia through a delayed and highly conflictual local field battle. Global in origin, the issue of human rights has been in the hearts and on the minds of diverse Colombian citizens for over a century. And yet in their efforts to institutionalize human rights at the state level, civil actors were both violently repressed and systematically excluded from political participation. Under such harsh conditions of repression, their grievances grew and the population began to mobilize. Through local to global linkages with international NGOs Colombia eventually came under the spotlight of international shame, and new political opportunities further galvanized a popular movement through one of the most violent decades in Colombia's modern history. The result of this dynamic "people-powered" movement was a phenomenal, broadly organized democratic Constitutional Reform that set into motion a new structural capacity for citizens to realize their human rights through formal state channels. Through the global lens, the Colombian individual became enshrined under the extension of new entitlements and legal privileges. From the local lens Colombia opened participatory power to a broadened and diversified constituency.

Of great importance to this human rights movement of both global and local orientations, the state pledged its commitment to securing the peace with its opponents and extending the human rights that would—in theory—put an end to rebel grievances and the dirty war. The form and the ways in which these human rights came to be naturally Colombian, followed an iterative process shaped by global–local networks and the flow of resources as much as by enduring conflicts among highly conflictual local actors. Unfortunately, there have been clear limits to this process of culturally constructing human rights at the local level. The same oppositional environment has shaped the persistent decoupling between the ideal of realizing human rights in Colombia and the reality.

In moving through the different stages of the domestication of human rights, several important outcomes illuminate how this process works in a state as ridden with violent conflict and deep-seated social problems as Colombia. First, the issue of human rights has long been a legitimate and highly sought-after resource among globally minded local actors who were historically disenfranchised from political participation and entitlements. It was not a resource that interested government elites or gained national saliency until the state was internationally shamed and called to defend its legitimacy as an upstanding democratic world actor. This local political opportunity was brought on by the castigation of a global moral authority (Boli, 2006) and points to the importance of the alignment of local mobilization with global–local political networks in bringing about state change. The state made efforts to defend its position as sufficiently politically equipped to deal with its own internal conflicts, but the efforts of the newly legitimated and broadly organized popular movement won out in this first stage of domestication. It was the intensity of the field battles that drove local populations to sharpen their thinking about how best to domesticate human rights, to publicize rights abuses to influential international actors, and to push the state through one of its historically most severe periods of repression to the adoption of a Colombian model of human rights that was believed to be the beginning of the end of the problems underlying the dirty war.

Then, in acquiescence to the move to expand the state's commitment to and instruments of human rights, a parallel process of cross-national comparison (and borrowing) and ontological actor creation fed into the realization of democracy in the Colombian political process. This pivotal event, marked by the changes following the 1991 Constitutional Reform that would later come to be defined as evidence of the dynamism of Colombia's own indigenous democratic capital, was a sure sign of the naturalization of global human rights as intrinsically locally emergent. But so much of this process, its structure and the cultural frameworks through which it was orchestrated, relied on a continued relationship between local and global civil society networks. In this purportedly indigenous democratic process a great deal of cutting and pasting from the global scripts on universal rights and democratic constitutions helped to fashion Colombian's modern commitment to equality, human rights, and the securing of peace.

In contrast to the macro-level approach to world polity enactment, I make the case for thinking about enactment as a highly conflictual and complex process driven by unique global–local interactions, constrained by the global–local exchange of resources, and made possible by the global–local development of new opportunities for how best to build a local polity from the outside in. What makes Colombia's internal troubles a dirty war is that a significant part of the country's social structures are at war with the other significant social structures; together these warring parties and their mechanisms of violence, corruption, exploitation, as well as resistance and efforts at change, constitute Colombia's global legacy, as does also the in-flow of forces for building up and expanding a structure supportive of democracy and human rights.

Notes

1 It is important to note that Colombian civil society is comprised of different local social dimensions embedded in global visions for world peace and progress. Among these, expanded secondary and university education provisions in the 1970s and 1980s saw more democracy and human rights discourse (following global institutional trends, see Schofer and Meyer, 2005). Religions have also historically been among the most prominent of Colombian democracy globalizers as they have built lasting ties with human rights INGOs (Deats, 2009). Finally, the expansion of international humanitarian aid in the area galvanized an "NGO boom" (Reimann, 2006), and Colombia, like other Latin American nations, experienced a growth in formal non-governmental organizations that played at first a marginal but later active role in shaping the polity's agenda.

2 There was another glimpse of hope in 1988, when Congress deliberated the possibility for reform, but then-President Barco withdrew his support following the introduction of a ban on the extradition of prisoners (a process he frequently employed). An editorial in *El Espectador*, a national newspaper, urged the people of the need for constitutional reform to curb drug and guerilla violence and gained widespread support, although the writer also soon fell victim to the wave of targeted political assassinations.

3 In fact, the 1991 Colombian Constitutional Reform represents one of the great efforts at democratic constitutional reform of the late twentieth century precisely because it so systematically incorporated a diverse host of never-before-represented social actors.

References

Americas Watch (1986). The Central Americanization of Colombia? Human Rights and the Peace Process. Washington, D.C.: Americas Watch.

Agence France-Presse (2013). Colombia, FARC rebels report progress in peace talks. Retrieved 4 August 2013 from http://reliefweb.int/report/colombia/colombia-farc-rebels-report-progress-peace-talks.

Alasuutari, P. (2009). The Domestication of Worldwide Policy Models. *Ethnologia Europea, 39*(1), 66–71.

Banks, W.C. and Alvarez, E. (1992). The New Colombian Constitution: Democratic Victory or Popular Surrender? *University of Miami Inter-American Law Review, 23*(1), 39–92.

Belnap, D.F. (1977, 28 November). Drug Smuggling Tops Colombia Crime, *Los Angeles Times*, p. A7.

Boli, J. (1998). Rights and Rules: Constituting World Citizens. In C.L. McNeely (ed.), *Public Rights, Public Rules: Constituting Citizens in the World Polity and National Policy* (pp. 271–293). New York: Garland.

Boli, J. (2006). The Rationalization of Virtue and Virtuosity. In M.-L. Djelic and K. Sahlin-Andersson (eds), *Transnational Governance: Institutional Dynamics of Regulation* (pp. 95–118). Cambridge: Cambridge University Press.

Boli, J. and Elliott, M.A. (2008). Façade Diversity: The Individualization of Cultural Difference. *International Sociology, 23*(4), 540–560.

Boyle, E.H. (2006). *Female Genital Cutting: Cultural Conflict in the Global Community*. Baltimore, MD: Johns Hopkins University Press.

Cárdenas, M., Junquito, R., and Pachón, M. (2006). Political Institutions and Policy Outcomes in Colombia: The Effects of the 1991 Constitution (Working Paper). Washington, D.C.: Inter-American Development Bank.

Coates, J. (1978, 27 October). Colombia: Economically Addicted to Marijuana, *Chicago Tribune*, p. B4.

Cole, W.M. (2006). When All Else Fails: International Adjudications of Human Rights Abuse Claims 1979–99. *Social Forces, 84*(4), 1909–1935.

Colombia, National Constitution. Retrieved 4 August 2013 from http://confinder.richmond.edu/admin/docs/colombia_const2.pdf.

Colprensa (2011). La Revolución de los Estudiantes. *El Colombiano*. Retrieved 4 August 2013 from www.elcolombiano.com/BancoConocimiento/L/la_revolucion_de_los_estudiantes/la_revolucion_de_los_estudiantes.asp.

Deats, R. (2009). *Marked for Life: The Story of Hildegaard Goss-Mayr*. New York: New York City Press.

Delaney, P. (2008). Legislating for Equality in Colombia: Constitutional Jurisprudence, Tutelas, and Social Reform. *Equal Rights Review*, 50–60.

Diehl, J. (1983, 13 May). Colombia Attempts to Pacify Guerillas: Racked by Violence for 25 Years, Nation Seeks End to Bloodshed, *Los Angeles Times*, p. C2.

Diuguid, L.H. (1980, 17 April). Colombia Accused of Torture, *Washington Post*, p. A22.

Dugas, J.C. (2001). The Origin, Impact and Demise of the 1989–90 Colombian Student Movement: Insights from Social Movement Theory. *Journal of Latin American Studies, 33*(4), 807–837.

Elliott, M.A. (2008). *A Cult of the Individual for a Global Society: The Development and Worldwide Expansion of Human Rights Ideology*. PhD, Emory University, Atlanta, GA.

Finnemore, M.J. (1996). Norms, Culture, and World Politics: Insights from Sociology's Institutionalism. *International Organization, 50*, 325–347.

Fox, D.T., Gallon-Giraldo, G., and Stetson, A. (2010). Lessons of the Colombian Constitutional Reform of 1991: Toward the Securing of Peace and Reconciliation. In L.E. Miller (ed.), *Framing the State in Times of Transition: Case Studies in Constitution Making*. Washington, D.C.: United States Institute of Peace.

Gill, L. (2004). Labor and Human Rights: The "Real Thing" in Colombia. Human Rights Committee of the American Anthropological Association.

Gonzalez, F.E. (2010). The Colombian Conflict in Historical Perspective. Retrieved 4 August 2013 from www.c-r.org/sites/c-r.org/files/Part1_ColombiaAccord.pdf.

Gordon, N. and Berkovitch, N. (2007). Human rights discourse in domestic settings: How does it emerge? *Political Studies, 55*, 243–266.

Grajales, J. (2011). The Rifle and the Title: Paramilitary Violence, Land Grab and Land Control in Colombia. *Journal of Peasant Studies, 38*(4), 771–792.

Hopgood, S. (2006). *Keepers of the Flame: Understanding Amnesty International*. Ithaca, NY: Cornell University Press.

HRW (2001). *The "Sixth Division": Military–Paramilitary Ties and US Policy in Colombia*. New York: Human Rights Watch.

Joxe, N. and Junqua, Y. (2004). They Killed a Man (Docsonline documentaries). Retrieved 1 March 2013 from http://docsonline.tv/search?input=they+killed+a+man&cat=all.

Kaplan, O. and Albertus, M. (2012, 9 October). Colombia's Rebels and Land Reform, *New York Times*. Retrieved 4 August 2013 from www.nytimes.com/2012/10/10/opinion/colombias-rebels-and-land-reform.html?_r=0.

Koenig, M. (2008). Institutional Change in the World Polity: International Human Rights and the Construction of Collective Identities. *International Sociology, 23*, 94–114.

Lopez-Gamundi, P. (2011). Colombia's Gold Rush: The Silver Lining for Paramilitaries and Guerillas: Council on Hemispheric Affairs.

Maidenberg, H.J. (1972, 4 September). Colombia Nudging Brazil in Economic Leadership, *New York Times*, 21.

Maidenberg, H.J. (1975, September). Colombia explains aid refusal, *New York Times*, 40.

McBee, S. (1977, 10 June). Mrs Carter arrives in Colombia: Drugs Top Talks Agenda, *Washington Post*, p. A20.

Onis, J. (1985, 16 June). Rebels Renew Colombia Fight: Betancur Blamed as Pacification Plan Fails, *Los Angeles Times*, p. A1.

Ortega, M. (2008). Deadly Ventures? Multinational Corporations and Paramilitaries in Colombia *Revista Electrónica de Estudios Internacionales, 16*, 1–16.

Reimann, K.D. (2006). A View from the Top: International Politics, Norms, and the Worldwide Growth of NGOs. *International Studies Quarterly, 50*, 45–67.

Robertson, R. (1992). *Globalization: Social Theory and Global Culture*. London: Sage.

Schofer, E. and Meyer, J.W. (2005). Worldwide Expansion of Higher Education in the 20th Century. *American Sociological Review, 70*, 898–920.

Sikkink, K. (2009). Comments on Colombia Chapters from the Perspective of Human Rights Theories. In E.F. Babbitt and E.L. Lutz (eds), *Human Rights and Conflict Resolution in Context: Colombia, Sierra Leone, and Northern Ireland*. Syracuse, NY: Syracuse University Press.

Soysal, Y.N. (1994). *Limits of Citizenship: Migrants and Postnational Membership in Europe*. Chicago, IL: University of Chicago Press.

UNHCR (2013). UNHCR Country Operations Profile: United Nations High Commissioner for Refugees. Retrieved 4 August 2013 from www.unhcr.org/pages/49e492ad6.html.

Wotipka, C.M. and Tsutsui, K. (2008). Global Human Rights and State Sovereignty: State Ratification of International Human Rights Treaties, 1965–2001. *Sociological Forum, 23*(4), 724–754.

Index

Page numbers in **bold** denote figures.

For Product Safety Concerns and Information please contact our EU
representative GPSR@taylorandfrancis.com
Taylor & Francis Verlag GmbH, Kaufingerstraße 24, 80331 München, Germany

www.ingramcontent.com/pod-product-compliance
Lightning Source LLC
Chambersburg PA
CBHW050431280326
41932CB00013BA/2069